WHAT
MOTHERS
LEARN without being taught

NAOMI STADLEN

piatkus

PIATKUS

First published in Great Britain in 2020 by Piatkus

1 3 5 7 9 10 8 6 4 2

A CIP catalogue record for this book
is available from the British Library.

ISBN 978-0-349-41244-3

Edited by Anne Newman
Typeset by Palimpsest Book Production Ltd, Falkirk, Stirlingshire
Printed and bound in Great Britain by Clays Ltd, Elcograf, S.p.A.

Papers used by Piatkus are from well managed
forests and other responsible sources.

Piatkus
An imprint of
Little, Brown Book Group
Carmelite House
50 Victoria Embankment
London EC4Y 0DZ

An Hachette UK Company
www.hachette.co.uk

www.littlebrown.co.uk

Naomi Stadlen has unique experience of listening to mothers. For nearly thirty years she has run weekly discussion groups, Mothers Talking, which meet at the Active Birth Centre in London. She is a qualified psychotherapist and author of the bestselling *What Mothers Do* and *How Mothers Love*. She is also a mother of three and a grandmother. Visit www.naomistadlen.com

Contents

With thanks

My warmest thanks to all the mothers who have talked to me. There is only room for a fraction of your observations here. Many that haven't been included have still shaped *What Mothers Learn*.

And thank you to my kind friends and family who have read and commented on chapters: Margaret Brearley, Merrill Carrington, Sarah Ereira, Elizabeth Long, Anne Manne, Jennifer Marsh, Rachel Montagu, Lauren Porter, Vera Salter, Anthony Stadlen, Lena Stadlen, Rachel Stadlen, Veronica and Richard Veasey. Special thanks to Rachel and Anthony Stadlen, daughter and husband, for their perceptive and invaluable comments; to Shoël and Natasha for discussions; and to Darrel for considering the front cover photo. To all my beloved family, Rachel, Eric and Tovi; Shoël, Natasha, Anya and Antoshka; Darrel; and my husband Anthony because, after over fifty years of my knowing you, time deepens the wonder.

My warmest thanks to Anne Newman for wonderful editorial suggestions and final 'diamond-polishing'. And my thanks for all the support and encouragement generously given by the editors at Piatkus: Emily Arbis, Zoe Bohm and Jillian Stewart.

Author's note

The identities of the mothers quoted in *What Mothers Learn* are confidential, so I have adopted the following system of referring to them and their families:

B indicates the name of a boy child.
G indicates the name of a girl child.
F indicates the father's name.
M indicates the mother's name.

The term 'mother' usually means the person who bears the baby, gives birth to him, and takes care of him afterwards. But today fathers and grandmothers especially may be the primary daytime carers. If the parents divorce and remarry, there may be step-parents taking turns. There may be adoptive mothers as well as biological ones. When a non-professional person stands in for the mother in this way, or takes turns with her, descriptions of what mothers learn may apply to this person also.

And the pronoun 'he' is used for general statements about a baby or child. This is to avoid confusion with the 'she' of the mother. So my apologies to girls to whom all general statements apply equally.

Mothers' words are usually quoted in order of the babies' ages. When a mother has two or more babies, the quotation usually uses the age of the youngest baby.

Introduction

There's plenty of information on what a mother *should* learn. But what do mothers really learn? Having a child isn't as easy as it looks. It can be disorientating. We soon realise how little we know and, for many of us, being a mother is a learning experience.

So *What Mothers Learn* isn't about what a mother 'should' learn. It's an account of what mothers have said they *did* learn. Mothers deserve to be heard. They discover aspects of themselves and their babies that are new and interesting.

Part of what mothers learn *can* be taught, such as how to bathe a baby. Topics like that could be summed up in a list, so that you could get the gist of it quickly. But what mothers learn without being taught comes to them gradually, and needs to be read gradually too. It's to broaden our understanding. It's not meant as a programme to tell another mother what she 'should' learn.

'It's a learning curve,' new mothers tell themselves. They realise that being a mother is hard at first, but that slowly they will get better at it.

So what do mothers learn on their 'learning curve'? They usually start by following received advice. Then, as they get to know their babies and talk to other mothers, they slowly venture forward with ideas of their own.

Some of what mothers learn is practical. But some of it is mysterious. We can sum it up as 'mothering'. Mothering is universal and ancient, and centres on the way that mothers relate to their children. Mothers discover *how* to relate. But these relationships often develop quietly with little to show for them. As the American writer Sara Ruddick said: 'The work at the centre of mothering, the work that children demand and that mothers do, remains elusive.'[1] In a materialistic culture like ours, people prefer to talk about quantifiable actions. These can be named and explained. If they aren't – and mothering isn't – it's easy to brush these relationships aside and assume that learning to relate isn't important.

Yet babies and children need mothering – plenty of it. And though, as mothers, we find that mothering requires a lot from us, we get back a lot too. Babies remind us of the wonder of being alive. It's eye-opening, and helps us to see one another from a gentler perspective. We often become more thoughtful members of the society we live in. Few societies acknowledge how much they owe to their mothers.

Mothering is often confused with childcare. But it's much more than that. Childcare can be paid for. When mothers say that they feel bored and frustrated, they're usually talking about childcare. Mothering is exciting and challenging, rather than boring.

Fathers learn a lot too. So does the mother's partner, if this is a man or woman other than the father. Shouldn't we look into what *parents* learn?

That would be a good idea for a different book. The roles aren't always interchangeable. When mothers, fathers and step-parents are all merged together as 'parents', the special experiences of each are lost.

Many women today can't afford to give much time to being mothers, and some don't see the point of it either. The qualities that enable a woman to get ahead in her career are different from those that enable a mother to connect to her child. Yet these motherly qualities add a whole new dimension to our way of being. Many women don't realise how much they benefit. *What Mothers Learn* is written to show, first, how learning to be a mother takes time, and then what a wonderful experience it can be. It also makes the case that, if enough of us agree that mothering is necessary, we must find a way to support those mothers financially who want to devote enough time to it – or simply time to *try* it.

For most of us, being a mother feels daunting at first. But just as 'morning' sickness shows how well the mother's body is adapting to pregnancy, so postnatal exhaustion and bewilderment are much more positive signs than they seem. They show that the new mother is realising how little she knows. Most learning starts like this.

A newborn already knows his mother's heartbeat, her voice and perhaps her moods. He may know more about her than she about him. Yet she is usually the first adult to create a relationship with him. He will learn what he can expect from other people by the way she connects to him. But it's not only he who learns from their relationship. Many of us completely revise our views on relating from being with our newborns.

It's odd that this whole area isn't taken more seriously because it can help us to understand what happens later. Children and adults describe the wonderful joy of intimate friendships – surely among the best experiences of our lives. Unfortunately, too many people today of all age groups grieve that their lives are lonely. They say they would like to 'find a soulmate' and 'be in a personal relationship'. Or, if they already are with someone, that they are anxious to 'make the relationship work'. But how is it, they ask themselves, that something they really want seems so difficult to achieve? Asking mothers what they have learned from their intimate moments with their newborns, and also their toddlers, growing children and teens might help to explain this.

Building relationships is a vital part of mothering. It's what distinguishes the mother from the father, other relatives and everyone else. The mother has carried the baby through pregnancy and given birth to him. After the birth, mothers describe feeling overwhelmed by strong emotions: 'Most mothers either fall in love with their babies, or want to, or wish they could, or regret that they have not,' wrote the paediatrician Daniel Stern towards the end of a lifetime's study of mothers.[2] Some mothers say they feel more protective than loving. Others feel numb at first, and their strong motherly feelings emerge months later.

Parents are legally responsible for their children. But, within the law, a mother is free to treat her child how she chooses. Cultures vary, and some are more restrictive than others. But mothering can't be handed down unchanged, even from mother to daughter. There are always times when the new mother has to decide what she believes is best. She may act on impulse, and only discover afterwards why she reacted as she did. Perhaps she tells her visitors: 'Shh! The baby's just fallen asleep.' So she has put her newborn's need for sleep above the excited chatter of her visitors. She may surprise herself by how sharply her words come out. She is learning what her priorities are.

Luckily, mothers aren't lumbered with a set of 'relationship milestones'. There are no supervisors to impress, tests to pass, or diplomas to be awarded on this. Instead, mothers are free to make choices, free to make mistakes, recover and learn. There is a lot to find out about relationships, and mothers often turn into life-long learners.

And yet, however much a mother learns from mothering, she will find that she gets little social recognition for it. Mothers rarely publish anything about their insights, so people dismiss their achievements as 'babycare' or 'childcare', which means the practical management – the *visible* side of mothering. The relational side tends to go unseen.

However, by the time mothers resume their paid work, they find they have learned so much. It's probably fair to say that each mother understands more than she did before having children. She has faced ethical questions, and countless temptations arising from being a more experienced person making decisions about a less experienced one. She understands more about vulnerability and pain. She feels much closer to creation than to destruction. Usually getting to know her baby means that a mother has learned to recognise some of the basics of human nature, and how far it is influenced by family patterns. Also, because a young baby can't talk, she has become perceptive at reading not just facial but subtle whole-body signals. On a practical level, she has learned how to save time, how to focus and how to plan ahead. Her baby may want her attention as suddenly as any employer, so she has learned to prepare for contingencies.

All this and more can be adapted for her workplace. So no mother should have to apologise for having taken 'time out' from her paid work to be with her children. Employers should head-hunt returning mothers and be thankful to have them on their payroll.

As mothers learn so much, you might think that what they learn has been the subject of many research studies. So it's odd to find that it has hardly been researched at all. There are some general results from studies which focus on other questions. For example, in 1954, a team of anthropologists, psychologists and sociologists set up a large project to visit and interview mothers in six cultures from Orchard Town, New England; Mixtecan mothers of Juxtlahuaca in Mexico; mothers of Tarong, the Philippines; mothers of Taira, Okinawa, Japan; Rajput mothers of Khalapur, India; and Gusii mothers of Nyansongo, Kenya. They coded and analysed their results, and published them in *Mothers of Six Cultures* in 1964. One conclusion they reached was that, in each culture, mothers were pragmatic and learned what to do, not from theories, but by solving problems resulting, for example, from family size, the composition of the household and the mother's workload.[3]

This is a significant result. It challenges researchers who believe that mothers are influenced by theories of childcare.[4] But one drawback of a large study is how unwieldy it can become. For example, researchers have to keep to the same set of questions for each group of mothers that they interview. It must narrow what they can find. An Indian researcher on a similar project wrote: 'Therefore the tone of the interview [between herself and mothers or caregivers] was conversational and informal, though I knew when to ... guide the conversation to make sure that all the topics in my agenda were covered.'[5]

Having an agenda makes a difference. One German researcher who was interviewing Gujarati mothers wrote: 'We were often confronted with questions like: "Why do you want to talk about babies for two hours? They have to be bathed, breastfed and cleaned. What else is there to talk about?"'[6]

Mothers don't always realise how much they have learned. If they start talking without a particular agenda, a discussion of bathing a baby can soon go beyond the practicalities. Mothers describe their feelings – their pleasure in the tenderness of the baby's skin; the realisation that he is also strong, and could wriggle so they might drop him; the terror that his wet body could suddenly slide from their hands and so easily drown – and then the whole experience of mothering deepens. Mothers realise that many of their individual experiences are shared. They often leave this kind of conversation saying: 'I thought I was crazy to feel things so intensely. Listening to the others, I realise I'm normal.'

I myself used to feel lonely as a mother. One afternoon, my friend and neighbour Janet Balaskas, founder of the Active Birth Centre, invited me to set up open mornings for mothers and babies. I started Mothers Talking on 30 January 1991. My children were already at school then, and the mothers who came had young babies. So I was at a different stage of mothering. And yet, right from the start, I noticed that there were essentials I shared, even with very new mothers. I recognise their questions and dilemmas, not just from my past but in my life today too.

It's wonderful to sit and listen to mothers without a structured agenda and without 'guiding the conversation'. I ask questions, but these are usually to clarify what a mother is saying. One mother may confess: 'I'm not the kind of mother I thought I would be.' Then I ask: 'Can you explain?' I discovered that most mothers think a lot and find it helpful to talk. They spend long hours observing their babies and have plenty to share. When a mother worries that she has 'nothing to say' this is usually because she is afraid the others wouldn't like to hear how she really feels. But becoming a mother is a humbling experience and most mothers are grateful to hear about one another's honest feelings.

My original plan was to use these meetings as 'background' for more structured research. But I soon wondered whether I would learn any more from using a formal methodology. True, I wasn't meeting a particular sample of mothers. The mothers who talk to me are self-selected, from many countries and from different family backgrounds. Some I see only once, while others I see weekly for several years because they return with second babies. Yet, from our informal conversations over several decades, I began to see patterns in what mothers were learning.

I am still finding fragments of what mothers learn. Each detail is important and has a place in the whole. I've tried to show how I think the details link up in the coming chapters. There is a lot to say, so I've had to cut and trim. There is much more that could be said by focusing on adoptive, single, immigrant and many other particular groups of mothers. And you may think of many more topics and examples that haven't occurred to me.

I think it's important to keep to the exact words that people use. I discovered I could train my ear to listen properly by chance at school. It was lunch break and raining hard, so we had to stay indoors. We all had rough notebooks, and I thought I'd write a story in mine. While I was sitting at my desk, wondering how to start, I heard a girl near by call out: 'O, O, O, where has my little dog gone?' I thought this sounded quite strange, so I wrote it down. And that started me scribbling down what the others in my classroom were saying. I noted everything I could hear. There were long silences when no one said anything, and then a rush of voices from different parts of the room. Soon I had pages of writing. It looked curiously alive, more than the stories I used to write. After that, I would often jot down what I could hear people saying. This taught me about the musical way they speak, their speech rhythms and how they often don't respond to one another directly. Now I am grateful because all this helps me to remember.

Later, at another school, and as part of A-level English, I studied the General Prologue to Chaucer's *The Canterbury Tales*. Here Chaucer introduces all the pilgrims who are going to tell stories on the long walk from London to Canterbury. When each pilgrim has been introduced, Chaucer suddenly speaks directly to us, his readers. He explains the importance of being faithful to the exact words the storytellers will use.

> Whoso shal telle a tale after a man,
> He moot reherce as ny as evere he kan
> Everich a word, if it be in his charge,
> Al speke he never so rudeliche and large,
> Or ellis he moot telle his tale untrewe,
> Or feyne thyng, or fynde wordes newe.
> He may nat spare, althogh he were his brother;
> He moot as wel seye o word as another.[7]

Although Chaucer's tales are fictional, there is wisdom in his words.

At Mothers Talking meetings, we sit in a circle with mugs of drinks, while babies and toddlers watch one another and explore. They are obviously learning as much as we are.

Their energy is amazing. Where did they come from, these

active young people with their reverence for life, their great hearts, their logic and intelligence? How have they been entrusted to *us*, with all our faults and weaknesses? We know what stupid things we do. How can we be good enough to look after them? It's this recognition of our responsibility and our fallibility that gives us a shared mothering base.

So as the Gujarati mothers asked: 'What else is there to talk about' every week? The themes are in the chapters that follow. There is some repetition because the subjects of some chapters overlap, and some themes have also been discussed in my two earlier books.[8] But one idea can belong to several contexts and can grow in meaning when discussed for a second and third time.

The more we talk about what mothers learn, the more its importance becomes obvious. And mothers learn so much that the rest of society needs to hear.

CHAPTER ONE

Intelligent work

Women who become mothers often feel as though they have crossed an invisible line. On the side where they used to be, they saw themselves as respected members of the working community. They only discover the unfamiliar other side as mothers. There, they find they have to work very hard to look after their babies. Yet they have lost their social standing as people who are seen as 'working'.

> My friends don't understand what I do at home all day. They say: 'You could take up a hobby.' [G, 2 months]

New mothers on maternity leave are surprised by how often they are asked: 'When are you going back to work?' People tend to put this question in a slightly impatient tone. They sound as if they consider looking after a baby an avoidance of 'real' work. It's true that mothers may also be told: 'Being a mother is the hardest job in the world!' But do people really believe this?

Some people are frank about what they think.

> I went into work and my boss asked me how I was. I said: 'Well, you know, it's quite hard work with two small kids.' And he said:

'Oh, come on! It's not *work*. All you have to do is change a few nappies.' [G, 3 years; B, 8 months]

The mother and her boss both spoke about 'work'. But the boss confidently claimed the word, challenging the mother to admit that she was wrong to have used it. Many people would share his reaction, though they might not have put it so bluntly.

Mothers can feel discouraged by this way of looking at themselves.

I feel so unimportant being at home with my girls all day. What have I got to talk about? My husband comes home and he's been involved in moving millions of dollars around. I've just been looking after two children. [1G, 3 years; 2G, 2 months]

This mother's view is understandable. Anyone who wants to know about the current view of mothers has only to look at our language. A mother, when she is employed for a job *other* than mothering her child, is called a '*working* mother'. But when she is with her child (sometimes after a long day's employed work, and with the prospect of broken sleep if the child needs her at night), she is said to be free or on leisure time. She's not working. Or she may be on 'maternity leave', which sounds like a normal holiday with a baby thrown in. Then she is classified as 'inactive', 'unoccupied' or 'a non-producer'. In this crude way, our language conveys the message that only 'working mothers' are pulling their weight – and then, only in their 'working' hours. It means that when full- and part-time mothers are with their children, they aren't perceived as doing valuable work.

People hurrying to their workplaces sometimes catch sight of a group of mothers sitting around a table in a café. Most have babies with them, and some have taken older siblings to school. One journalist voiced a common resentment towards them:

Moments after the morning school drop-off, groups of women [i.e. mothers] flutter to the nearest skinny latte . . . To use the fact of having once upon a time given birth as an excuse to hang around doing nothing else productive for the rest of your life does not mean you are a full-time mother ... it means you are a lazy mare.'[9]

You could defend mothers by arguing that they, like office workers, are entitled to a coffee break. But what do they need a break *from?* What have they produced?

Usually, if you ask, mothers will give you a list of their practical tasks. These lists do partly explain mothering, but they also belittle it. 'Churning out pasta and wiping noses,' wrote one mother.[10] 'Cleaning and cooking cupcakes and breastfeeding all the time,' wrote another.[11] Even Allison Pearson, mother, author and an outspoken journalist-defender of mothers, describes a mother's work as 'often numbing' and task-focused. Her list includes: '. . . the unsung and largely unacknowledged loving and often numbing work which millions of mothers do every day because it is the woman who carries the puzzle of family life in her head: that great 3-D jigsaw of birthdays, shoe sizes, packed lunches, nutritious meals, carol concerts and chickenpox.'[12]

Seen in this way, a mother's work sounds like one long succession of daily practical tasks. As Pearson says, they go 'largely unacknowledged'. Adrienne Rich sums it up in her pioneering book, *Of Woman Born*: '. . . the woman at home with children [i.e. their mother] is not believed to be doing serious work.'[13] The mother's work seems limited to doing menial tasks for her child. So it sounds necessary but not very exciting. A career suggests serious work that earns payment and respect.

This was the conclusion of Rebecca Asher, author of *Shattered: Modern Motherhood and the Illusion of Equality*. She argues that parenting should be shared equally between willing parent-couples. She contrasts this with her own unshared experience of mothering, which she describes as 'gruelling, unacknowledged servitude'[14] on behalf of 'our infant deities'.[15] She writes: 'I took my baby swimming, swishing him about in the pool as if washing a precious piece of cloth, while he blinked the water from his eyes and stared straight ahead.'[16]

Looked at this way, here is an intelligent woman, plunged into the apparently dull world of childcare where there simply isn't enough to interest or engage her. But looked at differently, surely this is an opportunity lost. Here she is with her baby, yet she doesn't seem to treat him like a person. It seems odd to compare him to 'a precious piece of cloth'. She describes taking him swimming as if it were one more act of servitude. If he 'stared straight ahead', it's possible that she wasn't making eye contact with him.

She sums up her time as a new mother:

> Having had a busy and purposeful life, I now occupied a universe where, apart from the grindingly repetitive tasks centred on feeding and cleaning my child, activity existed in the main simply to fill the time. I vacillated between a desperate hunger for tips on encouraging my child to sleep and a head-pounding boredom with this narrow entirely baby-centric world.[17]

Is this, then, the only possible reality of motherhood? Does being a mother mean entering a 'narrow' world? And does it have to be 'entirely baby-centric'? Couldn't it turn into a life that mothers and babies share? In a shared world, the whole work of being a mother could be the opposite of 'head-pounding boredom'. Asher's head might pound instead with all the challenging questions it puts to her.

Mary Wollstonecraft, the dynamic eighteenth-century writer, often called Britain's first feminist, was passionately in favour of women developing themselves and using their talents. But she believed this *included* becoming a mother. In her words, 'To be a good mother a woman must have sense, and . . . independence of mind'.[18]

What has 'independence of mind' to do with changing nappies

and all the other 'grindingly repetitive' routine chores of baby care? 'We *think* differently,' concluded Sara Ruddick, the feminist philosopher who wrote and lectured on maternal thinking.[19] She explained: 'Maternal work itself demands that mothers think; out of this need for thoughtfulness, a distinctive discipline emerges.'[20] Other women have made similar observations. 'Becoming mothers had given us more to think about,' wrote Camille Peri and Kate Moses in *Mothers Who Think,* the anthology they edited.[21] 'Children continually make you flex your brains,' observed Katherine Ellison who wrote *The Mommy Brain.*[22]

Nor is thinking a luxury confined to modern, well-educated mothers. 'I think a lot,' wrote an unnamed mother, more than a century ago, 'but cannot express it, as I had to leave school at the age of ten years to go into farm service.'[23] And in 2008, three American researchers published the results of a study in which they'd observed a sample of mothers and children at home. The title of their paper reveals their conclusion: 'Mothering: Thinking is Part of the Job Description'. 'Mothers', they wrote, 'were busy thinking as they accomplished their job.'[24]

> My academic friends say to me: 'Some of us would rather use our brains. We enjoy *thinking.*' It's hard to explain. I *am* thinking. [G, 23 months]

> I see red when people tell me they couldn't be a full-time mother because they like thinking. I feel like answering: 'Well, you swap with me, then, and have my kids for a morning, and see how much it gets you thinking!' [1G, 5 years; 2G, 2 years; B, 10 months]

The most challenging work usually requires a good deal of intelligent thought. But thought is not often associated with mothers. Indeed, many mothers complain that motherhood has changed them, and that now they *can't* think. The change starts in pregnancy when many have moments of being forgetful and dreamy. 'My brain has turned to mush,' they say. They feel shocked that they can no longer think in their usual problem-solving way. They fear that they have permanently lost the brainpower to manage their paid work.

Expectant mothers may have moments when they look as if they are daydreaming. Then, if someone asks what they are thinking about, they look startled and reply: 'Nothing.' But is it really nothing, or just hard to explain?

If mothers 'think differently', as Sara Ruddick argues, what (if anything) do they think about?

> I walked down the high street by myself, a week ago, and it felt *weird*. What did I used to think about before I had B? [B, 2 months]

> I'm never *not* thinking of B. He's always on my mind. But it's hard to put it into words. [*She was holding B and busy showing him a hanging mobile while she talked.*] It's the hardest work I've ever done. B keeps changing. All the time. I have such admiration for mothers now. What mothers do is silent. No one talks about it. [B, 3 months]

> G needs a special kind of attention, mental and physical. I'm always thinking of her. When I'm at work, I might feel tired, but I could always pull out one more stop. G switches on a special something in my brain. By the end of the day, there's nothing more I can pull out. I'm exhausted. [G, 16 months]

A lot of motherly thinking takes the form of questions. 'Question posing', wrote the American psychologist Mary Field Belenky, 'is central to maternal practice in its most evolved form.'[25]

> I have all these questions going round my head that I never had before having a baby. Like: what is a *person*? How do I do my best for G? [G, 15 months]

Whatever mothering choices you make, there are always times

when you doubt yourself and wonder if you're doing the right thing. [G, 3 years; B, 19 months]

Me: What about you, M? You have three children. Do you still ask yourself questions, or do you know the answers by now?

Mother: I keep asking myself questions. Every minute of the day. There is so much to question. [G, 5 years; 1B, 3 years; 2B, 11 months]

Everyone says that mothers 'know best'. How they get so much knowledge is not explained. Most mothers wish they knew more. They have many questions with no obvious answers.

It used to help me to say: 'I don't know what to do.' I'd say it to the children, and it saved me from having to be an expert. And it's still like that. You *still* worry with the older ones only over different things. My youngest won't study. He just won't. I don't know what to do about that. [G, 21 years; 1B, 18 years; 2B, 15 years]

Mothers are often accused of being too insular and of thinking only about themselves and their families. But this can't be right as their questions quickly broaden out into universal ones.

I look at older boys and think: B will be one of those. And it's made me look at gangs of teenage boys differently. Each one was a baby once. [B, 3 months]

You hear about people doing terrible things and you think: They were *babies* once. How did they get to that state? What happened in between? [B, 5 months]

When do you take risks for the future of the world that your child will inherit [*she was a journalist referring to politically dangerous areas that might be life-threatening for her*]? And when do you keep safe for your child's sake? I have no answer to that. [B, 21 months]

Mothers are usually sleep-deprived. They rarely have the energy to follow their questions through with clear analysis and research. They say they just have to 'get on with it'. But many of their questions do need answers. Often, answers emerge in stages, as mothers try something and see if it works.

A baby looks both wise and vulnerable, and his mother longs to do her best for him. But what is her best? She may have read a lot about what is 'good for babies'. But her baby usually has his own ideas – about, for example, whether he wants to be put down for a nap that he is supposed to need. When she lays him down and he cries in distress, her heart goes out to him and all her theories can seem irrelevant.

> I'm a health professional. I've got a lot of experience in child health and I thought I was well prepared. But when B is upset, I forget all my knowledge. It's gone to another part of my brain. Last week, I decided I knew *nothing* and I'd have to start all over again. So I'm starting by looking at B and trying to understand what he's trying to tell me. [B, 3 months]

There's a great difference between a professional understanding of child health and a mother's immediate emotional response. She may react quicker than thought. She may be deep in planning when her baby gives a loud cry. She picks him up at once. The cry startled her and she acted before thinking. But then she will wonder about what she did. Was it the right thing to do? Would her mother have done the same? Should a mother always react to her baby every time he cries? Mothering can feel like a cascade of questions without answers.

Do all mothers question in such depth? It's hard to know. However, it can be difficult for a mother to think about her baby if she is too worried about 'failing' as a mother. That kind of worry focuses her attention on herself. In an interesting essay, 'Learning to think', the educationalist Professor W. D. Wall identified anxiety as a major blockage to learning, especially anxiety about failure.[26] Many mothers describe exactly this kind of anxiety.

> I don't listen to B's voice. I am too busy with my own voice. I'm thinking: why is B crying? What do I do now? I don't know what to do. I don't know what he wants. But I have to learn to stop my voice and *listen* to what he is telling me. [B, 3 months]

So how do mothers listen to their babies? Can they learn, even if they are anxious? How do they start?

Here is a mother with her newborn. She has just fed him. Now his eyeballs roll up and his eyelids half-close. He gives a tiny sigh. He seems ready for sleep. She rocks him gently. But suddenly he's wide awake, mouth open, turning his head and urgently wanting to feed. But I've just fed him, she thinks. He can't be hungry again so soon. *I* wouldn't be hungry after a big meal. Well, I suppose I'm not a baby. Perhaps a *baby* could be hungry again.

This represents quite a jump in her thinking. She is an adult; it's a long time since she was a baby herself – yet she has made the shift from thinking how *she* would feel to imagining how her baby might. It's guesswork and she may have got it wrong, but she's trying. Professor Wall observed that learning begins when a person sees a problem that they want to solve. This mother saw her baby looking hungry as a problem. Another mother might think: 'It's the wrong time for my baby's feed,' by which she means that, in this situation, she has an answer, so she doesn't see a problem to solve or anything to learn.

This first mother started to solve her problem by asking herself how her baby might be feeling. It might not sound very much, but it's a big step forward as a mother. She is learning that her relationship to her child is not only based on their sameness. It depends on her realising that he will sometimes be different.

So now the mother is ready to accept that, yes, maybe her baby wants to feed. What should she do about it? Should she feed him right away? She was planning for them both to go out. Should she teach him to wait? She might not have time to question herself in words, but her actions will reflect a decision, and her baby will learn from her. The two of them are starting a 'conversation' together.

It might sound a very simple kind of conversation, but the baby depends on it. He is unlikely to have connected a painful bodily sensation with his desire for food. He needs his mother to guess what he wants and then decide if he should have it. And even if he isn't hungry, his mother can't sit back and forget about him. He needs her to keep observing and thinking about him while he is awake.

Eventually, this will bring the mother autonomy – not the autonomy of her previous way of life, but a new sort. The more she learns about her child, the less she will need to consult child-care manuals to tell her how to run her everyday life, or worry because her mother friends are making decisions that are different from hers. As she discovers more about her baby and her baby about her, the two of them can work things out together.

> When G was one month old, my husband went back to work and I found she wouldn't let me put her down. At first, I found that difficult. And then I thought to myself that I didn't *need* to put her down. I just thought that I did. But when I really *thought* about it, nothing seemed worth putting her down for. If she was happy, I could be happy. And holding her was an easy way to keep her happy. Nothing else seemed important. I mean, I didn't think it as clearly as I've just said it. But that's what I meant. [G, 15 months]

For the first few weeks, the baby will barely be able to raise his head. Yet he dislikes being bored and is eager to learn about everything. I have seen a mother reach into a toy box and pick out a silver bell or some bright beads – guessing with precision what her child would enjoy. He needs his mother to hold the object at exactly the right distance for him to study, because he can't do this for himself. When she does, his eyes grow round, and he kicks in excitement. Then his whole body goes still with interest.

In time, the mother is able to make observations like: 'I expect he's hungry,' or 'He's probably bored.' Her phrasing may be tentative, but she is *almost* sure. His needs and moods are starting to be familiar. She is beginning to understand him and to distinguish his signs of hunger from tiredness, or need for stimulation, and more. So they emerge from chaos into some kind of order.

> F was driving; it was a long journey and B was strapped in his child seat behind us, making a lot of noise. F and I both found the long journey difficult. And I suddenly realised that B did too. Then I could stop hearing what he was doing as making a horrible noise, and see from his point of view, that he found the journey as difficult as we did. [B, 6 months]

Each time she thinks about her baby and makes more sense of his behaviour, the mother experiences a burst of excited 'Oh-I-*see!*' energy. This energy, in turn, enables her to recognise him as a reasonable person like herself.

While thinking about him, she often has to put aside thoughts about herself. These can be basic, such as: 'I need a drink of water *and* I need to pee.' Or, 'Is there anything clean I can wear today?' These thoughts must wait until she has time for them. Then they can sound reassuring. They remind her of her own separate self.

> My friend rang and asked about coming to my [*university*] graduation. It's a good thing she reminded me. It was the very next day, but the date had completely gone out of my head. [B, 6 weeks]

Thinking about her baby in this intense way goes against the current belief that a woman should focus on her own interests, which requires her to keep her own perspective. But at first mothers seem to be doing the opposite, focusing so much on their babies that they almost forget about themselves.

> F keeps asking me how I am. And my answer is all about how B is. My head is full of B. I forget about myself. [B, 8 months]

All the while, as the mother focuses intently on her child, he is studying her and learning about her world. From his point of view, his thinking is very much about her. Making sense of her must be puzzling at first. On one occasion, he cries and finds he receives a good deal of sympathetic motherly attention. On another, he cries in exactly the same way, but is told to hush. At one moment, there seems a frantic need for them both to hurry. Then, a bit later, his mother stops hurrying and, for no obvious reason, he has to wait. Babies have to spend long stretches of time waiting, for reasons that they cannot understand. At these moments, mothers have focused their attention back on to their other responsibilities.

Not everyone chooses to be sensitive to a baby's feelings. When a baby cries, some people will dismiss him as 'only crying for attention'. By chance, one mother found herself in what might be similar to a baby's situation. It helped her to realise what a great difference personal attention can make.

> When I was in hospital last week [*with a painful gallstone*], I was left in a kind of cot-thing with all the staff hurrying past. I learned afterwards that they were doing everything necessary and that I was being well looked after. But I suddenly realised what a baby must feel when nobody has time for it. I could have done with someone stopping by to ask how I was. [B, 7 months]

It sounds a useful recognition. Babies, like adults, want to be in touch with the people looking after them.

A mother can usually give more personal attention than the staff of a busy hospital. When she thinks intensely about her baby, he seems to feel it. So why isn't this better recognised? Why isn't there a proper job description that includes thinking with the lists of tasks? The answer seems to be that thinking is invisible. Although many mothers learn to use their intelligence to make sense of their babies, they don't seem to notice what they have achieved.

> When G was one week old, my in-laws came to visit. They were all over G the *whole* time. After a bit, G started crying. I could hear that her crying had a desperate sound that I'd never heard before. Everyone was saying to her: 'Have you got wind?' 'Have you got a sore tummy?' I wanted to shout: 'No, it's *you*!' That's one thing I wish I'd done differently. [G, 7 months]

In other words, after just one week, this mother had already learned so much about her little daughter that she knew immediately that her baby couldn't be uncomfortable from wind or from a stomachache but from too much exposure to her visitors. Yet she didn't stop to appreciate her new understanding. Her overriding feeling was shame that she had lacked the courage to act on it to protect her daughter. She didn't recognise that she had *acquired* such intimate knowledge in the first place.

This knowledge has to be updated all the time. Babies develop in spurts that surprise everyone. Mothers often discover by chance that their children have taken a developmental leap, so they have to update their ideas. New questions arise at every change.

> I've moved to a new stage of being a mother. Now B can crawl, it's my job to keep him safe. I used to leave him to explore, because that was the way he would learn. But now he can reach more dangerous things. My dilemma is now that every time I rescue him and save him from hurting himself, I am *depriving* him of the chance to learn. [B, 9 months]

Because babies change, mothers learn to be adaptable. They

find they may have to change plans at any moment, and that it's pointless to fill the day with ambitious ones. And how do mothers adapt to several children simultaneously?

Me: How do you keep track of three children and yourself?

Mother: I don't. I don't know what 'keeping track' means. I am empathic to each. I can *feel* what each one would like. But whatever we do it never works for all of us. [G, 5 years; 1B, 3 years; 2B, 15 months]

And focusing on each child can mean having so much to think about that the mother is in a constant rush. Many describe chaotic moments when thinking about their children has got too much.

Going out is such an operation. There isn't even time to think about a coat for myself. Have I packed everything for B? Have I got everything G will need? Then I open my bag on the stairs to check I've got my bus pass and all the sandwiches I'd made for our lunch tip out over the floor. [G, 22 months; B, 4 months]

Going out means that a mother has to consider social values too. After all, she has a public role as well as a private one. The private role concerns her growing relationship with her child. But she also has to act as a kind of two-way shock absorber between her child and other people. She tries to pre-empt situations when her child might inadvertently annoy others, and she also tries to make sure other people will not overly distress her child.

G is quite loud. I noticed it on the bus. To me, it's a happy sound because G is enjoying herself. But I'm aware that, to people on the bus, it might seem just a noise. So should I shush her? [G, 7 months]

I was telling B off at the playgroup, when I suddenly realised I wasn't doing it for him at all. It was to impress the other mothers.

B couldn't understand any of it. It was to show the mothers that I was taking B's bad behaviour seriously. [B, 3 years; G, 9 months]

In some situations, a mother who knows her child well may find herself taking a lone stand for what she believes is best for him. It's not always a matter of fitting in with social norms at the child's expense.

This week [*the start of her son's first term at school*], I've had the whole school, it seems, putting pressure on me to say goodbye to 1B and leave him while he was crying. I've never *ever* left him like that. So I stood my ground. I've never stood my ground like that in my whole life. I told them: 'I'm trying to build 1B's confidence and make sure he *loves* school. I don't want him to develop a school phobia.' [1B, 4 years; 2B, 13 months]

Because she insisted, and put her concerns so well, she got the school staff to listen to her and give her time to calm her son every morning before she left him. Sure enough, just as she intended, he quickly came to love being at school.

All these actions – observing her newborn, learning to understand him, starting a 'conversation' with him, updating her 'risk list' to keep him safe, solving issues about how other people react to him – are part of mothering. They require constant intelligent thought.

However, is all this thought *really* necessary? Can it really be worth the time and energy of millions of individual mothers who delay their return to the workforce? Won't children turn out perfectly well with a quarter as much motherly care?

It's difficult to answer these questions, though researchers have tried. We can't key in a set of maternal actions and add them up to show that they produce a precise result – children are sensitive and respond to all kinds of influences. But neither can we discount all that mothers do.

Mothers have their own doubts about the value of their work.

B is lovely. But I never know if I have helped, or if it's his nature and he'd be as lovely as this anyway. [B, 10 months]

This brings us back to our earlier question about the mothers in a café: if they are on a coffee break, what are they on a break from? What exactly is their work? What are they producing?

Unlike many workers, mothers can't point to a precise outcome. There is no such thing as a 'finished child'. Yet mothers are continually working. They are in a position of great power over a dependent person. How they use this power is crucial. Each mother makes her own choices, whether consciously or not. These choices, which can seem trivial and hurried at the time, really matter.

With each child, the mother confronts the basics of human nature. Every baby is born with the potential to be both kind and cruel. A newborn is at his most sensitive, most inexperienced and most impressionable. If his mother treats him cruelly, he is likely to withdraw in self-defence and to put up a protective shield towards her and other people. (Though he may also withdraw because of other circumstances not connected with her.) If she is kind to him, learns to understand him and enjoys being with him, he will respond to her with all the passionate warmth of a new person.

Together, mother and baby build up a pre-verbal conversation. The baby is learning to understand his mother, and feels understood by her. This gives him the confidence to 'talk' to the rest of us. It's not a final outcome, because the baby will continue to develop. Still, his ability to communicate is an achievement. And yet there is no word we could use to show that his mother has helped him.

The mother has shared her child's history and thinks about his future. Through her, he has changed from being an unknown newborn into a person with a unique past and an unfolding life story. Her thinking has helped him to feel connected to her, yet separate, whole and real. And this helps him relate to others.

> I can remember what I was like when I was three. B is quite different. He is far more confident than I ever was. So at last I can see where all that mothering went. B is very sociable and outgoing. He talks to everyone. [B, 3 years; 37 weeks pregnant]

> I've had my head down for five years. Suddenly I can lift it up and see where it's all going. G can relate to other people. To me, it looks very intense. But I think: No! It's normal. G can relate to people normally. I still can't do that myself. But that's what all that mothering was about. [G, 5 years; 1B, 3 years; 2B, 14 months]

Children like these are warm and friendly. They can do for us what their mothers did for them: they can think about us. They can see how we are individual, yet connected. They can relate to us as people.

Long before he can talk, a baby can relate, sometimes to people who are complete strangers. 'Hel*lo*!' calls a passer-by. 'Excuse me, I couldn't help saying "Hello" to your baby. She gave me a very friendly look.' Or: 'Hi there, cheeky! What's that grin for?' Even a grumpy child still seems to give out social signals. 'Cheer up!' people say. 'You don't want a long face like that, do you, at your age?' Independently from his mother and from a very young age, her child has started his own relationships with other members of the human community.

At the same time, many mothers start to see themselves differently. Their perspective changes. Looking at their babies, they see how, for all our surface differences, we are akin. We share a 'common humanity' that connects us. This is what mothers discover for themselves. But it's rarely noticed. The journalist Lucy Cavendish quotes an angry full-time mother: 'No one pays us any attention. Working women look down upon us as though we are stupid and unfulfilled, chained to the sink. Well, we non-beings are the ones doing the hard job, bringing up the next generation with real values, manners and a sense of humanity.'[27]

Fortunately, there seem to be enough mothers who do bring up their children to recognise our shared humanity. These mothers are making an immense difference. The safety of our entire human civilisation, our politics and peacemaking, depends on enough people being able to think about others in situations different from their own, and to see that they are human too. It can be very difficult to bring up a child in a politically tense situation when the opposite side is portrayed as terrifying and subhuman. Some mothers in this predicament teach their children to demonise the opposite side. But enemy behaviour needs to be understood because it's not always what it seems. Aggressive threats may be no more than sabre-rattling. Submissive behaviour can be a form of passive aggression. Many of our crimes and wars are the result of people not understanding one another, misreading signals and reacting with hostility because they feel threatened and frightened.[28]

If we recognise what a good job these mothers are doing, and if we realise that we ourselves will benefit from a new generation of humane and sensible adults, we will have to accept that their work takes time. Of course, from an employer's or a colleague's point of view, it can be very inconvenient when a mother takes maternity leave; or only works for half the week; or suddenly decides to resign from her job.

So this leads to another issue: if mothering has true value, shouldn't mothers be entitled to financial grants for doing it? Shouldn't they be able to apply for funding? Not all mothers will want to. Some love their children, but feel mothering is not for them.[29] Others enjoy being with their children, provided they can combine it with paid employment. A minority can afford to look after their children without extra funding. But an uncounted number of mothers are distraught that they can't afford to look after them for as long as they want to. It's difficult for a mother to save enough money beforehand because, before her child is born, she can't predict how she will feel. Some mothers think they will get cabin fever looking after their children for six months, and then discover that even a year won't be enough; others can't wait to return to their paid work. A flexible system is urgently needed. It can't be right that so many willing mothers are prevented from doing this essential work for lack of money alone.

Mothering may look like an extravagance. Children want a lot of it at the beginning of their lives. But if we, as a society, can see that this will prove worthwhile, we should be calculating for the long term.

This can't be too difficult, so why has no one addressed the finances of mothers? At the moment, mothers are hampered from improving their situation because their work is misunderstood. It is perceived as a respite from 'real work', and a soft, playful, undemanding option. The amount of intelligent *thinking* needed for mothering has never been recognised. 'What is a great sorrow', wrote Sara Ruddick, 'is to find the task [of mothering] itself misdescribed, sentimentalised, and devalued.'[30] She published her paper back in 1983, but her conclusion is still true today.

Nancy Folbre, the American feminist economist, argued that 'primary caregivers' (by which she means mostly mothers) were doing necessary work and should receive economic support. 'Once [children] are brought into this word,' she said, 'we all have something to gain from fully developing their capabilities.'[31] However, Marilyn Waring, the New Zealand feminist, makes a sobering comment in her book with the significant title *Counting for Nothing: What Men Value and What Women are Worth*. Mothers, she says, 'are not even in the economic cycle in the first place'.[32]

If we want to change this, the first step must be to establish recognition for the true value of mothering. It should count for *something* and deserves the dignity of being classed as challenging work. It also needs to be distinguished from the work of professional child carers. From them, a child can learn important lessons – but different ones. What mothers learn to give, and what children learn from them, as we shall see in the next chapters, is distinct.

It's interesting that a person's work project may be called her or his 'baby'. People tend to be much more respectful and understanding when someone has a *symbolic* baby. They seem to accept that plenty of thought, emotional energy and time will be needed for it and that this will result in a valuable end product.

But a person's symbolic baby can't happen without mothers' work with real babies. All our transactions are founded on shared understandings and trust. They depend on enough mothers learning to communicate with their children. If too few mothers do this work, the hiatus may lead to a generation of adults who feel confused and suspicious of one another, impatient at listening to someone else's point of view and barely trusting any decisions but their own.

For a start, we could change our language. The expression 'on maternity leave' could be called 'doing maternal work'. And if – or more often *when* – the mother is doing paid work as well, whether part- or full-time, this could be acknowledged by a term such as 'dual-work mother'.

CHAPTER TWO

A special time

Babies seem to change when they reach three or four months. Up till then, mothers cradle their babies towards themselves, as if protecting them from too much stimulation from the outside world. But after that time, you can see a change. Babies seem to have 'arrived'. Mothers respond by holding them outwards to face the world – and babies seem excited to take in everything and to miss nothing.

Mother: B changed after about three months.

Me: In what way?

Mother: He became human. Before that, he seemed otherworldly. [B, 3 months]

A newborn's strangeness can disorientate his mother.

The first three months were hard. I lost all my confidence. I'm normally a confident person. Then I think B got more confident, so I did too. [B, 4 months]

So what happens during these early months? Babies can't tell us, but perhaps mothers can. Or can they? It's new for them too.

There's a particular time for young animals after their birth that zoologists call a 'critical' or 'sensitive' period. They are at their most impressionable then. Psychologists have noticed that human babies go through a similar period. And surely mothers are going through a 'sensitive' period of learning too.

Mothers start to change during pregnancy. Often, when they look back after giving birth, the expectant months seem unreal.

> I know that I *was* pregnant. I know it as a fact in my mind. I know
> I was getting bigger and more tired, and it was harder to get myself
> upstairs, and I kept needing to wee. But now I can't remember
> *any* of it. [G, 9 months]

Then there is birth itself, a momentous experience for most of us. Labour can remind us of a simpler way to be. 'The woman's body has to become soft, almost liquid,' said Ina May Gaskin, midwife and childbirth educator.[33] Contractions grow so powerful that we have to focus on them and stay in the present moment. For adults who are used to having all kinds of ideas and plans on the go, this can feel extraordinary. However, babies must be living entirely in the immediate present too. So when a mother has to focus on her contracting body, this may be the best possible preparation for meeting her baby for the first time.

> Birth put me in touch with my instincts. I don't think I understood
> what it meant to be a woman before. Suddenly money didn't
> matter, nor did power, success or . . . the only thing that mattered
> was my body and what I was feeling. [G, 4 years; B, 23 months]

People don't always realise how much these memories of the birth affect the mother afterwards. They can colour her early connection to her newborn. A joyous birth can make the relationship much easier. A traumatic birth can delay a mother's ability to turn her attention to her baby.

I was so looking forward to the birth. And it was traumatic. I still get flashbacks. [B, 6 months]

I'd had a lovely birth and I kept thinking about it while I was holding B. Those memories kept me going. [B, 19 months]

Yet, however it was, mother and baby have now met and are starting to get to know one another. Those first weeks can be intense, and, like pregnancy, hard to recall later on.

First mother: Everything's so blurry at first. [G, 4 months]

Second mother: Blurry, exactly, that's what I remember too. [B, 6 months]

Third mother: It's funny, I know I felt that too, but I can't even remember *that*. [B, 9 months]

The first few weeks were a *twilight* time. [B, 19 months]

It's not only first-time mothers who experience this.

First mother: No way after the birth could I just come down to everyday life. I was up in a cloud, in a haze. But I felt guilty towards B for enjoying it. [B, 3 years; G, 10 months]

Second mother: I *did* manage to enjoy the haze. It was lovely. [*Her firstborn was older.*] [B, 6 years; G, 3 months]

Looking back, one mother reflected:

Maybe that 'fuzzy' feeling is how it's meant to be. It makes you focus on what's immediately around you, and you feel very emotional, so you're more in touch with your baby. [B, 10 months]

One of the first things a mother may notice about her baby is how 'otherworldly' and peaceful he looks, especially when he is asleep. French obstetrician and writer Frederick Leboyer observed: 'The quiet, newborn baby radiates the most intense peace.'[34]

Mother: My baby didn't look like any of the names we had chosen for him when he was born. He hasn't got a name at the moment. [B, 4 weeks]

Me: What was wrong with the names you had chosen?

Mother: They were mostly warrior names. But when he was born, he looked very contained and peaceful.

Mother to the mother of a four-week-old: It's so lovely to see a small baby, so peaceful. G's not like that any more. [*Two weeks earlier, another mother had made exactly the same comment to this mother about how peaceful G had looked.*] [G, 2 months]

A newborn may get distressed if he is hurried from one place to another. But mothers often describe a social pressure to be on their feet quickly, acting 'normally'.

In the beginning, it was so hard to stop doing and just *be*. To find that stillness which is difficult to achieve when you are used to rushing around. [G, 4 months]

It's easier to think calmly when the baby is asleep. As soon as he is awake, the mother is faced with all the practical details of daily life. This usually means having to find out what her baby wants. A mother's mood can zigzag from bliss to anxiety, and from spiritual thoughts to very basic physical needs, such as feeding and cleaning.[35]

After nine months in the womb, babies usually want the warmth of being held by their mothers. This leads to practical concerns.

I'm afraid of my boyfriend going back to work and me being all alone with G. G doesn't like me to put her down. I don't know how I'll get to the toilet and look after myself . . . [G, 3 weeks]

If you sleep together, you don't dare cough in the middle of the night in case you wake them. [G, 4 months]

At first, G was so light that I worried that if I picked her up too strongly, she would go flying through the air. [G, 4 months]

In the early weeks, a baby can feel very uncomfortable and need a lot of comforting.

I'd forgotten a lot about my first baby – like the *hours* of crying over trapped wind. [G, 4 years; B, 4 weeks]

Many mothers feel they have been dropped in at the deep end.

It's wonderful, but it's all so new. If only I could have some time off. Just one day off! [B, 2 weeks]

It's mind-blowing. You don't get a simple version to begin with but something as complex as a real baby – and they let you go home with it! [B, 6 months]

Although in theory mothers have nine months to prepare, this preparation tends to be minimal. Usually mothers decide to continue at their work till their due dates, to maximise their maternity leave after the birth. In a work environment, the pressures and routines carry on as usual. So it's easy for a pregnant woman to get distracted and to forget that she will soon have a baby in her life.

After birth, most mothers leave the familiar working community to spend time at home. The privacy can be helpful in allowing mother and baby to have time to get to know one another. But it's a tremendous change of lifestyle. Mothers describe times when they look back on their pre-baby lives with intense nostalgia.

When we first got home with G [*from hospital*], I was terrified. I could hear the cool couple who were our neighbours talking in their garden, and I just wished I was like *them* – a couple without a baby. [G, 2 months]

I didn't like the chaos, the lack of sleep – and I thought of all the people having lunch at lunchtime when I couldn't. [G, 6 months]

I remember one night lying awake after midnight, before B was four months old. And I could hear in the street the 'tock-tock-tock' of high heels on the pavement. I imagined a young woman coming home late, looking gorgeous and glamorous, having had *fun*, and I felt so *jealous*. [B, 3 years]

Part of the difficulty of these first months is that there is a lot to learn. So you might expect mothers to be thankful when they emerge with some rudimentary knowledge and confidence. It's a surprise to discover that this is *not* how most feel. They say they feel more sad than thankful. They look back on those early weeks and see something that they didn't realise at the time.

First mother: Now those first days are over, I look at B and he's older now, and I feel quite sad. The early days were hard. But . . . they were . . . I don't know . . . somehow special. [B, 6 months]

Second mother: I know what you mean. I've felt it too. I don't know how to describe it, but I still feel sad knowing those times are gone. [G, 12 months]

There's a certain sense of loss when the baby stage is over. Even though you're glad your child has reached a new stage, you pack away the baby clothes with a sense of sadness. You can never get that time back. [G, 9 months]

First mother: I was in an odd state of *mourning* for the little baby that B used to be that I could just hold in my arms. [B, 10 months]

Second mother: I've felt that too. My daughter is quite independent now. Her horizons are stretching, and she's looking beyond me. She's not as dependent on me as she used to be. [G, 6 months]

This sadness isn't only true of first-time mothers. Second- and third-time mothers also describe it.

I feel sorry that my youngest is growing so fast. This special time is flying past and there's never enough time to enjoy it. I wish I could press the pause button and keep 2G the way she is. [B, 5 years; 1G, 2 years; 2G, 6 months]

What is it about this time that mothers wish they could keep? It seems hard to explain.

I've just come through a phase. My daughter isn't a new baby any more [*tears*]. I don't know how to describe what I have just come through. There are no *words* for it. I don't understand it myself. [G, 7 months]

Mothers perceive their dilemma more clearly when they see newer mothers struggling through these early months.

Newer mother: It's terrible to say it but I get so bored, waiting for G to fall asleep so I can do all the things I need to do. And these are all mindless repetitive tasks that take up all my time. By the end of the week, I can feel quite down. [G, 2 months]

More experienced mother: When I look at you holding your baby, I wish I had enjoyed it more myself. But, when G was that age, I was obsessed by keeping a clean house. Goodness knows why. [G, 10 months]

The mother's regret about her 'obsession' has been echoed by parents in a survey. More than two thirds of them said they wished they had spent more time cuddling their newborns instead of 'cleaning the house, losing their pregnancy weight and getting the baby into a strict routine'.[36]

Some mothers are distracted not so much by housework as with anxieties over their jobs and careers. Many sleep-deprived new mothers feel as though they will never be fit for work again. Others are troubled that their jobs will be restructured while they are on leave.

> I never really stopped working. My head was always full of work. I don't think I did myself any favours. [*Hugging B*] When I look back at the first months, I was always *so* stressed. [B, 11 months]

Writer Maeve Haran wrote a semi-autobiographical novel about a new mother that brings us closer to the problem. Her heroine, Liz, tried to combine her high-flying career with having children:

> Liz had loathed breastfeeding; she knew some people loved it, but it had always been hard for her . . . She'd prayed for the day the whole messy painful business would end. And then when it did, when she weaned them onto bottles . . . she'd felt an unexpected sadness so powerful she'd wept. A bond had been ripped through.[37]

'A bond had been ripped through.' This painful sentence is revealing. It sounds as though Ms Haran's heroine felt sad because she hadn't noticed how, while she was breastfeeding and therefore physically close to her babies, some kind of bond or intimate connection had developed between herself and them. Only when she had weaned them did she realise that she had inadvertently 'ripped' something that was precious to her.

What had been ripped? Surely these were the 'threads' of the relationship that had developed between mother and baby. There are long stretches of time when the mother is holding her newborn, rocking him, feeding him, comforting him and helping him to relax into sleep. It might look monotonous and repetitive, as if little is happening. But looks can be deceptive. The mother is discovering the feel of her baby, his smell, his different expressions of mood, and he is presumably getting to know her in the same way. Their future relationship will be built on what they first learn about one another.

The first few months, you are totally *immersed* in it. [G, 4 months]

First mother: I feel as if I went right down into deep water where I couldn't see anything. It was weird. Nothing was clear. And now, or maybe two months ago, I could come up and look around me. I feel so different. I've changed. And it may sound strange, but I feel free. [G, 5 months]

Second mother: I recognise what you are saying about going into deep water and coming up again. But coming up took me *six* months. [G, 8 months]

'Immersion' and 'deep water' sound good descriptions of living with a baby. But mothers need to feel safe enough to immerse themselves in this way. The psychotherapist Sue Gerhardt described her sense of being uncomfortably 'underwater':

Living with a baby, time took on a different rhythm from the busy, noisy life in an office that I was used to, dealing with colleagues, with paperwork, phone calls, machines. At the beginning, it was rather like being underwater in a fascinating, gloomily lit aquarium, struggling to move around and to get anything done at all.[38]

The 'gloomily lit aquarium' she describes sounds watery, so she seems to have felt immersed, though not in an enjoyable way. She was 'struggling to move around' and to get things done. She noticed how 'time took on a different rhythm', which is an experience that most mothers will recognise. But, like many, she didn't welcome it. As mothers explain:

In the first months, time seems very strange. A minute can seem to last for ever, and a bit later you find that several hours have drifted past. [B, 6 months]

How come time goes so slowly, but it's always full of things to do, and at the end of the day you are always so exhausted? [B, 3 years; G, 11 months]

In retrospect, mothers can see that these early weeks could have been a chance to relax into a very different rhythm of time. That would have helped them to get to know their babies. After all, most babies, during these first months, seem intently interested in getting to know them.

> After six months, I felt different, like a mole emerging from a hole. It feels good but different. The intimacy will never be the same again. [B, 7 months]

> It was intimacy, absolute intimacy [*during the first three months*]. I had never known any intimacy like it. [G, 2 years]

Some mothers try to pass this discovery on to mothers of younger babies who are struggling in ways they remember only too well:

> *First mother:* Last night, B woke up every hour. In the morning, we both cried. When I'm tired, I can't be as good a mother as usual. I usually chat to B all the time. [B, 4 months]

> *Second mother:* But perhaps he doesn't need so much. You are giving him your *presence*: your lap, your arms, your smell, your milk . . . He is getting plenty of his mum! [B, 11 months]

> *Mother, to a newer mother:* When you feel you're muddling along and not getting anything done, you are being *present* to your child. [*She was the first mother in the previous example, so this idea had obviously helped her.*] [B, 5 months]

What happens when a mother allows herself to feel less anxious, more present and to 'immerse herself' in the early months of mothering? Her feelings can surprise her.

> I didn't think I'd like being pregnant. I thought it would feel weird to have an alien being inside me. I was terrified of giving birth. I thought I'd schedule a Caesarean. I thought I'd give breastfeeding

a try, but I thought it was what Earth-type mothers did, not really me. But actually being pregnant was very nice. I planned for a natural birth. It didn't happen, but . . . And I *love* breastfeeding. [B, 2 months]

Before B was born, I thought it was important to be a bit detached from your baby. That's what I *thought*. Then B was born and my heart exploded open [*tears*]. I didn't know I could love so much. I love cuddling B and I love the way B holds on to me. [B, 3 months]

I feel so moved at the way G looks at me with her big undefended eyes. [G, 3 months]

These are accounts of intimate relationships that mothers discover with their babies. Mothers need to be relaxed enough to allow their own strong feelings to flow. For some, this takes months. Others say that they only feel safe enough with a second baby.

Becoming a mother was a shock the first time. I was terrified. I didn't know what to do when G cried. Having a baby hadn't been part of my life plan, but I fell in love with my husband and he wanted children. I did it for him, but I lost the whole of my identity. But with B, everything is easier. I feel like I think a mother is meant to feel now. [G, 18 months; B, 4 weeks]

I was thirty-nine when I had B. For the first three months, I was like this [*gesturing agonised tension*] because I was so afraid something might happen to him. But with G I was able to love her straight away. It's really nice. [B, 22 months; G, 4 months]

Most babies like to be carried a lot. Some mothers feel trapped by such physical closeness. Mothers might find it easier if they could be sure that this was a phase, not a permanent state.

I feel sad that these first months are over. I wish someone had told me that they wouldn't last. I mean, of *course* they don't last for ever. But I didn't know that, and somehow I thought B would always want me to carry him. I could have relaxed and enjoyed it more if I'd known. Now B has changed and he likes to play by himself. [B, 4 months]

G used to keep very close to me, and I used to feel it would be marvellous to get my hands free. Now she can move a little way away from me, and I feel so sad. [G, 10 months]

A baby's need for his mother can seem infinite. Adults usually indicate how much they want from one another. Each has certain limits, though these may be signalled rather than spoken. A baby has not learned such limits. Yet each baby *does* have limits of his own. A mother can discover them if she has the chance to slow down her busy life enough to notice. Mothers who complain that their babies' need for them is never-ending may not have done this.

They have their little rhythms. B likes to sleep after his morning feed. He's a very easy baby. If you look, he makes it obvious what he wants. You have to *look*. [B, 4 weeks]

G gives me little signs when she's tired like rubbing her eyes. If I miss that moment, she'll be wide awake again. But she does make it perfectly clear. [G, 3 months]

The early months can feel intense and mothers often say that they would like time away from their babies. But paradoxically, when they get time away, many report that they don't enjoy it nearly as much as they had expected.

My partner and I had a first evening out since B was born. My sister looked after him. She's brilliant with children, so I felt safe with her. But I noticed, in the taxi, that my heart was pounding. And I didn't like the restaurant as much as I'd hoped, and I spent the whole hour watching my phone [*in case her sister sent her a*

message]. We got back and B hadn't woken up. But I don't think
I'll repeat that for a while. [B, 4 months]

It's significant that she didn't want to repeat that outing, even
though her son hadn't woken up. Many mothers describe the need
to keep holding and touching their babies.

I went out with two friends and had two glasses of white wine at
a wine bar. Then they decided to go on somewhere else. But I
really needed G. Suddenly I felt *desperate*. I took a taxi home. When
I finally got back and took G in my arms, I thought: it's [*big sigh*]
okay! I don't mean I just thought everything in my home was okay.
Everything [*gesturing with her hands the entire world*] was okay.
[G, 4 months]

By being 'in touch' with her baby, a mother can continue a kind
of pre-verbal conversation. Going out for the evening may sound
like a treat, but can turn out to be more of an interruption.
    What kind of 'conversation' do mothers and babies develop?
Whatever have they got to 'talk' about? The next mother only
realised little details she had learned because she saw that her
partner *hadn't* learned them.

F was pushing the pram and B was crying. I said: 'Shall I just
check?' because I could tell from the crying that B needed attention.
F said: 'No, he's all right.' I couldn't help it. I had a peek and saw
that B's hat had slipped over his eyes. I pushed it back up his
forehead and B stopped crying. F said: 'Oh, you were right.' [B, 4
weeks]

Not all mothers find it easy to understand the signals of their
babies.

It was hard at first. I was so *frightened*. I was at home with B and
I didn't *know* him. I couldn't understand what he wanted. He kept
crying, and my mum and my partner and I thought it was trapped

wind. We kept taking turns to walk up and down with him, patting his back. But then I realised he was *tired* and we'd just been over-stimulating him. [B, 6 weeks]

To be honest, I didn't think I'd last three months at first. I couldn't work my baby out at all. Nothing made sense. I felt so *tired*, as if my head would burst. Then I sort of gave up trying. That's when little bits began to make sense. I completely 'get' her now. [G, 5 months]

Because this understanding takes a good deal of concentration, a new mother is in a very sensitive state. She bears the ultimate responsibility for the survival and well-being of her baby. A lot depends on her being able to understand him. So, as well as the joy and excitement, most mothers experience times of acute exis-tential anxiety about whether they will survive as mothers.

I don't want to wish this time away. I want to relax and enjoy it. But I *am* anxious. My chief fear, my *dread*, is that I might die. [G, 3 weeks]

First mother: I get so anxious that I've got F to sleep with G because he's calmer. My heart's pounding. I don't know what it's about. [G, 4 months]

Second mother: My heart used to pound too. I'm less anxious now. It's not gone, but it's not so much. [G, 7 months]

First mother: My midwife asks if I'm depressed. No, I'm not depressed. I look forward to things. So I call it postnatal *weirdness*. I have all these feelings – a burning chest, heart beating very fast and I keep dropping things – it frightens me. [G, 2 months]

Second mother: I'm so glad you said that. One time, I had a panic attack. It was just after I'd seen my midwife. She told me to do all the opposite things from what my mother was saying. That *totally* confused me. Suddenly I couldn't breathe. I was almost throwing myself out of the window, leaning out and trying to *gasp* in some air. [*Luckily her husband came in just then and got her to relax and breathe normally.*] [B, 4 months]

There may be external situations that make it especially hard for a mother to be able to focus on her newborn.

My dad died suddenly in an accident. I was seven months pregnant. I can't hide it from B. I often feel sad and cry. He's bound to see it. [B, 3 weeks]

A mother's mother and other members of her family can be a good source of support. But there must be many exceptions.

Mother: We had my mother-in-law come from abroad to stay. We have a new baby and we've just moved into a half-built house. If *my* mum was coming, she'd bring food, she'd stock the freezer, she'd ask how to help us. But F's mother – she sits and expects us to do her idea of normal.

Me: What's her idea of normal?

Mother: She wants to be served cocktails. [G, 2 months]

When G was six weeks old, both sides of the family visited, back-to-back. I didn't get any help. It was the opposite: they all needed a lot of looking after. I didn't have time for G – I believe they call it the 'special time'. I didn't get to gaze at her any more. I'm angry about that. [G, 3 months]

My brother-in-law said he was coming round to visit. He says he's B's uncle. But he's got chicken pox. I'm like: 'You *can't* come round! There's a new *baby* here.' [B, 3 months]

With so many reasons to feel anxious, mothers want to calm themselves. But this can be difficult. Usual methods, such as going out for a drink, to a party or even staying at home and watching television or making love are no longer easy options.

> I'm a very anxious person and all my ways of self-soothing are high energy, like getting on my bike for a fast ride. I can't do that now. [G, 6 weeks]

However, it can be a surprise to discover that the *baby*, even a very young one, can sometimes calm his mother.

> I went to the clinic. They weighed G and told me she wasn't putting on enough weight. I felt I must be a *terrible* mother. I felt such a *failure*. But on the way home G smiled at me, and it was such a happy smile that I felt much better. [G, 7 weeks]

> For two weeks after my son was born, I was on a catheter, stuck in my bedroom. Through the window, I could see other mothers with their babies out in the street. I didn't seem to be one of them. I felt as though I *never* would be. But then, when things seemed very black, I'd look at my son – he's such a nice little chap – and he was looking calm and peaceful. So I would think: There is still something good to be got from such moments. [B, 4 months]

Two aspects of life with a new baby can be especially stressful: crying and sleep. Some babies are uncomfortable and cry a great deal in these early months. We still seem to live in a culture where 'good babies don't cry'. A mother can feel inadequate if her baby starts crying in a public setting.

> I probably look quite calm, sitting here [*at a mother-and-baby meeting*] with my baby, but that's not how I'm feeling inside. I'm so afraid of him crying. At home, I just try to deal with it. But I'm terrified of him crying here and [*crying herself*] that I won't know what to do. [B, 7 weeks]

> I remember when G was very young and when she cried it seemed

world-shaking. I couldn't think of anything except how to stop her crying. It took me a long time to realise that, to other people, G's crying didn't matter. They were just getting on with their lives. It didn't affect them the way it affected me. [G, 14 months; 15 weeks pregnant]

It isn't always possible to discover why a baby is crying. However, it must be a comfort to the baby to find that he is not ignored and that his mother is at least trying to help.

Many babies find it hard to sleep. Modern life is very fast for a newborn – quick voices in the street or on the radio, the rushing sounds of traffic or even his mother's sudden panic when she realises she is late for an appointment – so that sensitive newborns are often overstimulated.

I thought babies just went to sleep. No one told me you had to help them. But that's a major part of my day now. B can be tired, but I have to find a way to calm him down for sleep. [B, 3 months]

B wakes up hourly now. It's much better than when he woke up every *half* hour. It's funny to think what you can be thankful for. [B, 4 months]

During the day, I know night waking won't be for ever. But it's different in the middle of the night. It feels terrible. I feel night waking will never end. [B, 4 months]

No one else knows those lonely, dark three-o'clock-in-the-morning moments. [B, 2 years; 14 weeks pregnant]

At difficult times, a mother may find comfort from other mothers. Some complain that conversation with another mother can be too competitive. But it doesn't have to be.

First mother: B is restless at night. I find it hard to sleep. [B, 5 weeks]

Second mother: In that case, cut yourself plenty of slack and don't expect too much of yourself the next day. [G, 18 months]

First mother: Has anyone here had that feeling when you pick up your baby and you *don't* feel that rush of love? Don't get me wrong. I love B to bits. But it was frightening. I picked him up one time, and I thought: *Where's* that feeling? That rush of love? It's gone. [B, 6 weeks]

Second mother: I can remember feeling exactly that – and it *is* frightening. [G, 11 months]

First mother: I'm a single mum and when G won't go to sleep, I feel desperate. Then I have this terrible thought. I'm so ashamed. I think I could take a pillow and put it over her face and then I would be able to sleep. [G, 2 months]

Second mother: I think it's so brave of you to tell us that. And I'm sure you will never do it. [*She was right: the mother didn't.*] [B, 23 months]

Other mothers long for practical help. One mother wanted this when her baby was younger but felt too proud to ask for it. Then her husband had to go abroad, and she decided to accept an offer from a friend.

F had gone to the States for his father's funeral. My friend said: 'I'll come over and sleep with you for two nights, so you needn't be alone.' She probably expected me to say no, but I said: '*Yes!*' B keeps waking up at night. At 2 a.m., I went into my friend's room and gave B to her. I said: 'You've *got* to take him.' Then I went down and locked myself into my kitchen. I was wound up and trying to calm myself down. When I went back upstairs, my friend was walking round the room with B, showing him things and talking to him. [B, 7 months]

This must have been a resourceful friend. But perhaps many friends could help if they were asked. People often respond well when they know their help is *desperately* needed. The sense of aloneness that some mothers describe may be avoidable.

Some new mothers experience extreme feelings. One day, they feel they are buzzing with too much energy, while the next they just want the baby to disappear so they can sleep. These feelings are often grouped together under the heading of 'postnatal depression'. Mothers are advised to seek professional help and are treated with medication and sometimes a form of psychotherapy.

But non-professional help can be effective too. Mothers seem very willing to comfort another who seems in difficulties. As one mother wrote, in a collection of memories of 'postnatal depression': 'So it just goes to show. People do help you out of that dark lonely hole. And it does get better.'[39]

'Postnatal depression' is sometimes described as a meaningless illness that afflicts some mothers. But becoming a mother involves a momentous change of lifestyle for which women today are poorly prepared. Most mothers describe the first months as difficult. In her book *Postnatal Depression* Paula Nicholson wrote: 'Postnatal depression needs to be reconceptualised as part of the *normal experience of most women when they become mothers*.'[40]

This is echoed by many mothers. As one wrote: 'I think every single new mum has a degree of postnatal depression or "baby blues" or whatever you want to call it – it's hideous for the first few months, and everyone struggles in different ways – your life changes and you do a complete 360° overnight.'[41]

It helps to acknowledge that these postnatal months are difficult for all mothers, and that some find this time especially challenging. The writer M. Sara Rosenthal concluded: 'Even when a depression seems to come from nowhere, it is your body and soul's way of getting you to *stop* and *think* about your life.'[42] Stopping and thinking, alone or with a compassionate friend, or psychotherapist, might enable the mother to piece together her understanding of why she feels as she does.

The whole of this early period is a learning experience.

> I wish I could speak to my younger mother-self. I'd say: 'Don't worry. You'll get through it. And, whatever it is, it doesn't last. [G, 12 months]

Yes, it's a pity a new mother can't be reassured by her more experienced future self. I find it helpful to notice when a mother says she feels very tired. That indicates to me that she can afford to relax more and think about herself.

> *Mother:* People don't tell you about all the anxiety you will feel as a mother. I'm just finding time now to think about myself and what I need.
>
> *Me:* So are you feeling tired?
>
> *Mother:* Yes. I keep yawning. Before now, there wasn't time to yawn! [G, 4 months]

This 'special time' or 'sensitive period' for both mother and baby is not acknowledged in Western societies. More traditional societies often do recognise it and have rituals first to prepare the mother before birth and then to support her after. The medical anthropologist Dana Raphael even coined a new word for this time: 'matrescence'.[43] Yet we in the West still expect mothers to bounce back to what is considered 'normal'. No wonder so many mothers find themselves worrying about practical problems. They are easier to think about than emotional ones.

What is the good of mothers learning too late that the early months could have been an intimate time? Why should they look back on them feeling sad that they hadn't enjoyed them more? Not all new mothers might want to use this time for intimacy, but there are many who do.

And what if a mother was too anxious or too busy or too ill to enjoy this special intimate time? Has the opportunity gone for ever? That particular time has gone, but later moments can become special too. Mothers often enjoy their new role more when they understand what their babies are doing, as we shall see in the next chapter. Older babies, small children – and even adult ones – often seek out moments of being close to their mothers. There are times when a child is ill or troubled or perhaps delighted, when only his mother will do. Mothers have described moments when they were able to establish intimate relationships with their children that hadn't seemed possible earlier.

Besides, many women know little about the practical side and haven't had much contact with a baby before their own. This would be easy to change. Expectant mothers could be encouraged to visit new mothers. A new mother might enjoy more company. Talking to her, seeing how she manages and perhaps holding her baby, can give an expectant mother some idea of how it will feel to have her own.

Ultimately, there can be no real training to become a mother. It's a unique experience. But that doesn't justify today's minimal preparation. Antenatal classes could include some information about the 'special time'. Mothers would then know about it. And they would have a better chance of feeling satisfied, not sad, when they emerge from it.

CHAPTER THREE

What babies do – especially when it looks like nothing

Newborns can look as if they are staring into space. Their faces are not yet as expressive as ours. To our eyes, they might look a bit blank, detached and remote. Perhaps this is why some people find them dull company.

> I didn't enjoy the first weeks at all. They were very hard work and I got nothing back from G. I thought: I can't do this. But I feel terrible saying this because *now* G is great to be with. [G, 4 months]

Most mothers enjoy their babies more when they can see meaning in their behaviour. They need time to observe their babies and discover what they are doing.

> I love being with G. I feel I'm like a birdwatcher or someone studying the lives of polar bears. I like looking after G and seeing all the changes. [G, 6 months]

> I feel G is a bud that has suddenly exploded into a flower. I can really see who she is now. [G, 6 months]

When a baby cries, the mother may respond immediately, while family members often try to calm her: 'Don't worry. It's just crying.

The baby will be all right.' But mothers have already started to learn what their babies are doing.

> I notice G's signals. A yawn, a sneeze, another yawn, another sneeze, and if you don't get her to sleep by the third yawn, you've missed her sleep window. Then she gets fractious. F says: 'All babies cry.' But they *don't*. You have to read their signals. [G, 3 months]

> When G's about to wake up, she pushes her little feet up and down. I keep looking to check. [G, 3 months]

Babies develop quickly and their communications become more sophisticated. Adults can reach great heights of sensitivity and intelligence. But how do we start to realise our immense potential? What are the early steps we take?

Developmental psychologists have demonstrated that babies are active and intelligent from the start. But psychologists study specific questions, usually in artificial settings. Mothers, on the other hand, are in natural surroundings and tend to make spontaneous discoveries. Without realising it, they may be breaking new ground.

> I read that research showed babies start to dream at 18 months, so B is right on cue. I actually thought he had been dreaming much younger than that, but I must have been wrong [*because of the research she had read*]. I expect he just used to *look* like he was dreaming. [B, 18 months]

Mothers often discount their observations in this way and trust professional researchers more than their own untrained perceptions. But perhaps they are being unfair to themselves. Surely, for millennia, mothers have looked at their babies and noticed significant details. A nineteenth-century Swiss mother described the behaviour of her son, aged six weeks:

> ... [His] soft murmurs are sometimes addressed to a bright metal

button; sometimes to a mirror lighted up by the rays of the sun; he seems to tell them how beautiful they are, and how much pleasure they afford to his newly awakened sight; sometimes he utters shrill but joyful screams as if to attract their attention.[44]

Observations like hers show a sensitivity that professional researchers might discount. For too long, mothers' descriptions have been undervalued, left unpublished and are therefore lost, from one generation to the next.

There is so much about early human development that we don't yet know.

A baby may be lying flat on his back. His neck muscles are still weak and he can hardly raise his head. He may only be able to see what is above him. So he may *seem* to be staring at what we assume to be 'nothing'. But babies are human. Like us, they don't like to be bored. If they are staring, surely it can't really be at nothing.

I look to try to see what B is looking at. He keeps looking at a corner of the ceiling. I don't know why. Well, maybe a *corner's* a wonderful thing if you've never seen a corner before. [B, 4 weeks]

Surely, yes, a corner *is* wonderful. It's a complex place where three planes and three lines meet at one point. So has this four-week-old baby already got some visual understanding of planes and lines? Is he trying to grasp the complexity of a corner? And entirely without language to help him?

After this mother had described her baby looking at a corner, I noticed how often other mothers mentioned their babies looking at corners too.[45] I hadn't prompted them.

First mother: B likes looking at pictures. If we walk into a room and there's a picture on the wall, he'll always look at it. Or maybe it's the frame he's studying. [B, 2 months]

Second mother: I remember G always had to look at corners at that age. We've got a photo of her staring up at the ceiling. [G, 8 months]

Third mother: So did G [*at that age*]. She would stare at a corner. I remember wondering what she was thinking about. [G, 23 months; B, 3 months]

These three mothers helped one another. It was only because of the first mother that the second mother remembered her earlier observation and only because of the other two that the third mother recalled what she had noticed nearly two years before.

At another meeting where none of the previous mothers was present, and I hadn't said anything about corners, a different mother said:

G loves patterns. We have a patterned pillowcase that we've taken off the pillow so she can see it better. And she loves a corner of our room. There's a bookshelf that almost goes up to the ceiling. She keeps gazing up into that corner. [G, 4 months]

Other mothers noticed how their babies were curious about patterns and repeated shapes.

G is interested in stripes. She likes a black-and-white striped picture we've got. And she stares at our bookshelves for hours, probably because they look striped too. [G, 6 weeks]

I was hurrying here when I suddenly stopped and let G look at some bricks [*of a wall*]. I could see she wanted to. I don't know why, but she was interested for quite a while. [B, 2 years; G, 3 months]

Light, shadows and reflections are all interesting subjects for babies. G looks at shadows and silhouettes. At least, I *think* that's what she's looking at. And she gazes at our faces for longer than she used to. [G, 7 weeks]

B was in his high chair, touching the empty tray in front of him. I suddenly saw that he was touching my moving shadow because the electric light was behind me, making a shadow on his tray. [B, 7 months]

B kept giggling. Then I realised he was looking at my reflection in the mirror. [B, 8 months]

All these mothers could see that their babies were not gazing blankly. They were actively looking. But what kind of conclusions were the babies drawing? Were they teaching themselves basic information about our complex world without a vocabulary to help them?

I can't imagine what G is thinking. She looks as though she's taking everything in. But how does she do it without words? [G, 5 months]

No wonder, then, that babies are so keen to be lifted and carried so they can look around them.

My mum keeps telling me: 'You've got to put that baby *down*.' But he likes to see what's going on, and he's happier if one of us is holding him. [B, 4 months]

Gradually, from months of lying flat, babies grow stronger. They get to know when their mothers are about to lift them up and start to raise their bodies in anticipation. I think this is what one mother was trying to explain:

G's armpits are stronger. I've noticed how, when I lift her up under her arms, her armpits stiffen. It's as if she's ready for me. Not floppy like a newborn. [G, 4 months]

Other mothers observe similar developments:

Mother: I thought babies just did things, like one day B would suddenly be able to sit up. But now I can see that he's already wanting to sit up, even though he's probably months away.

Me: How can you tell?

Mother: It's obvious. When I sit him halfway up, he's really pleased and wants to do the rest himself. [B, 3 months]

Once they can sit up, there is a lot more to learn.

G is interested in holes. When she was tiny, she used to spend ages putting her fingers through a metal air vent. [G, 10 months]

We must all have learned about solid surfaces that have holes in them. We can usually see holes without having to check out each one by touching it. But when did we gain such useful information? There is far more to understand about what babies are studying. And there must be many mothers who have noticed what their babies are studying but do not realise how important this information might be.

Babies seem to have a powerful curiosity about the world around them. We are curious too, but rarely with the eagerness we had as babies.

I might be curious about something but feel too lazy to get up and look at it. But G's not lazy. If she's curious, she's *got* to go and look. [G, 7 months]

I left my tea on the table, just where I thought it was out of G's reach. I went out of the room and then heard her cry. She had pulled the tea all over herself. Luckily it wasn't very hot. But she must have wanted my cup with every *fibre* of her being. [G, 8 months]

We've got some lavender hanging from a door handle. And I saw G stand up and reach out and stretch her arm and try with all her might to touch it. And I thought: If only adults could keep their curiosity and striving like G, there'd be no end to all the inventions and discoveries they could make! [G, 10 months]

How do we lose some of the intense curiosity we knew as babies?

I felt I had to get good grades at school. And it killed off all my natural curiosity. But G never stops. She is *always* curious, interested in *everything* and she is *never* bored. [G, 11 months]

After hours of excited curiosity, aren't babies tired and ready for a nap? Not always. But, even then, mothers can sometimes see the logic of their babies' behaviour.

The only way B'll go to sleep is if I talk a lot. [*Sure enough, B had just nodded off while she was talking.*] I think it's because I used to carry him in a sling close to me and I'd be on my phone. I think he associates sleep with the sound of me talking. Sometimes I pretend I'm talking to someone just so he'll go to sleep! [B, 5 months]

First mother: B can only nap in the day if I put him in the sling and walk very fast. [B, 7 months]

Me: Is that what you used to do during pregnancy?

First mother: Yes. I went for long walks.

Second mother: So did I. I wonder if many babies who find it hard to sleep had mothers who walked a lot in pregnancy, so they are used to the movement. [G, 5 years; B, 7 months]

These mothers found that their babies would fall asleep if the timing or the familiar stimuli were right. But one mother noticed that her baby didn't seem to like the feeling of going to sleep.

I don't think G likes the physical sensation of the transition from waking to sleeping. She looks as if she is going off, her eyelids droop, and then she starts crying and wakes up. [G, 5 months]

This may be true of other babies, and it would be interesting to hear whether more mothers have observed this.

Once children can sit upright, they can explore toys. At one meeting, a girl of ten months was turning over a set of chunky wooden beads, strung to make an irregular shape. Each bead was yellow, red or green, very faded, as if countless children had held them and turned them one way and another, as this girl was doing. I must have commented on her absorption, because her mother said:

Mother: Yes, G likes to spend a long time when she's interested. She really looks at things. She likes to turn a toy over and over, so she knows she has studied every bit and looked at all of it.

[*Pause while I considered her words.*]

Me: How did you realise that she was *studying*?

Mother: Because she looks serious. She doesn't like me to interrupt her, and she gets furious if I take away whatever she is studying. I've seen the same look on my husband's face when he's studying something. When G is smiling, it means she is playing. [G, 10 months]

This is an interesting observation. Many people, seeing a child with a toy, would take it for granted that 'playing' was the word to describe what he was doing. I haven't heard people use 'studying' in this context. But now I saw that turning a toy round and looking at it from every angle is the essence of studying. It's what we adults do with ideas.

This distinction between the two modes of playing and studying helped me to 'hear' what other mothers were saying at meetings. I wonder how much I missed before recognising that children don't only use toys for playing. Babies are given toys because they are safe, but, as I now see, they often use them for exploring shapes. One mother commented on how long her son was interested in some coloured stacking cups.

Yes, cups are the one thing that still interest him. Not toys. I never realised how much there is to explore in a cup. [B, 9 months]

Babies are also quick to notice that we don't usually play with toys. So they watch to see what we get up to.

G managed to pull the plug out of my laptop! [G, 8 months]

Should I be stimulating B more? But he's happy exploring an egg box under the kitchen table. [B, 9 months]

G does such lovely things. She's learning to put lids on things. She's just worked out there's a wrong way, and you have to turn the lid upside down. I never knew there was such a long stretch of fun to be had from an empty yoghurt pot. [G, 11 months]

Young babies seem fascinated by their mothers. They gaze steadily up at their faces, unsmiling and attentive. It is considered impolite for an adult to stare like this, and mothers often feel disconcerted, especially when it's an 'off' moment.

B is really looking at me now. Some days, I'm all bright and it's easy to be playful. But on other days I don't feel so great. I feel as if I should hide that from B. But then I thought it over and realised that hiding could be *more* cruel. Because then I'd be where B couldn't see me. [B, 7 weeks]

I remember when G was tiny she'd keep looking at me. Her eyes would follow me everywhere. And I remember thinking: G, can't you stop looking at me for *five* minutes? [G, 5 months]

B's interested in everything I do. Even if he's playing with a toy, if I turn a tap on, he whips his head round to see what I'm doing. [B, 8 months]

Then, by some mysterious process, the baby's expression changes from gazing at his mother in a grave and impersonal way into a radiant beam of love. And love doesn't seem to emerge slowly like most other developments. It seems to burst forth, almost too strongly for the smallness of the baby. Along what road have babies travelled? Is it the same way for most of them? And do some babies never experience this love?

Mothers need to enlighten us here. Mother–baby love is intimate. It might be hard to research in a formal laboratory setting. Mothers notice it in very ordinary situations.

G always seems so pleased to see me. If I come back into the room, she laughs and kicks as I come in as if to say: 'It's *you*!' [G, 5 months]

I remember when G would cry her heart out if I left the room. I'd say: 'It's all right. Mummy's just running for a wee.' And when I came back she'd give me these radiant smiles. [B, 3 years; G, 12 months]

B is very affectionate. He crawled under the table yesterday and I felt this kiss on my foot. [B, 17 months]

As children live through a range of emotional experiences, their faces become more expressive. Mothers notice differences, though these can be hard to describe.

Mother: I catch glimpses of B's personality already.

Me: What do you see?

Mother: Oh . . . I'm not sure. [B, 7 months]

There's more *of* her. I don't know how else to explain it. So much is new this week. There's more of her personality in every way. [G, 9 months]

G gave me a real *look* the other day. It wasn't like her lying-down breastfeeding look. This was much more of a sitting-up look. [G, 10 months]

Some mothers don't enjoy the early months because their babies seem so helpless. They feel happier once their babies can sit up and they can see that their actions are purposeful and rational.

> I didn't fall in love with G the moment I saw her. I was more anxious then. But, from about eight months, I started to love her more and more. I could see her experimenting and it told me how much her brain was developing. [G, 9 months]

Babies love experimenting. They want to understand how things 'work'. Once they have understood, their interests move on to something else.

> I keep telling B he can't do something, and then giving in. So now, when he wants to explore the electric toaster, I just unplug it and let him have it. He loves exploring what it does. [B, 15 months]

> *First mother:* B loves opening drawers and pulling things out and scattering them. [B, 17 months]

> *Second mother:* When G was that age, she wanted to pull all the saucepans out of my kitchen cupboard. At first, I said no. But she got very upset, so in the end I let her. She pulled out every saucepan and made sure the cupboard was empty. Then she helped me to put them back again. And then she shut the cupboard door and gave me a look as if to say: 'There. I've done that. I don't want to do it any more.' And she didn't. [G, 4 years]

> They have their little projects, don't they? I remember when B was interested in opening and shutting. He kept opening and shutting things. He was teaching himself about it. [B, 5 years; G, 16 months]

Babies also study their own bodies. Their hands are quite a discovery because they can move them and, at the same time, feel and see them move.

> I see G watching her hand as she brings it nearer to her and away again. She's interested in distance. [G, 6 months]

Mothers observe that hand control is learned gradually.

G can grasp things, but it's an accident. It's not her intention. She looks at her hand in surprise and she doesn't know how to get rid of the thing in it. [G, 3 months]

One day I gave G a piece of avocado, and she didn't know how to eat it. She found it too slippery to hold, so then she gripped it and it went all squishy. Two weeks later, I gave her another piece. You could *see* her thinking about it. This time, she took it in both her hands and held it more gently. [G, 7 months]

Then comes the excitement of being able to move their whole bodies by rolling, crawling, cruising and toddling. This progression has been explored by research scientists. However, mothers add something more – the reasons why their children learn.

B learned to roll over very quickly. It was because he hated going to baby classes where he was supposed to lie on his tummy. So he taught himself to flip over. [B, 4 months]

Any quick movement, such as rolling over, when the baby isn't used to it, must affect what they are learning to see. Shapes and colours probably merge into each other.

G wakes up every *hour*. I find it helps to think that she must be waking for a reason. I suppose . . . she's just learned to roll over. Her dreams . . . they must be *psychedelic*! [G, 5 months]

Some children seem to develop in spite of themselves. Their mothers report that they don't all enjoy it.

First mother: B is trying to crawl, even though he doesn't like being on his tummy. But I think he has a *drive* to crawl, even if he's not enjoying it. [B, 7 months]

Second mother: I've definitely noticed that. G didn't like crawling, but she also had a drive to do it. B is very different. [G, 2 years; B, 8 months]

How common is this? After all, many children are enthusiastic about their new abilities.

B has just learned to sit. Before now, he was so busy crawling that he didn't have much use for sitting. [B, 7 months]

B is so excited by crawling that he wakes up in the night and crawls down the bed with his eyes shut. [G, 2 years; B, 9 months]

Mothers have to keep pace with the thought-speed of toddlers. So much intrigues them that they rush from one exciting experience to the next. For an adult, used to taking longer over each one, the frequent switches of focus are tiring. But toddlers are no dilettantes.

G doesn't give up. If something's not working for her, she'll try to do whatever she wants to do another way. [G, 10 months]

Toddlers may have short attention spans for the moment. But G goes back to things. Like if she's been interrupted exploring a toy, she'll remember exactly what she was doing when she was interrupted and when she gets the toy again, she'll go on with it. [G, 13 months]

A modern home is full of dangers, so mobile children cannot be left alone, and their mothers are often exhausted. However, these mothers are usually aware of how much their children are achieving.

B likes to practise standing up about twenty times before going to sleep. Once, I felt too tired to wait for him, and tried to pull him down, a bit impatiently – and he just laughed at me. [G, 2 years; B, 9 months]

First mother: G is cruising. Actually, that's a funny word for it. [G, 7 months]

Second mother: Yes, 'cruising' sounds as though there's no effort. But G has to pull herself up. Then it's a question of finding her balance. She can't do that yet. When she can do that, she'll be able to move from chair to chair. [G, 10 months]

What about the inevitable accidents when toddlers miscalculate, and roll off the bed, fall over or down the stairs? Mothers notice an interesting pattern:

G fell down some stairs a few days ago. As soon as I'd comforted her, she wanted to go straight back and fall down those stairs again. With me ready to catch her, though. [G, 10 months]

B accidentally hit his head against a wall and cried. Then he kept deliberately hitting his head against the wall. I was worried he was developing a behavioural problem. Then I saw he was testing out how hard he had to hit his head before he hurt himself. [B, 13 months]

B fell down some steps. For half an hour, he wouldn't go *near* those steps. It was as if he was saying: 'I'm not talking to *you!*' But after that he went straight back to them. It was as if he was saying: 'Now, let's work this out.' [B, 14 months]

B was climbing on two chairs when suddenly he did the splits, fell off and banged his head. I rushed to pick him up, stroked his head – and then saw that there was blood on my hand. It came from a tiny cut at the back of his head. I washed it and he calmed down a bit. Then he wanted to go straight back to the chairs and see what had happened. I didn't. I was shocked. It took me *hours* to get over it. [B, 20 months]

This is interesting behaviour. Adults routinely investigate causes of accidents, especially major transport ones, and sometimes have to write up formal reports. We obviously learn a great deal in this way, and the results may help us to avoid similar accidents in the future. So it's fascinating to learn from mothers that this isn't only an adult preoccupation. Some of us start investigating mishaps as very young children. How common is this behaviour? In the last example, it's clear that the child must have taken the initiative. His mother didn't want to.

The long-term interests of mother and child are the same. Both want the child to be competent and capable. In the short term, the child is curious and experimental, and not all his plans are safe. Mothers who are reluctant to curb their children's joy in exploring decide to adapt their own plans.

> G wanted to learn how to climb down the stairs one day. And my head was full of my own agenda, like needing to empty the washing machine. That seemed important. But, when I really *thought* about it, none of my agenda seemed *half* as important as G learning to climb down the stairs. [G, 14 months]

> B is very restless unless we go out. He likes to be kicking a football or riding his bike. So I keep trying to get all of us out of the house. [B, 5 years; 1G, 2 years; 2G, 8 weeks]

Active children need a lot of supervision. Mothers find that they need to think at top speed to pre-empt risks ahead.

> *First mother:* B climbs up *everything*. I can't take my eye off him for a moment. [B, 16 months]

> *Second mother:* 1G doesn't do that now, but 2G does it even *more*. I've had to take all the chairs away from the kitchen table, and keep a constant watch-out. It's exhausting. [1G, 3 years; 2G, 19 months; B, 7 months]

> My reactions have got quicker if I think G's about to hurt herself.

My husband pointed it out to me. He said: 'Boy, I can't believe you jumped up so quickly.' [G, 10 months]

I spend my whole time running after G, trying to keep her out of trouble. [G, 17 months]

Children move quickly and it's not always possible to stop them from hurting themselves. What they find harder to understand is that, small though they are, they have the power to *cause* pain. Even a baby can hurt his mother. For example, if he is breast-feeding, he may inadvertently bite her. His gums are strong so he can hurt her even before his teeth come through. Then, when they do appear, new teeth are extremely sharp, and babies have to learn how to angle their mouths so they can breastfeed without hurting their mothers.

It is natural to be upset if someone inflicts physical pain, and a mother may respond to a bite with an angry: '*Ow!*' A moment's thought convinces her that her baby was too young to have meant to hurt her. But when does this change? Mothers sometimes say of their children: 'He *must* know by now that his hitting/biting/ kicking really hurts.' But they sound doubtful. It seems to take children a long time to develop this awareness.

At one meeting, where mothers sat in a circle and children played in the middle, one little girl put her hand on the head of a younger child. It didn't look forceful. But the younger child gave a startled wail, and his mother picked him up and comforted him. The little girl stood very still, staring at them.

Me, to the mother of the older child: Is G all right?

G's mother: Sort of. She's got her head on one side, as if she knows something's not right. She can't quite work it out. [G, 9 months]

So this mother realised that her daughter was puzzled. The little girl was concerned and observing carefully. I thought she had probably alarmed the younger child more than caused him pain, but even I, an experienced adult, couldn't be sure.

The American researcher Dr Allan Schore believed that a child's moral and altruistic behaviour naturally emerges, once the correct age has been reached:

> It is not until 18 months that the child first exhibits 'moral' proso-cial altruistic behaviour in the form of approaching persons in distress and initiating positive, other-orientated, affective and instrumental activities in order to comfort the other . . . The child, now capable of internally appraising her own negative affect, such as shame, can act as a distress modulator, an affect regulator for others.[46]

It is typical of well-known researchers to state an exact number of months for a stage in children's development. Perhaps they haven't observed the variations in age that mothers describe.

> One night, I was tired, I was crying, and G reached out her arm and touched me. She *meant* it. I *know* she did. [G, 5 months]

> I take G to several playgroups. There was a child at one who was crying, and G immediately went up to the child with open arms. [G, 15 months]

Moral awareness seems to develop gradually and in different ways. Children learn not only from adults teaching them how to behave but by noticing what adults themselves do in practice.

Mothers confirm that children remain puzzled about their ability to *cause* pain, for much longer than they would have expected:

> I don't think B knows when he hurts me. He laughs. He seems to think it's a joke. [B, 13 months]

> B hits me and then comes to kiss me better. I know he knows

Mum doesn't like hitting, but I'm sure he doesn't understand why. [B, 19 months]

However, eventually:

First mother: G knows that hitting hurts.

Me: How can you tell?

First mother: I'm not sure. But I do *know*. Sometimes she hits her own hand on purpose. [G, 22 months]

Second mother: B's like that too. He bites his hand. Once he bit it harder than he meant and he cried: '*Ow!*' [B, 3 years]

Both these mothers observed, independently, that their children were testing out pain on themselves. This convinced them that the children now knew that their own hitting and biting could cause pain. But until a mother can be sure, it is hard to know whether it is fair to be angry with the child for causing pain.

Once a child realises he can hurt other people, the mother may think she should teach her child to apologise.

We were having a horrible day. We'd gone to a fair and got caught in a downpour. I bought G some lunch, put her in the car and gave it to her. It had a little plastic fork to eat it with. As I was leaning over to strap her in, she jabbed the fork at my eye. I managed to turn my head in time, but I snatched away the fork and said: 'That's *it*. You *have* to tell Mummy you're sorry.' And she said: 'No.' I said: 'I really *need* you to say you're sorry.' She said: 'No!' So in the end we just drove home. But, two days later, in the morning, we were talking in my bed. She touched my eye and said: 'Mummy's *eye*.' So I said: 'Yes.' She said: '*Hurt* it.' I said: 'Yes.' And she said: '*Sorry*, Mummy.' [G, 2 years]

Listening to all of you talking about how your children won't do anything they're told, how they say 'Sorry' when you ask them to apologise, but they don't mean it and then they do what you've asked them *not* to all over again, I realise G's got through that stage. We're not in it any more. I don't know when we got through or how. But she was too young to understand 'Sorry' then, and now I know that she understands everything. [G, 3 years]

This is an interesting subject. A sense of justice seems to be innate in all of us. A child can feel hurt to be blamed for actions he did not know were wrong. So it seems important for his mother, or another person who knows him well, to keep track of his understanding.

Young children are also capable of being empathetic to their mothers, within the range of their experience.

G always notices the moment I'm upset. She says: 'What's wrong, Mummy?' When I was hunting everywhere for my bank card (because my husband had borrowed it and had forgotten to put it back), she said: 'Don't worry, *I'll* find your bank card for you.' [G, 2 years; B, 16 months]

I've cried in front of 1B. He was very curious, so I explained that I was sad and that it wasn't about anything that he'd done. He ran to get his drumsticks and he said: 'I'll play Mummy *happy* music!' [1B, 3 years; 2B, 7 weeks]

Mothers are often surprised at how young their children are when they show so much understanding. They don't seem to have deliberately taught their children to respond like this.

So far, everything that babies and children do seems to make sense, when mothers have time to notice what they are doing. But what about repetition? Why do children insist on repeating the same actions so often? Surely they can't be studying, because they know the results already. Are they trying to drive us crazy?

An early example, already discussed because it arises so often (see previous chapter), is that of night waking. Why do babies wake so often in distress? They must know that we are near by, that we are keeping them safe and that frequent waking is tiring for all of us.

One mother remembered her own repetitive waking:

> I don't mind being there for G at night. My parents did that for me. I'd fall asleep, and that was fine. But then I'd wake up and see shapes in the night. They were coming after me to get me. My parents would always come in and comfort me. I didn't do it for their attention though. They *gave* me attention anyway. I cried at night because I was terrified. [G, 8 months]

This mother said it took years before she learned not to be frightened, and was grateful to her parents for being patient with her. But how did she learn to stop being frightened? Do most children learn to overcome night fears?

As well as night waking, adults get irritated when a child keeps repeating actions that seem inconvenient and unnecessary. But, however odd it looks, the child is trying to communicate something.

> It took me months to notice, but whenever we get home 1B seems to get bad-tempered and want my attention. So I'd have to stop rushing off to make a meal, and attend to him. As soon as I real-ised it was a problem, I could start to think what to do about it. [1B, 4 years; 2B, 10 months]

It sounds as though her older son was responding to the sudden change of energy in his mother. She was in a hurry to make a meal, and perhaps he felt a bit deserted. If she kept repeating her actions, it would make sense that he would repeat his too.

And what about all the times when children want *us* to repeat something?

> Sometimes it can be boring. It's a relief to admit it. Like if I'm singing a song and B thinks it's the most amazing song in the

world. At the same time, to you, it's just a nice song, and it gets boring to keep repeating it. [B, 8 months]

This demand for repetition may also arise over a storybook, or an action. It's easy for mothers to feel exasperated. Whatever is the point of so much repetition? This only becomes clear if the adult has the patience to keep repeating what the child has asked for. He might have been frightened or startled by an event, a song or a book, and wants to be told the 'story' of it. Then there is too much information to take in at one telling, so the child wants many repeats of the identical story. Eventually, the adult discovers that the child has learned the whole story, or song, or sequence of behaviour by heart. Once the child is satisfied that he has got everything he needs from it, he no longer asks for that particular repetition.

Without this kind of understanding, it is difficult to sympathise with the child. So instead of the renewal of energy that comes with understanding, the adult feels drained and exhausted. The journalist Sam Leith wrote in London's *Evening Standard*:

> You often feel, as you collapse into a stiff gin, like your main achievement has been getting through the day. Kids do say the funniest things. But they say them over and over again. It is not sufficient stimulation for most adult brains to spend twelve hours a day agreeing over and over again that crocodiles go SNAP and that moocows go MOO.[47]

Why was his child repeating the sounds of crocodiles and cows? Presumably there was a reason. It might have been connected to himself. His child might have been repeating the words to get him to give another laugh. Perhaps the child thought there was too much paternal gravitas. Or maybe the repetition was his child's tried-and-tested way to get his busy father's attention.

Mothers describe all kinds of daily repetitive situations in which they try hard to be understanding rather than judgmental.

> G likes taking things out of the washing machine. I can see she is trying to be helpful and copying what she sees me do. But someone else might perceive it as 'being difficult'. [G, 9 months]

Do these examples suggest that all repetitive behaviour is rational? This has to remain an open question. We need many more mothers to share their observations.

What about laughter? A sense of humour seems to develop at a young age.

Mother: G used to chuckle in her sleep.

Me: At what age?

Mother: Early. Like six to seven weeks. [B, 4 years; G, 8 months]

Adults usually like to share a good joke they have heard. Babies seem to notice how much we enjoy sharing a laugh. So they join in and laugh with us, though they are far too young to understand what the joke is. I noticed a girl of ten months laughing enthusiastically together with her mother and myself. She looked meaningfully at both of us, as if wanting us to be sure that we were including her.

Children seem to reach all kinds of milestones, but not necessarily at the same age as each other. Mothers can show us how uneven a child's understanding can be.

> I'm amazed that G is so mature in some ways and then there are other things that she just doesn't understand. [G, 21 months]

> I thought B's development would be linear, but it hasn't been like that. [B, 5 years; G, 12 days]

Children's understanding develops as they learn to talk. Mothers find that talking doesn't happen in a linear sequence either. Examples are in the next chapter.

If babies and young children are expending so much energy in study, do they have any left for play? Yes, and it's interesting how many of their early games are unplanned. They arise spontaneously through a playful kind of repetition of actions that mother and baby are doing anyway.

> I was lying beside G on the bed, and I opened my eyes and she opened hers and saw me. Then I closed mine, and she closed hers, because then I opened mine and saw she opened hers again. It was great. It was like her first real game. [G, 2 months]

> *First mother:* I was hanging up the washing and I suddenly found I could play hide-and-seek around it. Both children enjoyed it. [1G, 2 years; 2G, 5 months]

> *Second mother:* I've done the same, hanging up bedsheets. I play peek-a-boo. [G, 8 months]

> B crawled to the edge of the bed, so I grabbed his heels. And he laughed and laughed, and wanted me to do it again. So we repeated this for about half an hour. It was his first real game. He initiated it himself. I suppose the desire to play is innate in all of us. [B, 8 months]

Many games seem to be of a construction/destruction sort. One mother remarked:

> B builds things with his blocks. But when he's done that, he likes to kick it over and send everything flying. [B, 21 months]

How young are children when they start to use memory and imagination in their games?[48]

> We had a lovely holiday. We'd take G to feed a horse at the end of the lane. We used to pick grass specially for the horse. A few

days later, at home, I was in the garden, hanging out the washing, when I turned round and saw G picking little bits of grass and pretending to give it to the horse, just as we did on holiday. It's the first time I realised that she doesn't live only in the present. She's got her own world of memories. [G, 15 months]

1G makes me cups of tea with her tea set. I hear her going: '*Shhhh!*' as she pours the 'tea' out of the pot, and then she pours the 'milk' in, and then she adds 'powder', which is what she calls sugar. Then she stirs it all round and then she gives it to me. [B, 5 years; 1G, 2 years; 2G, 8 months]

I hope it has become clearer that, though babies may look blank, they may well be busy, working on something. And although a knowledge of, for example, corners and holes will undoubtedly be useful to them when they are older, they don't seem to be studying corners, holes or anything else for practical purposes. They couldn't foresee these purposes. Instead, they seem motivated by curiosity and the desire to learn for learning's sake.

Mothers who notice details about their babies have a great deal to tell us. Researchers on child development spend time ascertaining results that have long been obvious to mothers. They usually say that mothers' observations are unscientific and 'contaminated'. Scientific research, they claim, is impersonal, relies on questions that can be measured and compared and experiments that can be replicated by another researcher to check the conclusions.

This sounds good in theory, but apparently is not easy to do in practice. Psychology research often cannot be replicated. An international team of 270 scientists repeated 100 experiments published in reputable psychology journals. Only 36 per cent of their results were the same as those of the originals.[49]

Mothers' observations are based on individual anecdotes, so these can't be replicated either. But they describe everyday behaviour in the baby's ordinary environment. Other mothers may have had that experience. Nearly every example in this chapter has been greeted by the laughter of recognition or the nodding heads of other mothers.

A scientific researcher has to explain his methodology and his grounds for reaching his conclusions. Mothers don't have to. But perhaps they *could*. In my discussions, when a mother describes an observation, I often ask: 'How do you know? How can you be sure?' She usually replies that it's hard to explain.

People often attribute a mother's knowledge to 'women's intuition'. The writer Agatha Christie challenged this idea. She gave the following lines to her detective Hercule Poirot: 'Women observe subconsciously a thousand little details, without knowing that they are doing so. Their subconscious minds add these little things together – and they call the result intuition.'[50]

Is she right? Are we registering thousands of small details without realising it? If so, perhaps we could try to remember the details that we used to reach our conclusion. We should then be in a much better position to justify our observations. We may be able to provide a great deal of 'missing' information on what babies are doing.

Does it matter? It may do. Just as children have no idea how useful it will be when they study corners, why they fall over and that they can hurt people, we cannot predict how valuable mothers' data may turn out to be.

CHAPTER FOUR

'I don't feel desperate any more'

The essential work of a mother is to relate to her child, which means learning to understand him and to create a two-way conversation together. Very soon, her child finds he can communicate with others. Professional teachers can take over later on, but their work is difficult if the mother hasn't prepared her child first.

The hardest time is at the beginning when mother and child don't know one another yet. As a new mother explained at a meeting:

> I feel so frightened when B cries. Is it food? Is it wind? Is it a tummy pain? [B, 3 weeks]

Soon he did cry, and she almost threw him into the arms of her friend. The friend had two children and was more confident. She held him against her shoulder and walked to and fro, patting his back. The new mother had thought of good reasons to explain why her baby might be crying. She just didn't trust herself to guess which one it was. If she had, she could have calmed him herself. The baby took a long time to stop crying in her friend's arms, perhaps because he sensed that his mother had panicked.

It's easy for a new mother to feel desperate when her newborn is crying. With experience, she can be calmer. Mothers learn in a similar way to a nurse who is caring for a very ill patient. The patient, like a newborn, might be unable to talk. Florence Nightingale, pioneer of good nursing, addressed this problem when she was in charge of a team of nurses during the Crimean War. The soldiers arrived at her hospital with serious injuries, and she was horrified to hear her nurses troubling them with streams of questions. She wrote:

> A good nurse scarcely ever asks a patient a question – neither as to what he feels nor as to what he wants. But she does not take for granted, either to herself or to others, that she knows what he feels and wants, without the most careful observation and testing of her own observations.[51]

This is exactly what new mothers learn to do. Their babies, like patients, feel distress but don't always know what would make it better. So mothers also have to observe, and then test their observations. Both nurses and mothers have to stay calm enough to read body signals. Their patients and babies depend on them. But a nurse has been trained and is usually part of a team. A mother is on her own. And babies differ from wounded soldiers. A soldier can hear and understand useful messages like 'I'll be back in a moment'. A baby won't be able to understand this sentence for months.

Observing and testing is the way mothers start to learn. Friends and family members may not realise that a mother is concentrating intently on her baby. It's not just for the first couple of weeks. For at least the first year, she may need to stay focused on him.

> My friends visited and talked to me, but G had tongue tie and I was worried she would wake up and need feeding. I'd see my friends' mouths moving up and down, but I just couldn't *hear* anything they were saying to me. [G, 4 months]

> When I am in groups of people, 50 per cent of my attention is on

B. It *has* to be. I tune out other people like you tune out the sound of a radio. I'm trying to concentrate [*on other people*], but I couldn't do a whole conversation.' [B, 6 months]

If I had a friend with me, I wouldn't be able to have a conversation. I'd have to keep [*jerking her head from left to right*], looking out for B. [B, 11 months]

The reason for not being able to concentrate on adult conversations is that the mother is focused on 'conversation' with her baby. This conversation works partly by touch, partly by visual signals. It probably starts before the baby is born, when she can feel how active he can be. After birth, visual signals are added to their communication. Understanding a newborn can take time, especially if the birth was difficult, and mother and baby were separated because one or both were ill.

One mother told me that she was seriously ill after giving birth and was hospitalised for two weeks. Her own mother looked after her newborn for that time. One day, after she and her baby were reunited, she was getting ready to feed him. It occurred to her that she could easily prop up a book and read while he fed. She quickly found a prop, arranged her book and sat down with her baby. As he started feeding, she was about to look across his body to read when she glanced down and saw him gazing up at her with wide-open eyes. It felt wrong to read, so she gazed back. This made feeding him feel personal. Suddenly she could believe she was his mother. In this way, they both recovered from the first two weeks of separation.

Slowly mothers learn to recognise a range of signals.

A big change for me was realising that B was getting overtired. He would get grumpy and we wouldn't know why. Then I noticed he'd give a harsh cry when he needed sleep. If I put him in his sling *then*, he'd be asleep in ten minutes. [B, 3 months]

You hear a little squeak, and you know from experience that if you ignore it, it'll escalate into loud yelling that takes longer to calm down. It's better to get there quickly. [G, 6 months]

Sometimes B's crying and nothing makes it better. It's usually when he's overtired. So I've discovered it's all right to let him cry. It's counter-intuitive and F finds it even harder to listen to than I do. But I've timed it and it's only for one minute. And then he's calm and ready for sleep. [B, 7 months]

A mother who has learned her baby's signals is a great help to him. To a group of friends or family, who each want to hold him, the baby may look excited and happy. But his mother can see when it's getting too much.

I've seen G give everyone her best smiles at being handed round a room of people. Then she sees me and she's angry. To me, she is saying: 'It's too much. I've had enough.' [G, 4 months]

Gradually, from sounding tearful and confused, mothers have moments of feeling more confident.

One day I wake up and think: Hey! I can do this. Another day, I think: It's too hard. [G, 4 months]

I feel I've got a tool kit now for when B cries. At first, when he cried, I used to go to pieces. [B, 6 months]

I don't feel desperate any more. Now, if G cries, I know what she wants, or I usually do, and I know I can comfort her. I don't know when it changed. A few weeks ago. Recently. [G, 8 months]

When they have learned these essential basics, mothers often feel guilty that they are not 'working harder' at it all. Instead they have times of comfortable togetherness. It's difficult for her to believe that, for her child, this can be enough.

I was walking along with B when I suddenly thought: Hey, I should be talking to him. I'm not helping him to develop. Do you have to keep pushing yourself? I was quite happy just walking along, not talking to B. [B, 10 months]

Even if a mother is not directly interacting with her child, she is observing him to make sense of his actions. A passer-by might not realise how much understanding is going on between the two of them.

G and I are in sync in a way that other people do not see. [G, 19 months]

At one meeting, a mother gave me an example that puzzled me at first. She said she didn't know whether she was doing the right thing by staying at home with her children. Playing devil's advocate, I asked: 'So, by being with your children, are you wasting your time and ruining your career?' She answered: 'I don't know. I wish someone could tell me.' I said: 'But didn't you decide to be with your children for a reason?' Her reply was hardly audible: 'I think it's the relationships.'

I asked her for an example of when she felt related to her children. The answer she gave me didn't sound very helpful at the time. It was only going home on the bus afterwards that I realised what a good example it really was. She said:

The other day, I spent half an hour in the street with my son while he looked at a poster of a giraffe. There was also an elephant and a zebra and he looked at those too. I thought: Should I be doing this? But I decided it was okay. He was getting a lot out of it. I felt okay about it. [G, 3 years; B, 15 months]

It sounded to me an odd example of a relationship. There was no intimate dialogue. They weren't even making eye contact.

But an hour later, on the bus, I could hear behind me another mother talking to her child. 'What's *that* called?' she asked. Her child didn't answer, so she gave the reply: 'It's a zebra, isn't it? And what's *that*? A tiger. And what's this? It's a monkey.' She must have been turning the pages of a picture book.

The second mother was teaching her child to match words and pictures. I'm sure anyone listening would agree that she was doing something productive. Teaching a child is seen as important work.

But it would be easy to walk past the first mother with her child looking at the giraffe poster and think that she was doing nothing at all. She wasn't teaching her child to recognise the giraffe. He seemed to be absorbing the animal images on the posters himself. She *thought* about it and decided that this was 'okay'. This was a silent but definite decision. Unlike the mother with the book, she was letting her son take the lead, and she supported him by waiting for him. It would be good to have a term like 'mother's understanding' to honour all the sensitive, silent work that mothers do.

Mothers usually feel much more confident once conversation becomes two-way. It's exciting to hear their children talk. We talk about a person's 'mother tongue'. Do mothers have a special method of teaching language to their children? From what mothers say, it's a casual, almost playful process. As we saw, it starts soon after birth and long before the child can use words. But eventually the child will be able to manage complex adult dialogue.

From early on, babies make deliberate sounds. Not every mother enjoys this. Some get irritated and hear the sounds as meaningless babble. But are they meaningless? I used to be puzzled when mothers said they could hear their babies 'talking'. I wasn't attuned enough to these babies to hear what their mothers meant. But so many mothers have drawn my attention to what they can hear that, even though the babies are young, I am now convinced that their mothers must be reporting accurately.

G isn't newborn any more. Her language skills are developing. She's making different sounds. [G, 2 months]

G can say vowel sounds and she can do the vowels of 'Hello'. There! She just did it. [*I couldn't hear this at all.*] [G, 3 months]

Children today are born into a very verbal society. They need a lot of help to get launched into the first stages of communication, and after that come all the nuances of the culture in which they grow up. It would be easy for a child to feel bewildered at having so much to learn – and perhaps many children do. What helps them is the pre-verbal learning period when the mother or another person is 'listening' and making space for them to talk. Talking depends on people taking turns, one talking, the other listening. But it teaches babies even more. They learn that, young though they are, their 'opinions' matter. They aren't being brushed aside because they can't talk properly yet. This surely helps them to feel they belong to the 'talking society'.

I talk to B and I leave pauses for him, and then I talk some more. Of course, he can't answer but he's very chatty. [B, 3 months]

F laughs because I say you can have a real conversation with B. But you *can*. I tell F that, if he just waits for B to speak, B *will*. He *loves* dialogue. [B, 3 months]

Conversation is two-way. It's not just a question of B making meaningful noises to me. It depends on me noticing the particular noise and responding to it. Otherwise, if I don't respond to his noises, he'll learn that there is no point in making them. [G, 3 years; B, 4 months]

Mothers discover that part of helping babies to learn language is through silence, through listening to them. When a baby notices that his mother isn't continually talking but listens to him, he has taken a significant step to becoming a good communicator.

But mothers aren't teaching this formally. I hope no one will
ever invent a curriculum for them. The whole point is the easy,
spontaneous way in which they introduce their children to the
rhythms of language.

> I've talked to B since he was born. I say: 'Isn't it time for a coffee
> now?' Things like that. And when my family come round and it's
> all adult conversation, B certainly thinks he's part of the party. [B,
> 8 months]

> B likes to know exactly what we are saying. He leans forward and
> asks my sister: 'What are you and Mummy talking about?' [B, 2
> years; 21 weeks pregnant]

At a young age, some mothers notice that their babies seem to
make regular sounds for particular communications. How far
these are intentional is hard to know. And other mothers may be
responding to these early sounds without being aware of it.

> After about two months, I could tell B was crying *to* me [*i.e. not
> just crying*]. [B, 5 months]

> At first I thought G always needed to be picked up when she was
> awake. But sometimes I've noticed that she isn't giving me signals
> of wanting to be picked up. Then I realised that she is happy to
> be by herself. When she wants me she gives one loud cry. [G, 4
> months]

> G gives a special kind of cry when she's a *bit* hungry and she'd
> like a snack. Don't ask me too much about it. I've only just worked
> it out. [G, 10 months]

When mothers are attentive, they are astonished at how soon
their babies start to communicate their own independent wishes.
They don't always 'agree' with their mothers.

> I lay G down to change her nappy and, if she doesn't want me to,

she cries and wriggles and – this probably sounds weird – but I'm sure she's saying: 'Why *should* I?' [G, 3 months]

G has become assertive. She can tell me what she really wants. I'm very proud of her because I was never allowed to be like that. [G, 8 months]

B can't talk yet but he can 'tell' me what he thinks. He has an opinion on absolutely *everything*! [B, 2 years]

Mothers discover that already they can start to 'negotiate' with their babies.

G hates having her face wiped. But if I stop to ask her *permission*, I've found she lets me and I can get two wipes in! [G, 6 months]

I put G on the bed and she's: 'I don't wanna lie on the bed.' Then I put her hat on, and suddenly she's: 'Oh, I get it, we're going out.' Then she's excited because she loves going out. [G, 8 months]

It can be awkward to deal with young, strong-willed, independent thinkers. They haven't yet got the experience to realise that they may be objecting to something we are doing for their benefit.

At what age can a baby think of the future? I offer G a glass of water and she's: 'No. I don't want it.' Then, about two minutes later, she points to the water because it's exactly what she needs. But when is she able to predict that? [G, 10 months]

It's hard for a mother, then, to know whether her child has a reason for not wanting something, or whether it's more of a whim. Understandably, mothers sometimes get it wrong.

G refused to put her shoes on. We once spent more than an hour on a doorstep with her refusing. But now I think they hurt her feet. [*Crying*] I got some new shoes for her, and they were fine. I feel so mean, making her wear shoes that hurt. [G, 19 months; 36 weeks pregnant]

The transition from pre-verbal signs and sounds to language can seem imperceptible. Mother and baby already understand one another well. Researchers have studied the complexity of language development, but they may not be aware of its long 'pre-history'.

I've been noticing G's language development. First she used to say the first letter of the word she meant. There's an awful lot of things that start with a 'B'. Then she added a vowel and the consonant-vowel-consonant. Now she points to things, and I think she *wants* them, but she doesn't. I've just peeled her a banana, but she's walked away. She didn't want to eat it. She just wanted to hear the *word*. [G, 17 months]

Children's speech, at first, can be hard to follow to anyone who doesn't know them well. I often have to ask a mother what her child is trying to tell me. Nearly always, the child's mother will know. She also has a good idea of how much her child can understand. And this needs regular updating.

Children understand things but you have to find the language that they can manage. 'Potty training' has no meaning for G. But I say: 'We need to keep our undies dry.' She has no trouble understanding that. [G, 21 months]

Children's understanding is usually ahead of their ability to speak. They have strong emotions and, at first, mothers have to work out what the emotions are all about. But, by now, it's much easier to identify than it was at the beginning.

G gets stressed if I only go out of the room for a moment to fetch B a clean nappy. Her stress was getting to me and making me stressed. Next time it happened, I looked at her face and I asked: 'Are you feeling *frightened* if I go out?' And she stopped crying.

It's made a huge difference to me. I think I have to make it better for her. But what she really wants is for me to *understand* her. [G, 21 months; B, 8 weeks]

B has tantrums and F says it's the 'terrible twos'. But I've found he calms down when I understand him. I say: 'Are you upset because you wanted a bath?' And he . . . [*gesturing her child's emphatic nod*] and then he's all right with it. [B, 23 months]

2G has food allergies, and she cried all day for most of her first year. I had to keep holding her. I thought this must be hard for 1G, and tried to see it from her point of view. So, when 2G was a few months old, I said: '2G won't always be like this.' And I was glad I'd said it because I could see from 1G's face that that was exactly what she *did* think. [1G, 3 years; 2G, 15 months]

But even an attentive mother can't understand everything. As children develop, they often have ideas that are far too complex to explain. A typical situation arises when a child asks for something. He wants it for a particular purpose but can't verbalise his complicated plan, and his mother doesn't realise how important it is to him. It would mean extra trouble for her, and besides she is short of time, so she gives a brusque: 'No.' Her child may feel frustrated and furious. However, if he has learned from experience that getting angry still doesn't achieve what he wants, he may resort to whining. To his mother, whining, especially after a clear 'No', is very irritating.

The one thing that really gets to me is whining. G does whine. I tell her that I'll always give her what she asks for, if I can, if she asks for it nicely. [G, 3 years; B, 6 weeks]

But one mother suddenly saw her son's whining from his point of view.

I get very annoyed when B asks for something in a whiney voice.

But then I stopped to ask myself how it looked from his way round. And I realised something. B's a child. He feels powerless. He whines when he thinks he's *never* going to be able to get the thing he wants. [B, 2 years]

Social life, even at home, is complicated. Mothers don't always appreciate how many 'rules' they have which seem obvious to them but not to their children.

B is very keen to do the right thing. When he found out he wasn't supposed to draw on the wall, he cried and was very upset and tried to rub it all off. [B, 2 years]

Mothers also often don't realise how carefully their children listen to what they say, and how they enjoy repeating their mothers' words. But a mother's words can sound different when a child says them.

When my friends ask G how she is, she says: 'I'm *amazing*.' It makes me realise what she hears me say about her. To me, she *is* amazing. [G, 24 months]

Once children become good at language, they think of original ideas of their own.

I see it as my job to give G a good day. But she opposes me over *everything*. One morning, she got up saying: 'Today, I'm going to have a *sad* day!' [G, 2 years; B, 11 months]

1G asks me if I am going to die, and where is Heaven, and who is God. I feel I'm like a scientist, trying to find the answers that will satisfy her and not be frightening, but which are also true. I'm not going to tell her that I won't die. But she gets very worried and lies in bed, thinking about it. And if I say I don't know the answer to what she's asked me, she'll say: '*Try!*' [1G, 3 years; 2G, 11 months]

My mum was telling me about when her father died. B overheard her and asked: 'What did she say? Did someone die?' I said: 'Yes, your great-grandfather. A long time ago.' B said: 'Am I going to die?' That question took me by surprise, so I said: 'Yes. But not for a long time.' Then B said: 'I don't know what death *is*.' And walked off. I was *amazed* at his thinking. [B, 3 years; G, 13 months]

Children also like to know how things work. Mothers often find they aren't sure of the answers themselves. They start to check, and brush up on their education on science and technology, sometimes discovering information they never knew before. The children want the answer immediately, and are usually on to another subject long before the mother has found the answer to their earlier question.

Eventually, mothers can see how articulate their children have become. Those non-verbal newborns have gone for ever. Here are people who can tell you what they are thinking.

The early days weren't easy for me. But my children are wonderful people. They all talk a lot. It's exciting for me to hear them. They have interesting thoughts and they put them so well. [G, 21 years; 1B, 18 years; 2B, 16 years]

What about speech-impaired children, unable to talk at all? It may be difficult to communicate with them, and their mothers may feel desperate. But many learn to observe them. They then discover that these children, too, still manage to give signals. It must be vital for a disabled child to feel noticed and understood.

One mother, writing in the *Guardian*, remembered understanding her daughter who had cerebral palsy and epilepsy, and died aged four:

Megan was a star. She was never able to speak, but she could certainly communicate. She had a huge smile and told us with her eyes what she wanted – she'd point to things, and if she didn't like something, she'd poke her bottom lip out . . . Others might not have been able to tell what she wanted, but we always knew.[52]

And the mother of a five-year-old with severe cerebral palsy wrote:

Without language [Ailsa] communicates in cries. If she is hungry or thirsty, she sticks out her tongue. Recently we had a small breakthrough: she has developed a 'pretend cry' for when she simply wants a cuddle.[53]

Another mother of a seven-year-old with such severe cerebral palsy that his only mode of communication was through his eyes, wrote:

I'm currently fighting with the educational psychologist. I believe my son understands everything, but she disagrees.[54]

It seems surprising that an educational psychologist would disbelieve the observations of a mother, especially one who has to attend to her son night and day.

It's exciting to learn from mothers that speech-impaired children want to communicate not just basic but complex ideas.

When children notice that their mothers understand their early efforts to talk, they can't wait to talk to other people. They have the confidence to persevere, even if the other person doesn't immediately understand what they are saying. They keep trying, because they know the satisfaction that comes from getting their message across.

Not every mother has the time or, perhaps, the patience for this. Then the child's father or an older sibling, a grandparent or even a professional may take on the role of being the first person to initiate the child into conversation.

Children who spend time in daycare have more to learn. They work out how to behave in a group, how to get attention when they need it and when it's better to fit in without a fuss. This learning is very important. But it would be a mistake to see communication in a group as a substitute for what a child learns from his mother.

What happens if a mother keeps dismissing her child's early efforts to communicate? Some people dislike the sound, and snap at the child to 'talk properly'. If no one supports the child, he may withdraw from saying anything but a few essentials. He may decide that this whole area leads to humiliation. He may shut down his social antennae and become difficult for other people to reach.

Researchers in Britain and the United States have found that some mothers hardly speak to their children. They point out that these children start reception class at their primary schools virtually unable to talk. These researchers discovered that this was not because their mothers were immigrants with their own language problems. No, these mothers were simply too busy or too tired to talk to their children.[55, 56] However, not getting practice at talking is a serious deprivation for us. As David Attenborough, the well-known broadcaster and naturalist, put it: 'Man's passion to communicate and to receive communications seems as central to his success as a species as the fin was to the fish or the feather to the birds.'[57]

Then what about the countless mothers who put in years of sensitive work and enable their children to become capable talkers? Many of these mothers taught themselves what to do. They weren't trained. Yet their achievement goes unrecorded. When children start school, those who have difficulty in communicating will be allocated remedial help, if it's available. The rest of the children will be absorbed into school life, as if they were mysteriously able to manage complex communication without any help. Isn't this an important time to recognise and appreciate all their mothers' work?

And what happens when a mother has a second child? Is this a much easier beginning because she has already got to know her first? Some mothers do feel more confident with their second child.

> I am enjoying it so much more this time. I am *letting* myself enjoy it. I am able to relax because I know I can do it. So, this time, it is quite a different experience. [G, 2 years; B, 2 months]

But for another mother, having a second child was harder.

> I thought it would be easier having a second child because now I'd know what to do. But a second child brings up different issues. I don't know how to divide myself between the two of them. I was brought up by a single mother and I was her only child. Being a mother means you are on a constant learning curve. [G, 3 years; B, 6 months]

Many mothers go through a new learning curve with their first child after the second one is born. They notice how 'difficult' the older child has become. Because the mother is tired from looking after two, she may find her older child unreasonable. Even though he can talk, his feelings may be too strong and confusing for his vocabulary. More than ever, he needs her help.

> *First mother:* G keeps whining. She can complain for hours. I don't know what it's about. [G, 21 months; B, 2 months]

> *Second mother:* Is it because she doesn't like waiting? B had to be patient while I breastfed G until I could give him what he wanted. Then suddenly his patience would go, and he'd have a tantrum if he had to wait two seconds for me to put a cup down. [B, 3 years; G, 7 months]

> *First mother:* G doesn't like having to wait.

I remember one mother saying that when her second baby was born her little boy changed overnight from being her wonderful three-year-old into a child who kept doing annoying things, so she kept hearing herself shouting: 'No!' I remembered that, so I've tried very hard not to get angry with G. It can be difficult sometimes. [G, 3 years; B, 6 weeks]

However, although mothers have to give their immediate attention to their newborns, they say they continue learning about their older or oldest one.

When your second child is born you think: well, that's a baby, I know how to do that. So you still go on worrying about the older one. [B, 3 years; G, 11 months]

First mother: With a new baby, you feel you know some of it. It's nice. But you *still* worry about the older one. [B, 6 years; G, 4 months]

Second mother: Yes. The older one keeps meeting new situations. [B, 3 years; G, 11 months]

I'm starting to worry about when 1B reaches his teens. [1B, 10 years; 2B, 7 years]

It sounds as though mothers often give their firstborns a more anxious kind of attention right through their childhoods. Many mothers have said that when their new baby is born, the older one looks huge in size and seems nearly adult in maturity. But he is still a young child, and he still needs his mother. Mothers discover that giving time to the older one may turn him from a 'difficult' child into an easy one again.

B was asleep so I had an hour with G to herself. I don't think we've done that since B was born. It's made a huge difference to G's behaviour. I'm going to have an hour alone with her more often. [G, 2 years; B, 6 months]

B was being very difficult, always testing the boundaries. But then I gave him some one-on-one time. It's made a lot of difference to his behaviour. [B, 5 years; 1G, 2 years; 2G, 3 months]

As the siblings grow older, mothers are surprised to see how much they are affected by one another. Typically, the younger child closely studies the older one.

> B doesn't need toys. I offer him G's old toys, and that's not what he wants. He is completely absorbed in watching what G is doing. [G, 23 months; B, 4 months]

> 1B hates brushing his teeth and creates a big fuss. But 2B watches and he's *very* keen to brush his teeth. He wants to do everything 1B does. So if I don't give him his toothbrush when I am helping 1B to brush, he gets very upset. [1B, 4 years; 2B, 13 months]

And it's fascinating for mothers when siblings can talk to one another.

> G is much more responsible when I'm out of the room. I hear her saying: 'Be careful, B,' and, 'I'll have *this* and you have *that*.' [G, 2 years; B, 13 months]

> I heard 1B tell another boy: 'Don't hit 2B's head!' He's protective of his brother. Mind you, *he* hits 2B on the head. [1B, 3 years; 2B, 12 months]

> I was out of the room for a moment, when I could hear 2B crying. I heard G say: 'I'll get Mummy, and you [*1B*] tell 2B he'll be all right.' [G, 4 years; 1B, 2 years; 2B, 4 weeks]

How much have mothers learned from having more than one child? In a revealing study of experienced mothers, researchers were surprised to hear them say that, even with more experience, they didn't think they had become more competent. But when the researchers studied their results, they realised that because mothers of two or more children had more challenges, their expectations of themselves had increased. So they simply didn't perceive how competent they had become.[58]

As they become more capable, mothers catch sight of the interesting people that their children have become.

G and 1B went to spend two nights with my mum. I watched them walking down the road with her, talking to her, one on each side, holding her hands. It was amazing. They both looked so separate and independent. They are real *people*. [G, 5 years; 1B, 3 years; 2B, 14 months]

B is starting school next week. He's ready for it. He's very keen to learn everything and he loves the company of other children. But I'll *miss* him [*tears*]. I was saying this to one of the teachers and she said: 'Don't worry. You'll soon meet other mums and go for coffee mornings.' I know she meant well. But I've met other mothers. I'll miss B. [B, 4 years; G, 8 months]

I wonder whether there should be a celebration for mothers when they feel their children have reached the stage of needing them a little less. I don't know what the markers would be. And there are sure to be future challenges ahead. But couldn't mothers have a special time to celebrate? These early years are the hardest work. They have learned so much. It's easy to blame themselves for what they didn't know at the time. But, every so often, a mother reaches a moment to marvel at her child and in the same breath to see herself as an essential part of his journey.

CHAPTER FIVE

Anger from deep inside

Many women only learn how angry they can be when they become mothers. When they do get angry, it's often a sudden outburst that startles them, as well as their children.

> B wouldn't go to sleep on Tuesday night. I was *incandescent* with anger. I really lost it. [B, 6 months]

This mother had wanted her son to feel secure when he fell asleep, so she always lay down beside him. On the Tuesday when he stayed awake, it must have seemed as though she had kept her side of the 'deal', while he had reneged on his. She knew she wasn't being fair because he couldn't possibly have known what a deal was, but she was still furious.

It's easy for a mother to get angry with her child for not doing what she wants. We have all been children ourselves. Probably most of us can remember times when adults expressed anger – physically, verbally or silently – to us when we were little. A mother's anger is especially powerful. Even years later, a chance event may remind us of it and we immediately feel 'small'. Generations of daughters turn into mothers and pass this experience on.

The fourteenth-century poet Dante was about thirty-five when he wrote his poem on Purgatory. He wanted readers to understand how he felt when he finally met his beloved Beatrice there. So, for this extraordinary meeting, he chose an ordinary experience that he was sure his readers would recognise. When Beatrice reproached him, 'Mine eyes drooped down,' he wrote. 'So doth the mother seem stern to her child, as she seemed to me.'[59] His reaction still sounds recognisable, seven centuries later.

All through history, writers have been clear that anger can be destructive. The Roman philosopher Seneca devoted one work entirely to *De Ira* (*On Anger*). He said anger was 'the desire to take vengeance for a wrong'.[60] He gave examples of the futility of getting angry, followed by ways of avoiding or controlling it. He was writing primarily for men and about men, so he didn't discuss angry mothers. 'The greatest cure for anger is delay,' he wrote.[61] This sounds good advice for any angry person.

But anger isn't always about 'vengeance' for a wrong. Anger is a natural response to a wrong, but the angry person may not be seeking vengeance but justice.

The trouble with trying to 'cure' anger is that the perceived wrong, which evoked it, will probably get lost. A fictional example of a mother trying to cure her anger is Mrs March in Louisa M. Alcott's *Little Women*. The 'little women' are the four March sisters. In one chapter, two of them, Jo and Amy, reacted to one another with a fury that Seneca would have recognised. But Jo was shocked at herself and confessed to her mother how guilty she felt for her hot temper. To her surprise, her mother told her that she too was often angry.

> 'I've been trying to cure it [*her temper*] for forty years, and have only succeeded in controlling it. I am angry nearly every day of my life, Jo; but I have learned not to show it; and I still hope not to feel it, though it may take me another forty years to do so.'[62]

Why was Mrs March angry 'nearly every day'? One example is given: "'. . . when I had four little daughters round me, and we were poor, . . . I am not patient by nature, and it tried me very much to see my children wanting anything.'"[63] There might have been very little she could have done about their poverty. She was a full-time, and therefore dependent, wife and mother in nineteenth-century America. But her anger at the unfairness of her situation is understandable. Why should she cure herself of that?

She was being unusually honest in confiding to her daughter that she felt anger that she tried not to show. Jo resolved to emulate her mother in trying to subdue her own anger – and the novel, published in 1868, has had great international success. So how many millions of girls have read this exchange and identified with Jo?

Today, when mothers of young children talk to one another, they often admit to getting angry. Like Mrs March, they feel guilty for it. But they don't usually describe large issues like poverty. In fact, to an outsider, the reasons why some mothers get angry might seem ridiculously trivial. No serious wrong has been done.

> When B cries and I can't calm him, I get violent inside. I'd never do anything to B. But I feel like hitting my head or banging it against a wall. [B, 5 months]
>
> I get so angry when G whines. [G, 2 years; B, 4 months]
>
> I feel everyone needs me and I can't give to everyone. I was getting angry and feeling that I wasn't being the mother I wanted to be. [1B, 3 years; 2B, 2 months]

These situations don't sound very stressful. In each case, the mother felt upset that she couldn't satisfy her child or children. But surely this is unavoidable. A mother is only human and can't always do what her child wants. Does she need to get angry about that?

The daily life of a mother can be full of frustrations. Often, her child will do things that create extra work for her. He didn't mean to. And perhaps, each time, it only meant a little extra trouble. But these little extra troubles can add up to a lot of time spent doing annoying tasks. Her child is too young to appreciate any of this and, to cap it all, may complain of boredom while she is cleaning up after him. There may be no one around to sympathise. It can feel unfair.

F had a day off work today. He said he was tired and I could see that he was. Anyway, I gave him a lie-in. [*This seemed to mean taking their two children out for a walk to make sure they did not disturb him.*] I was trying to get G to sleep in her sling. Then B found some dog poo. I told him to walk round it, but somehow he got a bit on his hand. Then he started screaming and that woke G up. And I felt this *huge* wave of fury go right through me. Who was I furious with? I've no idea. Maybe with the whole situation. [B, 2 years; G, 5 months]

My sense of humour seems to have gone. 1B thinks it's a huge joke to pour his orange juice through his fork so it splashes down on the kitchen floor, or to put cornflakes on his toast, or to squirt the washing-up liquid. [1B, 3 years; 2B, 3 months]

When I'm kneeling down to clean food off the floor, my head gets kicked and the thing that annoys me most is sticky hands in my hair. It's nearly always the day after I've washed it. [1G, 4 years; 2G, 23 months]

Again, nothing outrageous happened. Yet mothers are surprised at how angry they felt. Those who have returned to paid work might have more reason to be under stress. But these three examples were from mothers on 'maternity leave'. Surely they have plenty of time to deal with a few minor setbacks. Why did they get so angry?

It's not ordinary anger. It comes from deep inside. Like being
possessed by a demon. [B, 2 years]

Often, a mother describes getting angry after she has already
held back her temper several times. In the end, a small incident
tips the balance. The mother's anger might seem out of proportion
to the latest event, but makes more sense when understood as the
point at which her frustration suddenly outweighs her patience.

I find it hard to be consistent. G does things in the morning and
they don't bother me at all. But when she does the same things in
the evening, I find them *so* annoying. [G, 2 years]

When we got out of the park, a string got tangled round the
pushchair wheels. It was the last *straw*. I didn't control myself then
because I . . . [*She gestured stamping both feet in frustration.*] It was
a childish tantrum of my own. And B remembered it. To my *shame*.
In the evening, F asked B if he'd had a nice day, and B pointed to
me, stamped his feet and laughed. [B, 2 years; G, 4 months]

I feel so *terrible* when I get angry with 1B that I forget all the times
before I got angry when I was patient. I think I need to remind
myself or keep a diary. [1B, 4 years; 2B, 13 months]

It might sound as if the mother is angry with her child. She
may feel, in an angry moment, as if her anger is all his fault. But,
if her child really was the culprit, then expressing her anger would
bring relief. Instead, mothers keep saying that they feel guilty at
voicing anger towards their children. They find relief when they
are clearer about why they are so angry.

Frequently a mother runs out of patience because she needs a
break. There may be no other adult with her who could take over
for a few minutes to let her recover.

First mother: G usually falls asleep if I carry her up and down the
stairs. But I've got really angry when I've walked up and down

the stairs five times with G and she still won't settle. I feel like throwing her out of the window. It doesn't last. As soon as I calm down, I'm fine. But I feel so *guilty*. [G, 10 months]

Second mother, with quick understanding: Is it because you were hoping to do something else? [G, 14 months]

First mother: Yes. And the more she cries, the more the cup of tea or whatever I'm hoping for becomes *desperately* important.

It's easy to see, from a back-seat-driver position, how the first mother's longing for her baby to sleep so she can make a cup of tea is likely to be felt by the baby in her arms. It's hard to fall asleep if someone is angrily waiting for you to drop off. So the mother may have inadvertently started a spiral of anger and wakefulness between the two of them.

Mothers don't get statutory breaks and are often alone with their babies, so their time can seem to stretch ahead endlessly without a breather and chance to rest. This situation is recent. The old support systems that seemed to have worked well in the past are now unavailable. Husbands, grandmothers, siblings, cousins, neighbours and friends are usually working far away. Working people may be free when they come home in the evening, but then they too feel in need of a rest.

It's easy for a mother, alone with her baby, to 'overstretch' and to overlook herself in wanting to give her best to her baby. After all, a baby's needs are usually basic and it is possible for a mother to meet most of them. Moreover, her baby's needs sound urgent, whereas she has learned to wait. So she can easily lose touch with herself.

I know how old G is to the exact week. But I was sitting on the train wondering how old *I* was. I couldn't work it out. Finally, I got out my calculator. I'm thirty-four. [G, 12 months]

I never dreamed I could be so angry with B. It's easy to lose track of *yourself* when you're focusing on your child. [B, 13 months]

This partly explains why mothers get angry over apparently trivial frustrations. In overstretching and forgetting to think about themselves, they have 'overbalanced' in the child's favour. Their angry outbursts make sense as an effort to redress the balance by swinging an equal amount towards their forgotten selves. But it doesn't achieve justice because neither extreme feels right.

There is a particular kind of exhaustion, unique to mothers.

I wish I could have a whole day off. I wish I could go to a hotel, and go to bed and *sleep,* and there'd be no one clutching at my boobs [*to breastfeed*], and no one waking me up in the night. Then I could wake up in my own time, go to the loo entirely by myself, have my shower without having to listen out and have a whole breakfast to myself without sharing anything and no one taking bits off my plate. [G, 12 months]

I crave time to do nothing. [G, 18 months; 17 weeks pregnant]

Stillness. Stillness and silence. [G, 21 months]

And what seems a modest wish:

I think: If only you [*husband and children*] would all go away and leave me to have a cup of coffee for *ten* minutes to get myself back again. [B, 2 years; G, 5 months]

But don't most mothers have friends or relatives who offer them 'time off' while they take over babycare? They do – but is 'time off' the right term for it?

I don't like 'time off'. Those words make me angry. It doesn't *feel* like time off. It's time I *need* to feel like myself again. [G, 7 months]

Mothers may feel that a quick outburst of anger would clear

the air after hours of frustration and self-restraint. But it doesn't. And, once started, it's not a quick outburst. Mothers say they have lost control of themselves. Their angry voices seem to be rushing on without their own consent.

> Once the anger starts, I can't stop it. It feels horrible, being out of control, and I know I shouldn't be like that. I can hear my voice saying things that I know I shouldn't say. [B, 2 years; G, 5 months]

> There's a very fine line between coping and not coping. When you're coping, it's like it's all easy and you can go on like this for ever. When you fall into not coping, it's dreadful. I've said things to 1B that I told myself I'd *never* say. [1B, 3 years; 2B, 5 weeks]

> I find you get days when everything is going well, and you feel amazed at the amount of patience you can find in yourself for your children. And there are other days, usually when you are tired, when you say horrible things, and you wish you'd never said them, and you try to stop, but the whole day seems to unravel like that. [B, 5 years; 1G, 2 years; 2G, 7 months]

> When I get stressed, I find I shout, even when I don't mean to. I try to get calm, but this voice comes out. It's not my voice. I've *lost* my voice. [B, 6 years; G 13 months]

These examples are from mothers of several children, but mothers of one child have made similar comments. Whose voice was it if a mother doesn't feel it was her own? There are aspects of ourselves that we hardly know until we experience considerable stress. Under exceptional stress, our behaviour becomes exceptional and unfamiliar too. So the strange voice might not seem like the mother's usual one, but it is still hers.

Are mothers, then, under exceptional stress? As mothers at home, they have no boss, no deadlines, no appraisals or presentations. True. But people under these workplace pressures earn social respect. Most women become mothers after being part of the working community and have enjoyed the respect that comes with it. So it is a shock to discover that, as mothers, they have been socially 'demoted'. If they delegate the care of their babies to professionals and quickly return to work, they can regain their previous status. But if they leave the workforce temporarily to look after their babies themselves, they can feel like social nonentities.

A mother gets very little affirmation for her mothering. So when she goes out with her baby, to go shopping or for a walk through the park, she contacts a 'social world' where she is barely respected. She is often treated as someone who is 'not working', in contrast to the bus driver or shop cashier, park attendant or whomever else she talks to.

A mother can cope with this if she and her baby are in harmony. Then she feels vindicated for the life she has chosen. But she and her baby may have been 'at odds' all morning. Usually, when a mother says she is angry with her baby or child, it turns out that he has done something at an inconvenient time for her, or won't stop crying, whining or grumbling. It's easy to feel he is criticising her mothering and has turned against her. A niggling voice asks whether she is any use as a mother anyway. Someone else might do it all better, perhaps a trained professional. Yes, and perhaps she really ought to be back at her job. So when he is discontented, despite all her efforts, she can feel betrayed by the very person all her efforts are for.

There is a constant temptation to get angry with a small person who cannot defend himself. And when that same person has been grumpy all morning, giving in to that temptation can be easy.

Yet one reason that many mothers feel so guilty is that they were themselves daughters of mothers who got angry. They know exactly how hurtful it can feel to be a child on the receiving end.

My mum used to get very angry, and I spent most of my childhood being afraid of her. Even now, I always look at her face to see if she is in a bad mood. I can never relax. [G, 8 months]

My parents got angry with me and I did *not* find it helpful. [B, 14 months]

Some parents went beyond verbal anger.

Both my parents hit me when I was a child, as a punishment. And I was wondering if it did me any harm. I think the *real* harm is the damage it's done to my relations with them. Now we are not close. When you realise how angry they can be with you, you keep your distance. [1B, 3 years; 2B, 6 months]

After the mother had spoken, nearly every mother in the circle admitted that she too had been hit by one, or both, of her parents, and that she had distanced herself in similar ways.

However, other mothers came from families where no one got angry. For different reasons, they too felt that they shouldn't show anger.

In my family, no one ever got angry. It wasn't done. I've only been angry once, no, maybe two times in my entire life. And both times it was traumatic. I'm sure it would have been much better if I'd been allowed to be a *bit* angry. [B, 3 months]

I was always told I was being very silly when I was angry as a child. So now, when I feel angry, there's a secondary feeling of being very silly. [G, 2 years; B, 6 months]

Perhaps these early experiences explain why some mothers express their feelings indirectly.

I think I react by withdrawal. I do what G wants, but it's like: 'All right, we'll go into the other room if you *insist*.' I guess that's not great for her. [G, 17 months]

Some mothers manage to avoid expressing anger to their children, and instead vent their feelings on to inanimate objects.

> G keeps waking up at night. She gets hungry and I can't blame her. But I felt I couldn't keep it together any more. So I picked up my phone and threw it across the floor. It broke and it's ruined. I don't usually get angry, but I actually felt good about throwing my phone. [G, 5 months]

> The other day, I was breastfeeding and B bit me. I managed to stay calm. But the anger was still in me and I had to let it out. Later, I went to the kitchen door and slammed it – about eight or ten times. I got the anger out of me. [B, 6 months]

> When G was small, I felt so frustrated I'd wait till she was asleep and go down to the kitchen and smash cups. [G, 21 months]

These mothers resorted to physical actions to release the tension caused by anger that they thought they shouldn't be feeling. Throwing or breaking something seemed to be a way of releasing tension by 'hurting' an external object. So their actions gave some relief.

Shouting or throwing something can get rid of anger, but doesn't help to identify the underlying sense of injustice that has usually given rise to them. People aren't roused to anger for nothing. Are there more basic reasons why mothers get angry?

> I have times when I feel so angry, I throw cushions around. I feel very bad about it. I'm not angry with my baby. It's always something . . . something inside your*self*. [B, 13 months]

What kind of 'something' is it?

> *Mother*: My anger seems to come from nowhere. But, if I'm not too tired to look back, there's nearly always a trigger, which usually has a 'should' attached to it: I 'should' be able to manage something.

Me: Does it help to find the trigger?

Mother: Yes, it's a definite help. I feel relief. And then I'm not angry any more. [B, 10 months]

Many mothers get angry with themselves because they feel they 'should' be managing better. Their anger bursts out from a build-up of self-criticism and seems like a kind of self-flagellation. However confident a mother seems, she is sure to have had moments of self-doubt.[64] There are so many important decisions to make in bringing up her child.

The real difficulty is not B. B's lovely. It's me. It's the self-doubt. I have good days and other days when I just don't know if I'm doing it right. [B, 7 months]

When I've decided I've got to work [*freelance at home*] and then B needs me, I get furious with him. But I realise: okay. You don't know how to deal with him. Once I admitted to myself that I didn't know, I stopped being angry. [B, 15 months]

Mothers are in an odd position. Sometimes they feel sure that mothering is responsible work, and that they are making crucial decisions that will benefit their children's future. The results will become more obvious as their children grow older and go to school. But this conflicts with their awareness of pervasive social disrespect. Everyone knows that 'real' work is paid. So if mothers think they are doing important work, well, that just shows how deluded they must be and how out of touch they are with the 'real' world.

Mothers often seesaw in mood between feeling responsible and feeling useless. People need social affirmation for the value of their work. When it is absent, many mothers become extremely self-critical.

I think when you are a mother your 'inner voice' gets louder. I'm always thinking: Am I doing it right? [B, 4 months]

I think everything should be perfect for this perfect baby, and then I feel so guilty if I lose my temper when I'm with her. [G, 7 months]

First mother: If I make one mistake and get one thing wrong, I know perfectly well that it's irrational, but the *feeling* is that it means there is something wrong with me and I'm a bad person. And *that's* when I get angry. [1B, 3 years; 2B, 4 months]

Second mother: I like everything to be perfect too and I feel responsible when it isn't. I can *so* relate to what you are saying. [B, 5 years; 1G, 2 years; 2G, 6 months]

Mothers can then recognise anyone else in this painful self-critical position:

I heard a mother shouting at her baby of about six months: 'I *told* you it was hot.' He'd knocked her tea over, but he was all right and didn't seem scalded. She said: 'I'll have to put my mug up *here* now.' Her baby couldn't have understood a word of it. I could hear she was telling *herself* off. [G, 18 months]

A mother who has only conceived after a long time, or who conceived by IVF, or who adopted, may feel under extra pressure to be a 'perfect' mother. So she may feel especially guilty if she gets angry.

I had so many miscarriages that I was in my forties by the time I had B. I love him so much. But I don't understand why I keep getting *so* angry. It's probably myself I'm angry with more than B. But I never used to get angry. I'm a very gentle person. [B, 18 months]

It's incredibly confusing. You've got a baby through IVF which is what you wanted, so you feel you should be perfect and never complain, and you feel unable sometimes to ask for help. And your partner can say unhelpful things like: 'Well, you've got what you wanted, so what on earth's the problem?' [G, 8 years]

However, once mothers can see that they get angry because of tensions in themselves, and that their children provide the triggers rather than being the whole reason for anger, they also see that their feelings didn't erupt out of 'nowhere' but escalated.

> I made myself check my feelings every hour, and that helped. I found there was a pattern. At certain times of day, I got angry more easily. [B, 13 months]

> I reach a certain stage and then I flip [*from calm to anger*]. I don't think that's good for B. So I'm trying to catch myself at an earlier stage. It's very difficult. I've no idea what sort of thought processes I go through before I get there. [B, 2 years]

Thoughts like these help mothers to see that they could find ways to cope with their angry feelings at an earlier stage, before losing control and blaming their children.

> B wakes in the night all bright and ready to go. Sometimes I can cope, sometimes not. When I feel angry, it's so physical. I have to do something to let those feelings out of me. Also, I want to model to B how to get angry. I want him to be able to manage his own anger and not be afraid of it. So I make 'Brrrr!' noises [*demonstrating and shaking her head in rhythm*]. B thinks it's very funny. But I hope he can see that I'm letting my anger out as well. [B, 9 months]

> I try not to shout when I'm angry. I walk out of the room. Or I *sing*. I find I can't sing and be angry at the same time. [G, 13 months]

> B was ill and I was disappointed in myself. He was whining and I knew he felt terrible. But where were my motherly instincts? Where were my empathy and compassion? I felt so angry I just wanted to run away. After I'd admitted it to my partner, I could accept myself and could respond better. [B, 13 months]

It is obviously important for her child that a mother is more in control of her feelings. But there is always a risk that calming herself, or even identifying her individual reasons for getting angry, will mean that she doesn't recognise the underlying injustice that aroused it. We haven't yet accounted for the depths of motherly anger.

> I feel *angry* at how hard it is for mothers in our society. There's nowhere for my anger to go. There's nothing I can do. [B, 6 months]

> I have a right to be angry. I'm a mother alone all day at home with a baby. That's something real to be angry about. [B, 8 months]

> We've been sold a lie. We were told we could have it all. And it's not true. We can't. [B, 11 months]

The writer Rachel Cusk would have agreed. Mothers, she wrote, 'may have cared beautifully for their children but their politics have been left to wrack and ruin . . . So their anger is in itself a little startling, coming as it does out of the (politically, at least) noiseless realm of modern female domestic life.'[65] This is a useful observation. Mothers' anger from the 'noiseless realm of modern female domestic life' is a significant description.

Women have only recently demanded a political voice. But not yet as mothers. For millennia, mothers have been politically silent, dependent on the goodwill of their husbands. Some mothers managed to exert their influence indirectly. But that can't be as empowering as having the right to a political voice.

One mother, Vanessa Olorenshaw, challenged this situation in her spirited pamphlet 'The Politics of Mothering', now available online.

> The valuable work we do [as mothers] is ignored and devalued and our voices are not heard or heeded, given the fact that we are effectively consigned to the cupboard, at home, with no respected

public presence or influence. When no political party speaks to us or for us, we are rendered effectively disenfranchised. When we feel unable to make our voices heard, we are disempowered.[66]

Isn't this good reason for mothers to be angry? Can we expect modern mothers to stay calm in the middle of mounting daily frustrations, when they sense that their motherly achievements are 'ignored and devalued'? At the moment, all the British political parties are trying to 'help' mothers return to paid work. *Motherly* work receives no recognition. And isn't part of the trouble that mothers themselves are usually too busy and too tired to think beyond planning today and tomorrow, so they don't see that there are political issues at stake? Have their unfamiliar, angry voices, often misdirected to their children, been diverted from a legitimate sense of injustice?

If so, mothers are not only angry because of daily frustrations. They are balancing their relationships to their children with their responsibilities to the society they live in. There is no Minister for Mothers to speak up for their concerns. Their responsibilities are many, but they receive only minimal support and recognition in return.

Their daily lives are affected. A mother may be in the street, looking 'normal', but feeling raw. Her whole morning has been exasperating. The smallest friendly comment from another adult can soothe and restore her. I wonder if passers-by realise how calming their words can be.

I was in the park and I took B out of his sling. A man walking past said: 'You did that nicely.' And I floated on that remark for twenty-four hours. When B woke up at night, I found I wasn't angry. [B, 12 months]

I feel tense all the time. I get no praise, so I'm always criticising myself. My friend visited and I thought she would think I was a bad mother. She asked: 'How are you getting on at uni?' [*The mother was finishing her university course.*] I said: 'Well, I know I'm trying to do too much and being rubbish at all of it.' My friend said: 'I actually think you are doing everything well.' That was so nice. [B, 12 months]

I keep noticing people's kindness to myself. Sometimes I'm on the phone trying to sort out my taxes, and people can be really rude. I can be on the phone for half an hour and it's frustrating to get nowhere. And I find myself taking it out on B. But if someone talks to me kindly it makes a *huge* difference. [B, 16 months]

If mothers were better understood and supported by people around them, they might feel less angry when their children grumble and whine.

There may be times when a mother can justify her anger with her child, usually an older one. That kind of anger is quite different. She doesn't usually feel guilty after expressing it. She and her child both know he is responsible for something within his power to control, such as a promise to be home by 10 p.m., which he fails to keep. It's not like the one-sided bargains she made when he was younger. Her anger here is to strengthen her case, not to get rid of tension.

Many mothers worry that their young children will be 'emotionally scarred' or 'damaged' by their frequent outbursts of temper. They also wonder what they are teaching their children about dealing with their own angry feelings.

When a mother is furious, her child may feel as though their relationship has broken down. So it helps when a mother makes it clear to her child that she did get angry, but knows that she shouldn't have unleashed her feelings on to him so forcefully. Then her child seems better able to accept it as a blip in their usual trustworthy relationship.

My mum used to get very angry, and I spent most of my childhood being afraid of her. I get angry too, and I want G to know that Mummy can get angry, but G's not going to get hit or punished. It's a *safe* anger. And I tell her when Mummy's feeling better. [G, 11 months]

You're allowed to get angry. One little burst isn't going to cause massive damage. My mum used to stay angry for days and days. [G, 9 years; 1B, 7 years; 2B, 4 years; 3B, 20 months]

When there are several children, the siblings can support one another. Provided the mother hasn't terrorised them all with a really brutal anger, a posse of siblings can offset the edge of their mother's furious temper.

My children make me so angry. I've turned into a shouter, but they still don't listen. I get fed up when I've asked them to come and put their tights on *five* times and they still won't. One day, I got so furious I was literally jumping up and down with rage. And they just *laughed* at me. They say: 'Remember the time when Mummy jumped up and down?' [1G, 4 years; B, 2 years; 2G, 11 months]

Children can be moody and angry themselves. But they can also be surprisingly compassionate at times when their mothers feel distraught.

The other day, I shouted at B. He seemed to know I was irritable, and he came to offer me a cuddle. I felt so undeserving. I cried when I told my husband about it, that evening. Because I know that if I had made my parents angry, I'd have been frightened. I would never have cuddled them. [B, 22 months]

I was shouting to B: 'Can't you see I can't play with you? I'm looking after your sister.' And he said: 'Yes, I know, Mum. You haven't got lots of legs like an octopus.' [B, 3 years; G, 6 months]

Children are much more forgiving than they are given credit for.
[B, 6 years; 1G, 3 years; 2G, 13 months]

Children can also be helped to address the reasons for parental
anger, and to sort out whatever has gone wrong.

My parents used to get very angry with my brother and me. And
that was sort of the end of it. They didn't help us to see how we
could do anything better to improve the situation. That's one of
the main things I've learned as a parent. Things may go wrong.
But I say to my children – or I try to: 'Well. Where do we go from
here?' [1B, 4 years; 2B, 14 months]

However, children can get confused if their mothers blame them
for 'making' them angry. Adults say this often and don't always
see the wrong of it. The reality is that one person, however young
and provocative, still does not have the power to 'make' another
person angry. Getting angry is a choice, however swiftly it is made.
So then children may sense that their mothers are blaming them
unfairly, but can't explain why.

'It's your own fault,' a mother may say to her crying child. 'If
you did what I asked, I wouldn't need to be angry with you.' But
what had the mother asked? 'Come on, hurry up,' she may have
said. She didn't add: 'But don't fall over.' To her, that was obvious.
Her child was more literal and thought she wanted him to hurry
up at all costs. Many outbursts of a mother's anger are the results
of this kind of misunderstanding.

Mothers sometimes say that their children were 'so naughty
that they made Mummy angry' and so she 'had' to walk off to
another room. This may calm the mother, but can be frightening
for her child. The mother is blaming the child for her own actions.
Besides, the safety of their relationship can feel at risk. In a warm
relationship, children seem to prefer their mothers to keep
connected to them, no matter how angry they are.

I sometimes walk out of the room to stop myself from shouting. But G gets terribly upset. She'd probably *prefer* me to shout at her. [G, 2 years; B, 6 months]

I said to B: 'Would you rather I stayed with you and got angry or withdrew to the bathroom when I feel like that?' And do you know what he said? He said: 'I want you to stay with me.' But I'd *much* prefer to withdraw. I don't like being angry. [B, 4 years; G, 6 months]

It's not only mothers who get frustrated and angry. There can be times when their children are angry too. This is interesting because in nineteenth-century England, for example, adults had much greater authority and children, even very young ones – and especially little girls – were trained to be obedient and to suppress their tempers. In 1836, when her daughter Marianne was a mere ten months old, the novelist Mrs Gaskell wrote: 'I think she [Marianne] is now as sweet-tempered as ever in general; though at times her little passions are terrible and give me quite a heavy heart.'[67] The children's author and essayist Alison Uttley remembered: 'When I was two years old [in 1886 or 1887] I was reprimanded by my godmother for throwing my little slipper on the floor . . . It was most important to her that I should be taught obedience at the earliest age.'[68]

This traditional culture of teaching children that they are 'naughty' if they show anger still continues. However, when mothers do allow their children to express their anger, they discover that their children copy them.

G throws things when she's frustrated. I've been known to throw things when I'm fed up, myself. Anyway, today G threw a pan from her toy stove on to the floor, and she said: 'G is *cross.*' [G, 22 months; 34 weeks pregnant]

And mother and child may both be angry:

The other day, I was angry and 1B said to me: 'Stop shouting! I am warning you.' And I realised that's the sort of cross thing I say to him. It didn't help my angry mood at all. So no wonder that's no way to talk to him. [1B, 3 years; 2B, 2 months]

Many mothers today allow their children to be far more expressive than Mrs Gaskell, or Alison Uttley's godmother or the fictional Mrs March would have thought right. They let their children, even daughters, express anger, both in words and actions. But this doesn't mean giving permission to act out in raw anger. Mothers find ways to protect themselves from being helpless victims of their children's feelings. With younger children, anger can be physical.

First mother: G hits me from behind, and it hurts quite a lot. [G, 2 years; B, 9 months]

Second mother: I've taken to saying: 'Are you having a hard time?' to G when she hurts me. That helps me to see it from her point of view and stops me just getting angry. [G, 19 months]

Sometimes G needs to express her anger. I say: 'Are you angry? Do you want to kick Mummy?' Then I cover my legs with a pillow and I say: 'All right. You can kick Mummy now. Go for it!' and she does. But she's not allowed to kick me when I'm clipping her into her car seat. [G, 2 years]

Slowly, children learn that they can use words to express their feelings.

G gets furious with me. Inside myself, I feel so *proud* of her anger. I wouldn't have dared to talk like that to *my* mother. And, in two minutes, she's said it all and she calms down. [G, 2 years; B, 8 months]

My mother wanted everything to be perfect. Anger, sadness, negative emotions weren't allowed. I find it more helpful to listen to what my children say. I let them feel *anything* they like. I say that's absolutely fine. [G, 21 years; 1B, 18 years; 2B, 15 years]

So mothers seem to be discovering 'middle ways' of allowing their children to express their frustrations, but safely.

A mother may fear that her angry outbursts have ruined her child's chance of happiness for ever. But anger has a positive side. What matters is what mother and child learn from it afterwards.

After G was born, I worried that I was getting so angry with B that I'd traumatised him for life – oh God, yes! But now I *know* I haven't. In fact, I think he's better off and has gained from the whole experience. [B, 3 years; G, 6 months]

I'm afraid I've got so angry I've ruined my first child. In fact, I said to him: 'I'm very sorry, 1B. I didn't know how to be a mummy at first. I've made some mistakes, and I regret it.' Then, a few days later, 1B came to me and said: 'Mummy, I did something just now with my Lego people that I think was wrong, because it was cruel and probably sexist, and now I really regret it.' [1B, 7 years; 2B, 3 years]

So this little boy had learned from his mother that it was safe to be honest, to admit to (what he thought was) wrongdoing and to allow himself to be genuinely sad about it. As some mothers discover, getting angry need not end with the closing down of the angry episode, or 'burying' it quickly as if it shouldn't have happened. They find they can talk to their children about it and both of them learn something new.

Have we accounted for the depth of motherly anger, the sense of being out of control and shouting at their children in voices that they don't recognise as their own? Their anger sounds disproportionate to whatever their children have done. People get angry when they don't feel heard. Most mothers were once women in paid jobs, and even the poorest of them looked for ways to speak up for themselves. As mothers, they feel disorientated. Mothers are an enormous group of people who are short of language to explain their work. It can be confusing to receive only token respect because they are not paid for mothering. And, as we have seen, they have no political outlet as mothers. The writer Vanessa Olorenshaw has demonstrated this in *Liberating Motherhood: Birthing the Purplestockings Movement*, and has suggested economic solutions.[69] But perhaps she is ahead of many mothers today. Mothers seem to sense what is wrong without recognising that they are justified in wanting change.

It's true that, as Seneca wrote, an angry person can be destructive and vengeful. But mothers' anger doesn't sound vengeful. The shout of an angry mother sounds more like an inarticulate cry for justice. She may have directed it against her child. But usually he has done no more than trigger it. No wonder that she feels guilty after an angry outburst. It is good for her to discover her unused angry voice. But the power of her anger needs to be directed towards adults.

Too many people not only fail to understand her: they completely *misunderstand*. While there is such a dense barrier of disrespect for the value of her work, a mother is right to be angry.

CHAPTER SIX

'Am I still a feminist?'

Why do so many mothers ask if they can still call themselves feminists? The short answer is that the feminist movement has two strands. The better-known one was inspired by feminists who saw that women must be liberated from 'careers' as wives and mothers. No longer should they be 'the weaker sex', financially dependent on their fathers and husbands. With a proper education, they could earn their own livings and choose from a full range of exciting careers, including those that used to be thought the exclusive province of men.

The struggle for equality with men is not over, but an essential point is proven. Women have now been so successful in so many fields that they can no longer be presumed to be inferior to men. This has required an immense change of outlook. However, it has also led to a shift in the perception of mothers. Many feminists regard mothering as a risky step backwards to the domesticity from which women have barely been liberated.

The other strand of feminism – less well known – is a redis-covery of mothering, and the recognition that childbirth and breastfeeding can be empowering. Feminists who write about the satisfactions of mothering have been less well publicised. No wonder, then, that many women, who learned about feminism in their teens, and felt it supported their career aspirations, ask themselves if they still 'belong' to the movement when they become mothers.

Rebecca Walker, feminist daughter of the feminist novelist Alice Walker, became especially conscious of this inconsistency when she became pregnant herself.

> To stop working and raise children, to be weighed down with tots like so many anvils around my neck, none of these were acceptable. They smelled of betrayal and a lack of appreciation for the progress made on behalf of women's liberation. Worse, they suggested a kind of ignorance about the truth of the gendered world, which was that unless women refuse, their children would enslave them. Which was that the myth of blissful motherhood was just that, a myth, and the reality was much more banal.[70]

Rebecca finally challenged this outlook that she had imbibed from her mother when she discovered how much she loved her newborn son. Motherhood, she found, was not banal.

But women who grow up with less exposure to feminist ideals also feel less able to challenge them.

> I tell people I'm working hard as a mother. But the feminist inside me doesn't believe myself. I feel what I'm doing isn't real work. I always make sure F has a good night's sleep because he'll be going to *work* next day. [B, 4 months]

> I don't tell some of my feminist friends that I come to this [*mothers'*] group. It would raise too many issues. I'm afraid of being misunderstood. [1G, 2 years; 2G, 4 months]

Many feminist mothers see their independence threatened – exactly as Rebecca Walker described – by the expectation that they should shelve their careers and turn into all-giving mothers who are slaves to their babies. Feminists, whether child-free or as mothers, counterattack these expectations with a special fury.

An early example of this can be found in the work of the existential philosopher Simone de Beauvoir. As a young woman, she refused to live by conventional standards. She took charge of her own life, and then saw how many other women seemed trapped in theirs. She wasn't impressed by motherhood and didn't become a mother herself. In *The Second Sex*, she wrote: 'He [the baby] is like a tyrant; she [the mother] feels hostility for this little individual who threatens her flesh, her freedom, her whole self.'[71] She concluded: 'What is beyond doubt is that until now women's possibilities have been stifled and lost to humanity, and in her and everyone's interest it is high time she be left to take her own chances.'[72]

I witnessed some of this fiery feminist anger at first-hand. My husband, Anthony Stadlen, invited the feminist (and child-free) writer Kate Millett to give an all-day seminar in London.[73] We sat round a long table in a conference room and she spoke in a throaty whisper, so we all craned forward to hear her. But suddenly she raised her voice in a hoarse shout: 'When a woman becomes a mother, she's finished, *finished*!' WHAM! went her fist on the table, so our teacups jumped in their saucers and many of us jumped too. 'I've seen it happen,' she said more quietly. 'Countless times.' Several of us, myself included, were mothers, and could have protested at being thought of as 'finished'. But there seemed so much pain in her voice that no one questioned her.

How common is a negative view of mothering in feminist literature? There are signs of it in *The Feminine Mystique* by the American Betty Friedan – a groundbreaking feminist book, published in 1963. In the opening paragraph, she describes an American suburban wife: 'As she made the beds, shopped for groceries, matched slip-cover material, ate peanut-butter sandwiches with her children, chauffeured Cub Scouts and Brownies, lay beside her husband at night, she was afraid to ask even of herself the silent question: "Is this all?"[74] This is brave and moving. At the same time, it's revealing to notice how Friedan describes her mothering. She lists the impersonal household tasks of making beds and matching slip-cover material. Then she adds her relational motherly acts, such as eating peanut-butter sandwiches with her children. So, without directly complaining about her children, she implies that they, just as much as household chores, filled up her time and limited her life.

Born in 1921, Friedan opened the eyes of a generation of mothers to question the restricted lives they were living. She went on to create for herself the kind of active life outside her home that she had thought impossible. Her work inspired the next generation, and today schoolgirls are educated to develop into women who see themselves as equal to men, able to earn their own living and to be creative outside the home.

But what happens to a creative woman when she becomes a mother? Shared parenting will be discussed in Chapter Nine, and hasn't yet become the norm. Most new mothers discover that they are expected to look after their children, at least while they are babies. Some mothers feel divided, loving their babies as much as, or more than, their paid work. No wonder many describe feeling confused. Isn't this the kind of dilemma that a feminist woman was taught to avoid? If she pays for babycare, she may judge herself, or feel judged by others, as a 'bad mother'. But if she shelves her career to fulfil the needs of her baby, won't she risk turning into a doormat? Why should her baby's needs take priority over her own?

Rebecca Asher describes her perplexity:

I am . . . driven by an overwhelming love to nurture my adored child, who drains me of my strength in order to build up his own. A few months later, I appraise myself in the landing mirror on the return leg from a night feed . . . I still look deathly. My dressing gown is covered in an appliqué of baby snot and nappy cream. My T-shirt, an old Fawcett Society number, is stiff with stale breastmilk. I look down. Among the stains it is possible to pick out a slogan. It reads: *This is What a Feminist Looks Like.*[75]

Through the image of her T-shirt, Asher is able to convey her sense that signs of being a mother (the T-shirt, stiff and stained with stale breastmilk) are *not* what she thought a feminist should look like. She feels angry, but trapped. 'I am . . . driven . . .' she says, as if she is in the passenger seat rather than doing her own driving. Her 'overwhelming love' seems to work against herself. Whereas her son seems to act for himself. He 'drains me of my strength in order to build up his own'. So, as she sees it, she is in an either-him-or-me struggle for her strength, and compelled by her 'adored child' to let him win.

'The best mothers always put their kids' needs before their own, period.' So write Susan J. Douglas and Meredith W. Michaels in *The New Momism*.[76] The word 'period' expresses the authors' anger. They question whether it is 'best' for either mother or baby if the mother is putting her child's needs first but resenting it.

And yet, the mother is in control. Her baby has no power to make her do anything. Nor is he able to see both sides of a situation. But a mother can think about her baby's 'side' as well as her own. Then whose needs should she prioritise and why? Would it be better for both of them if she put herself first sometimes, to avoid feeling resentful?

The feminist writer Clare Potter recognised that, as a mother, she was free to make the choices that suited her. She described a particularly challenging moment when her child 'screamed the roof off' but she left her child to it (she doesn't say whether girl or boy) 'because a poem wants writing and I can't lose it to you'. When she came back, she found her child awake but making calm sounds.[77] Potter wrote a second poem to record this situation and to show that she had learned how, even with a screaming child, a mother could still decide to use the moment for herself.

Another feminist mother found that she could recover lost control.

> I think I have been giving too much authority to G. She was sounding like a tyrant. I can't be authoritarian. That's not my way. But I thought about it and realised that I am the one who has authority. [G, 5 years; B, 18 months]

Mothers find different ways of balancing their control. It's an important topic and one that will form part of the next chapter.

Some mothers feel more in control if they feed their babies at set times. However, if a baby is breastfed, clock-timing isn't helpful. It's best if he breastfeeds whenever he is hungry. But this, protest many feminists, limits his mother's freedom to control her time. Feminists divide over breastfeeding. Some who value it discover a different kind of control because they learn to predict when their babies will be hungry.

It's amazing that in our technological society, maternal breast-feeding still seems the best way to feed a baby. Research has added to our recognition of its value. A baby can be bottle-fed with a formula or with the mother's expressed milk. However, formula milks can't imitate breastmilk which adapts to the needs and the age of the baby, provides some immunity to diseases common in the baby's society and prepares the baby for the tastes of solid food. Expressed milk can provide these, though it becomes homog-enised in the bottle and loses its sequence to aid digestion. Also, the baby's jaw movement while breastfeeding seems to prepare him for speech development.

Anyone who complains about breastfeeding might do better to examine the social circumstances which make it so difficult. Breastfeeding mothers need an 'infrastructure' for it to work well.

They need enough food and drink, a secure home and reliable financial support to enable them to spend time breastfeeding their babies. In many societies, both rich and poor, the infrastructure is completely inadequate. When this happens, it's usual to complain about breastfeeding, rather than to acknowledge how poor is the maternal support.[78]

Mothers also need information about breastfeeding. Here, they themselves have organised it. La Leche League, for example, is an international breastfeeding charity. It collates data about how mothers have solved breastfeeding difficulties, and trains mothers to offer information about it that has been tested and found to be safe. I like its basic philosophy of offering support when mothers ask for it, so I trained to become a 'leader' and have led the Central London Group since 1990.

However, some feminists see breastfeeding, and therefore La Leche League, as a threat to a woman's independence. Élisabeth Badinter, a much younger friend of Simone de Beauvoir and herself a French feminist, published a book with the title *The Conflict: How Modern Motherhood Undermines the Status of Women*. The middle third of the book is entirely made up of a furious attack on La Leche League.

'Conflict' is a good word for the quandary that feminist mothers face. But Badinter hasn't taken much trouble to find out about La Leche League, so her argument rests on misrepresenting it. For example, she claims: 'The league's supporters have clearly declared war on bottles and formula, and implicitly on mothers returning to work.'[79] She doesn't give her source for this, and it would be difficult to find one. A typical La Leche League guideline reads: 'The decision on how to feed a baby is a very personal one and LLLGB recognises that some women choose not to breastfeed.'[80] Badinter also doesn't seem to have heard of the League's book *Hirkani's Daughters: Women who scale modern mountains to combine breastfeeding and working*,[81] published in 2006, well before her French original, *Le Conflit*. So she has identified the difficulty mothers face in combining career and fulfilling the baby's needs. But her attack seems misplaced.

La Leche League is a grassroots mother-led organisation which sounds feminist in itself. So it's odd to see that it was given a misleading entry in the *Encyclopaedia of Motherhood*, an impressive three-volume work edited by the Canadian feminist and publisher Andrea O'Reilly. In Volume 2, under La Leche League, there's a claim that the name 'La Leche League' was chosen 'in order to demonstrate a commitment to Marian worship and devotion'.[82] La Leche League has always said that it does not 'mix causes', and surely someone should have checked such a strange statement before it was published. There's an extra paragraph headed 'Criticisms'. There aren't many 'Criticisms' in the *Encyclopaedia*. La Leche League seems to have been singled out. And the criticisms look unclear and unjustified too.[83]

It seems illogical for feminists to argue over breastfeeding. After all, most of them agree that mothers have the right to make their own decisions. Some women discover how much they enjoy it and how empowered they feel. Feminist childbirth educator Sheila Kitzinger wrote *The Experience of Breastfeeding* to show how breastfeeding works, to inform women rather than leaving them to think they should know about it 'by instinct'.[84] Vanessa Olorenshaw, a lawyer and feminist mother who became a La Leche League leader, saw breastfeeding as integral to feminism: 'Because when it comes to the use of a woman's breasts for the primary purpose for which they exist, it is nothing short of radical to see breastfeeding as a feminist issue.'[85]

Kitzinger, Olorenshaw and many mothers in La Leche League are part of the lesser-known 'strand' of feminists, who embrace mothering. They found ways of adapting to their children rather than feeling enslaved by them. Shortly before she died Kitzinger wrote:

Motherhood is never what you expect. It is an incredible adventure. You discover a lot about yourself. I don't think it can be for any woman exactly what she thinks it is going to be. I thought I would be in control somehow in bringing up my children, whereas, in fact, you find that they bring *you* up. Motherhood is a magical mystery tour and you soar to the heights of elation and swoop into depths of despair. It is one of the best forms of education there is if you are prepared to learn from it, and you learn along with your children.[86]

Kitzinger was fascinated by childbirth. She was an activist, who wrote and taught, and brought up her five daughters as well. How did she manage? She experimented. She bought a large playpen, put herself, her books and papers inside it and allowed her little girls the run of the house.

The American psychotherapist Daphne de Marneffe was another feminist who enjoyed being a mother and didn't see herself as subordinate to her children. For many women, she wrote, a woman's desire to be a mother is 'a desire anchored in her experience of herself as an agent, an autonomous individual, a person'.[87]

The 'desire to be a mother' seems common in every society and mothers have found ways to be autonomous, whether wealthy or poor. A feminist, single mother in the United States, Heather Jackson, and a British researcher, Val Gillies,[88] studied mothers who were poor. Heather Jackson concluded: 'I realised that other poor mothers make me feel empowered because they work so hard and do so much for their children. And I am a poor mother, too. It takes courage, strength and intelligence to raise children when a person is poor.'[89]

All these feminist mothers realised that their work was undervalued. De Marneffe said: '... they want the enormous importance of their nurturing to be acknowledged.'[90] Olorenshaw wrote: 'There has to be a recognition, somewhere, that seeing to our children and home is valuable work and that there are plenty of people who want to do it, at least for a few years.'[91]

Not all mothers can afford to stay at home and, for many, working part-time offers a good compromise. But does this mean that their loyalties are divided between paid work and children? Nancy Folbre, the American feminist economist, saw that a mother's love for her children could give her a motive for working well. 'Most people don't think about children in economic terms,' she observed. 'But love for others can be just as powerful an economic motive as self-interest.'[92] She has made an unusual point, and it would be interesting to hear whether mothers agree with it.

A different way of combining a career with mothering is to build up a group of reliable people who can look after the children when the mother is working. Two ambitious feminists, with three children each, both developed this idea in similar ways.

'A feminist standpoint on mothering', wrote Andrea O'Reilly, founder of the Demeter Press which specialises in books about mothers, 'affords a woman a life, a purpose and identity outside and beyond motherhood; as well it does not limit childrearing to the biological mother.'[93]

Then who else did the childrearing? O'Reilly and her partner had their three children while they were 'penniless fulltime students',[94] yet both pursued academic careers and she became a professor. 'Empowered mothers', she wrote, 'look to friends, family and their partners to assist with childcare and often raise their children with an involved community of what may be termed co-mothers or othermothers.'[95]

'Othermothers'? This is an African–American concept which O'Reilly first read about in *Beloved* by Toni Morrison.[96] She quotes Morrison: '"I don't think one parent can raise a child. I don't think two people can raise a child. You really need the whole village. And if you don't have it, you'd better make it."'[97]

This sounds a moving idea. Some of the poorest women seem

to have evolved a system of shared support. 'Othermothers' sound similar to Western traditional neighbourhood communities.

The American anthropologist and primatologist Sarah Blaffer Hrdy came up with a similar solution she called 'allomothers'. Like O'Reilly, she had three children and combined mothering them with an academic career in which she researched primates. She said she was 'supported by a steadfast partner, resilient children, and the generous hearts of alloparents – all the individuals other than me and my husband who helped us rear our children'.[98]

'Othermothers' and 'alloparents' or 'allomothers' sound creative solutions for mothers who need time away from their children to do paid work. But not all mothers want this.

'People really are different; they want different things. There are as many forms of feminism as there are feminists,' wrote Daphne de Marneffe.[99] She didn't think 'allomothers' would suit everyone. 'But for many mothers the problem is a prior one; it is the very giving up of their *own* proximity to their child, *regardless* of how loving or consistent their [allomother] replacement is.'[100]

It's wonderful to hear her acknowledge that there are different forms of feminism. Every form of feminist mothering is a delicate balancing of priorities.

Anne Manne, feminist Australian writer, described very simply how she felt about her daughters as young babies: 'I experienced an overwhelming desire to be with my baby. There was a kind of bodily anguish to it. It felt right when we were together and wrong when we were separate.'[101]

Mothers today feel awkward admitting to feelings that used to be *de rigueur* for them, only a century ago. Keren Epstein-Gilboa, a Canadian feminist, made an interesting observation. She researched and interviewed mothers of infants. 'When mothers seem to trust the researcher or therapist,' she wrote, 'they gradually and shamefully disclose that, despite their exhaustion and need for time alone, they are overcome by a strange and erupting desire to remain close to their infants at all times.'[102]

Why should a mother be ashamed of how she feels? Lawyer and feminist mother Miriam González Durántez pointed out how often women were criticised for *whatever* choice they had made. She protested:

> If we do not have children, people assume we are 'frustrated'. If we stay at home taking care of our children, it is said we are 'not working'. If we have a job, we are portrayed as just 'part-time mums', and sometimes even as bad parents. If we succeed in our professional lives, we're branded 'scary'; if we follow fashion, we're 'shallow'; if we like science, we're 'geeks'; if we read women's magazines, we're 'fluffy'; and if we defend our rights, we're 'hard'.

These are 'absurd labels' she said, but they can be difficult to deal with.[103]

A good way to deal with these 'absurd labels' is for all women to unite in the struggle for our rights. Women don't need to be mothers or regard themselves as feminists to see how little provision is made to accommodate them. We need only think of menstruation, or pregnancy, miscarriage, birth, breastfeeding, care for older children, the menopause. These are all normal life stages for women, and we have the right to want allowance for them in daily life. The mothers who speak to me usually have their heads 'down' trying to organise the next few hours of the day. But the rest of us surely have the time and perspective to appreciate that this is an essential part of our struggle, if women are to stand as equals to men.

Can we feminists learn to accept ourselves with our differences so that we can combine our strong points in the unfinished struggle for equality and choice? We haven't yet, but perhaps we will. It's painful to hear one feminist attack another for not being 'feminist enough'.

When I told a feminist friend I was being a mother to my son, she said: 'Why? What's happened to your feminism? What a waste of all your education.' But that's odd because I'm working harder than I ever have in my whole life, and my work seems more valuable than anything I have done up to now. [B, 9 months]

The claim by some feminists that being a mother is a waste of her education is a serious one. Western women have had to fight to ensure that girls receive a good education, and in some countries this struggle continues today.

Is mothering a waste of a woman's education? Or do children require us to *use* it? Profound issues arise when we have children. Children themselves come up with astonishing philosophical and scientific questions. So a mother needs to know where to find information, and she also needs the confidence to assess, and double-check what she has found. 'How', asked Virginia Woolf, in a moment of despair as she tried to find out about women from a collection of books she had ordered in the old Reading Room of the British Museum, 'shall I ever find the grains of truth embedded in all this mass of paper?' The man sitting beside her seemed to know how to study. She, daughter of Leslie Stephen, a well-known Cambridge academic, had no idea.[104] She shows us that it's not enough to have books of information. We need to learn how to use them.

When G was born, it made me think: What is a woman? I realised that all the literature I read was written by men. I didn't know anything by women. So, for the first year of G's life, I *only* read books by women. [G, 4 years; B, 9 months]

Fortunately, this mother knew from her education how to access the literature she needed. It's a small example of how much mothers need a good education.

*

So can a mother still call herself a feminist? Feminism can't represent women unless it includes mothers. Many women identify as feminists before having children. They then have the difficult task of learning how to combine their feminist aspirations with their mothering. Even if mothers today haven't yet found ideal solutions, their efforts must entitle them to continue calling themselves feminists. And the feminist movement needs to accept them.

CHAPTER SEVEN

Is mothering a spiritual experience?

Mothers today have no difficulty in recognising the down-to-earth physical aspects of life with a baby. But many are suspicious of claims that it can be spiritual too.

There is good historical reason for this. For centuries, motherhood has been described in religious terms such as 'a holy duty' or 'sacred work'. Today these words anger many women. They suggest a sugar-coated pill that has seduced mothers into being trapped at home to care for their children. Few people thought that women should be able to access any of the freedom and excitement of working in all the professions that men did. So mothers tend to avoid using words like 'holy' or 'sacred'. If they want to describe a more spiritual moment, they say it is 'beyond words'.

There is one spiritual word that mothers find useful: sacrifice. It was originally used in the context of religious occasions, practised in nearly every culture, and often attended only by men. Today it has gained a secular meaning as well. Its literal meaning is 'to make something sacred'. We will come back to this at the end of the chapter. Its secular meaning is more negative. It describes the act of giving up something precious.

In the secular sense, mothers have made personal sacrifices for their children for millennia, and have been admired for making them.[105] Some of these are major and tragic. Others are smaller but made daily.

> My parents were very strict. They had to be, there were so many of us. But I always felt secure and loved. They gave up everything to give to us. I used to see the parents of other children in expensive clothes. My mum only wore poor clothes. They spent all their money on us. [B, 5 years; 1G, 2 years; 2G, 8 weeks]

This sounds a long-term sacrifice, yet lovingly given. However, with the spread of feminist thinking came a tremendous reaction against these maternal sacrifices. No mother, feminists say, should have to deprive herself. Why should she be expected to devote the best years of her life to satisfy the needs of everyone in her family except herself? Surely children can feel loved without such heavy sacrifices. So now you may still hear the words 'sacrifice' or 'self-sacrifice' and even 'martyr' used about mothers, but usually with disapproval to describe a mother who 'overdoes it'.

> Does a proper mother have to forget about herself? My own mother sacrificed her needs to us four children. I don't think that's a good way to be. [B, 7 months]

Most mothers would agree that they should remember their own needs. But in practice it's not easy. Babies need a lot of attention, and panic if they have to wait. At first, mothers find they are constantly looking after them. This can feel exhausting, especially when, after a long day, babies are wakeful at night.

> G is such hard work. She thrashes about at night so it's hard for me to sleep. I wonder how long it will be till I lie face-down on the pavement and say: 'I can't *do* it any more!' [G, 7 months]

> I am so *tired* of being tired. I thought it would have got better by

now. G wakes in the night – and she's *wide* awake. There's no end in sight. How much sacrifice is too much? My friend put her child in a separate room at night [*to 'cry it out'*]. Should I do that? [G, 17 months]

Many people would reply to this mother: 'Yes, of *course* you should put your child in her own room at night. She's seventeen months. She'll cry for a bit and then fall asleep. She'll be fine.' This is the 'Don't sacrifice *yourself!*' view. Many mothers recommend it to others. So why don't they all follow this policy?

When I was pregnant, I thought I was going to have a baby. But, as soon as 1B was born, I saw that I had given birth to a *person*. So I see his behaviour as part of the way he's going, and cherish even the inconvenient bits as part of the whole of him. [1B, 4 years; 2B, 18 months]

Not all mothers see their newborns as persons, but those who do face a dilemma. They describe an overwhelming desire to treat these persons well. But where does this leave themselves? As young women, most were brought up *not* to sacrifice themselves. They were encouraged to put their needs first. Having a baby can feel very confusing. Perhaps now it's the baby's turn to come first.

I'm knackered. When do you think about yourself and when about your child? If I see things from G's way round, of *course* she wakes at night and needs feeding. So then I feed her and everything seems all right. But then I look at me and think: What about my life? My creativity? [G, 5 months]

This mother's bewilderment is understandable. Although feminists have protested at the ideal of the selfless mother who always puts her children first, a mother who sees her child as a person discovers that she wants to respond as a person. The trouble is that the work of mothering has no upper limit. There's always more a mother could do. She may spend long stretches of time alone with her baby, and everywhere she looks there are baby-related tasks that she hasn't done yet.

I don't know when to say 'No' to B. I don't know where to set the boundaries, what's me and what's him. I'm afraid if I give in to B's wants, there'll be nothing left for me. [B, 12 months]

Nor can her baby appreciate how much she is doing for him. This can remind mothers of working for a demanding employer.

Breastfeeding is enjoyable but sometimes you wish . . . I used to work as an artist's model. You're not allowed to move, and you have to keep absolutely still for hours, for someone else's benefit. I'm surprised that I sometimes feel like that about breastfeeding. [G, 6 weeks]

The discipline needed for sitting still to breastfeed reminded this mother of her work as a model. However, artist and model have agreed on a contract. A baby is too young to do this. The mother is in control, even though she might not feel it. She hasn't been paid to sit still. She is free to move any time she chooses. If she believes her baby will stay asleep at her breast, and keeps still to make sure he does, this is her own decision. But, if her back starts to ache and she needs the toilet, at what point should she prioritise herself?

How much giving is too much? Where does it all end? The child psychologist Dr Margot Sunderland gives the example of a mother of a three-year-old.

Imagine a typical day of looking after your three-year-old child . . . when he asks you to watch him for the eighteenth time, it's starting to feel a bit wearing. Despite this, you know that attention and praise is so good for establishing positive chemical arousal systems in your child's brain, so you do it again and again.[106]

But is this repeated 'attention and praise' going to work? Won't the child's brain be sensitive enough to pick up his mother's real feelings? Mightn't he soon realise that she is finding him 'a bit wearing'? And mightn't his 'positive chemical arousal systems' then be offset by the sense that his mother isn't enjoying it?

The paediatrician and psychoanalyst D. W. Winnicott told mothers: 'If you are there enjoying it all, it is like the sun coming out, for the baby.'[107] But what if the mother is there but not enjoying it? Does the baby sense that the sun is missing?

Mothers frequently describe times of discomfort when their children are enjoying themselves while they are not.

> *First mother:* I take B to children's groups and he loves it. He goes from room to room of wonderful toys. But there's nothing for mums, nowhere to sit, no hot drinks. I get a migraine and think: Do I really have to stay here for another two hours? But if I go early am I depriving B? [B, 15 months]

> *Second mother:* I recognise that. It's when you go somewhere that your child loves but you *hate*. You start to feel that grey cloud descending . . . [1B, 3 years; 2B, 3 months]

Mothers of two children, especially if they are close in age, can sound desperate.

> I feel on the edge of getting depressed. It's as if I am filled with sand. I start the day with a bit of a plan, and then B and G both want me, and it all starts to go wrong, like a sandcastle collapsing and going all over the place. I'm not doing anything. Perhaps I should give up trying. [G, 2 years; B, 3 months]

> I feel a *shell* of myself. I'm tired. 2B wakes up about five times a night, and usually he needs breastfeeding back to sleep. In the day, 1B is very sociable and likes me to play with him. [1B, 4 years; 2B, 19 months]

These mothers sound overstretched: 'that grey cloud descending', the 'sandcastle collapsing' and feeling 'a shell of myself' – these all sound like warning signs that the mothers could become depressed. Aren't they already sacrificing too much of themselves for their children?

Some of the most stressful situations are described by mothers of several children. It's usually when everyone seems to need attention at the same moment.

> I feel I've only just got myself back from the abyss. I feel everyone needs me and I can't give to everyone. [1B, 3 years; 2B, 11 weeks]

> [*Tears*] I've lost my*self*. That's what it feels like. When the children all need me at the same time, that's the hardest. Sometimes I wish I had a robot that would do all the tasks I have to do, like washing yogurt off everyone's faces. But that wouldn't work because a robot wouldn't feel about my children what I do. [1G, 3 years; 2G, 19 months; B, 7 months]

> It sounds a terrible thing to say but sometimes I *forget* I love G [*tears*]. B keeps breastfeeding and seems to need me a lot. It's hard for G. She keeps asking me questions, every moment. And I'd *love* to be able to answer all her questions. But sometimes I get annoyed and I just can't be patient. [G, 3 years; B, 17 months]

So mothers learn that they can't please everyone.

> You can't do it all. When 1B and 2B both want me, someone doesn't get what they want. [1B, 4 years; 2B, 13 months]

I was interested to discover that these last four distressed mothers were all firstborn children themselves. As babies, they had been used to their mothers' undivided attention. I am curious to learn whether mothers who were later-born children are less troubled when they are needed by several children at the same time.

How can a mother recover herself if she feels overstretched? One way is through humour. A frustrating situation can be turned into comedy and told as a hilarious story to other mothers. This allows mothers to laugh at themselves and to feel connected to one another. Their shared laughter creates a warm sense of sister-hood. They get into the most absurd situations, they say, for the sake of their children. As one journalist wrote:

> Jeez, I can't *wait* until they grow up! I'd think, crawling across the floor to put the jigsaw puzzles away every night, picking glitter out of the crevices on my forehead, folding mountains of tiny items of clothing, reading *The Gruffalo* and doing all the voices for the 1,000th time until my neck snaps and my eyes turn to dust and crumble onto the *Star Wars* duvet cover, taking the nappy bins out, scraping the scrambled egg off the kitchen floor and trying to get a rain cover to stay *on the damned buggy*.[108]

Just don't ask who gave these children all the jigsaws, the glitter, the mountains of clothing and so on. This is comedy, after all, in which mothers scurry after their children like humble servants.

Some mothers, however, go beyond the bounds of comedy. They describe feeling exploited by their heedless despotic children. The psychoanalyst Rozsika Parker has written several strong versions of this attitude. For example: '[A mother] can feel anni-hilated, devoured and devastated by a child's apparently wilful determination to humiliate her and frustrate her needs.'[109] Here, the mother sees herself as her child's victim. A number of mothers describe this kind of relationship.

However, is the child really trying to frustrate his mother?

> What people don't say is that being a mother is wonderful – but it's very hard work. But my point is: G doesn't *mean* to be hard work. She's just being a baby. People often talk as if it's the baby's *fault*. [G, 9 months]

Yes, babies are hard work. And it *can* feel unfair for a mother, alone at night, when her baby keeps waking. She doesn't want to leave her baby distressed or hungry. But what about her exhausted self?

Some mothers learned that they could manage their 'workload' if they changed how they felt about it. This helped them to feel back in control.

> At first I really resented the way G kept waking up at night. Then I thought: Well, G's not going to go away. She's here. So now I *accept* that I feel resentful. It's not G's fault. [G, 3 months]

> I was getting bad-tempered because G keeps waking up at night and wanting me. It made me ask myself: what is so hard about looking after G at night? I decided the worst thing was everyone saying if you don't get a decent night's sleep you won't be fit for the next day. But I haven't got a next day full of appointments. So now I am calmer at night. [G, 22 months; 34 weeks pregnant]

> F had gone abroad and for two nights G wouldn't go to sleep before 3 a.m. I was getting very irritable. But then I thought: I'm the mother G's got. She hasn't got a choice of mothers. She's only got me. So that made me realise that I've got a duty to be a *nice* mother. She doesn't deserve a horrible one. That would be awful. *I* know what that can be like. [G, 2 years]

Other mothers discover that they don't always need to put their children first. They learn to their surprise how accommodating young children can be.

> It helps when it's not all about G. Sometimes you think: I'll go with her and do everything she wants. But sometimes she doesn't feel happy about that and she's more contented doing things with me. [G, 4 months]

> I was with G in a playground and I was getting bored. So I said

to G: 'I know you are happy but I want to go home now.' And G immediately put out her hand to me and started walking towards the gate. But she only did it that once. [G, 16 months]

With my first child, I forgot about myself. I wasn't aware of sacrificing my own needs. I used to make things nice for B and F. If they were happy, I felt happy too. But with G I found that if I stated my needs, they could be accommodating. So now I state my needs and I'm happy – and that sends a little *glow* round them because Mum's happy. [B, 4 years; G, 4 months]

Is it wrong of a mother to put her own needs first, even when it doesn't suit her child? She has the power to prioritise herself at any time. But when is it the right thing to do? Mothers seem to make choices without spelling out the logic behind them. Essentially a mother and child are on the same 'side'. In the short term, their interests may collide. However, thinking long-term – which a mother can do, but her child can't yet – their interests are the same. The child needs a functioning mother, not an exhausted, burnt-out one; if a mother is prioritising herself because she needs to, even if it doesn't please her child, in the long run this will be good for them both.

If I hadn't come to this meeting, I'd have stayed at home and G would have napped for an hour and a half. Now she'll be tired. But what am I supposed to do? I'll go *mad* if I stay indoors all day. [G, 10 months]

Mothers talk about 'self-sacrifice' and feeling like 'martyrs', but hopefully they are using the words as metaphors. A mother could actually risk her health and well-being if she never gave herself any attention.

A good antidote to overstretching is to decide on boundaries. A boundary is a territorial word to indicate the limits of one person's property, separating it from that of a neighbour. This literal meaning doesn't apply to mothers. However, all mothers learn that they have limits. They also discover that the limits they *thought* they had before having their babies ('I won't be one of those mothers that feeds her baby at night') are different from the more flexible ones they adopt once their babies are born ('I try to have my shower at some point in the day').

The old territorial boundaries were usually agreements between two landowners. Mothers are often told that they must 'set' boundaries for their children. But children are not passive. Even a baby can protest as vehemently as any landowner if he thinks the boundary is unfair. The mother can either insist or do her best to negotiate.

Negotiations depend on a shared understanding that mother and child have built up together. If they haven't got that, then the baby's protests will sound like a meaningless noise or even deliberate 'naughtiness'. Once a mother understands why her child is finding her boundaries difficult, she can look for a compromise that will suit them both.

> My first child forced me to be the mother he wanted. Reasoning with him didn't work. He was physical, so I had to develop a more physical way to be with him. He needed me to set physical boundaries. Once I did that, he'd calm down. [1B, 8 years; 2B, 4 years; 3B, 2 years]

This seems to have been a pre-verbal arrangement when her oldest son was very young. However, even when children can talk, they may protest in rebellious actions rather than complain in words, because they sense that something about the boundary is unfair, but it's too complicated for them to spell out.

> 1B never did anything I asked. Then I realised I was rushing past him, telling him what to do. Of *course* he didn't do it. I made a point of making proper eye contact with him. So then he listened. [1B, 3 years; 2B, 5 weeks]

I've been getting very frustrated and angry with B. Something happened this week that made me question my boundaries with him. When I have tight boundaries, B pushes against them and I get angry with him. But if I relax the boundaries and think: B's bored but he's not doing any harm – then I feel much less angry. Everything is easier. Just this morning, when he was pouring orange juice into 1G's cornflakes, I couldn't help shouting: '*No!*' [B, 5 years; 1G, 2 years; 2G, 6 months]

A mother may find herself enforcing particular boundaries without giving them a second thought. They may be boundaries she herself had been taught as a child. It can be an eye-opener to find that they aren't as important as she had been trained to believe.

Should G be able to do everything she wants? She wanted to drip water from her sippy cup on to the kitchen floor. At first, it was 'No!' *I* wouldn't have been allowed to do that. But what was the big deal? So I let her drip the water and gave her a paper towel, and she wiped it up and threw the towel into the bin. She's learned a whole new useful sequence. [G, 16 months; 24 weeks pregnant]

Should children be allowed to do whatever they want? Mothers often ask themselves whether their boundaries will damage their children. After all, many of them aren't self-evidently right or wrong. Instead, there are considerations to weigh up every time.

I've been reading a book about unconditional love. It says you should love your child even when he does things that you don't like because your disapproval might hurt him. B does things I don't like and I get annoyed with him, so I was thinking perhaps I'd damaged him. But then I thought: Surely the book's not right. B needs to learn what is acceptable behaviour for me and also in social situations. [B, 3 years; 30 weeks pregnant]

This is a good example of when it can help to recognise the strength of the mother/child relationship. Disapproving of her child's unacceptable behaviour in no way contradicts the mother's unconditional love. She may get annoyed with something her child does, but her love for him remains unshakeable. Her child has probably long got used to her honest love and anger. He might be a good deal more confused if he sensed that she saw him as fragile, and that she was withholding her disapproval for fear of 'damaging' him.

The boundaries between a mother and her child can be friendly. The mother discovers that she can balance what her child wants with what she can manage.

> Some days G keeps complaining and nothing I do is right for her. Usually I feel guilty that I'm not being a good mum. But the other day I thought: I can't always make things right for G. So I try to break it to her gently: 'We won't do *this*, we're going to do *that*.' Maybe that's life and she just has to learn it. [G, 12 months]

> I take my children to do things that I enjoy. That way, we all have a good time. I don't do imaginative play and I don't bounce with them on bouncy castles. I've noticed other mothers doing both. [1B, 6 years; 2B, 2 years]

That still leaves sleep as a problem. Sleep can't be negotiated. A child can't fall asleep at will, though some can be trained by a graded programme. But the training doesn't suit all children.

> G seems to think that sleep is for losers. She doesn't nap and hardly sleeps. [G, 6 months]

Many babies wake up at night, crying desperately for their mothers. After all, maternal sacrifices can look pointless. Why do mothers make them? Many babies don't learn to sleep through the night, however much sleep their mothers give up.

But people don't make sacrifices for nothing. They decide to give up certain things for the sake of something even better. Is there really something better for a mother than her much-needed sleep?

I'd no idea my baby would be such a *person*. We have lovely times together. She loves me talking to her. She's become my new friend, my *friend*. [G, 6 weeks]

Me: What keeps you going when it's so difficult?

Mother: G does. Nights are exhausting. But in the mornings, she smiles at me, and then . . . [G, 8 months]

By the end of a day with B, I'm so tired I'm completely *finished*. But B and I are the best of friends. [B, 12 months]

Some writers opine that a mother must not be her child's friend. A mother's role is different, they say. And clearly a mother–child friendship is not the same as one between peers. Peer friendships are more reciprocal. A mother does things for her child that he can't do in return. So it can look as though babies only take without giving anything. But even a very young friend can give back something, and it's this that mothers prefer even to getting enough sleep.

What can a baby give back? A newborn, especially when asleep, conveys a strong sense of peace (see pages 33–4). Then, after a few weeks, babies suddenly give radiant smiles.

I feel G has got a well of happiness inside her. It shows when she smiles. She has lovely smiles with a beginning, a middle and an end. [G, 8 months]

Next, they learn to laugh. There's no sound quite like that of a baby laughing – nothing malicious, cruel or mocking about it. It's light, joyous and catching. So his mother will usually laugh too. It can lift her mood, even though she is tired. In all these moments, she is receiving something special from her baby.

If a mother has shared peacefulness or joy with her child during the day, she feels his distress if he cries at night.

> I get up for B at night. He never needs very much. Just a breastfeed gets him back to sleep again. But lately it's been every hour-and-a-half. I'm very tired now [*tears*]. Sorry, it's just I'm so tired. My partner says: 'Why don't we sleep-train B?' And I can't explain. I just don't want to. I've worked for seven months to get to here. I can't explain why I don't want to sleep-train. [B, 7 months]

Yes, it's difficult to explain. The relationship between mother and child is very much a work in progress. Sleep-training, which works for some babies, would mean changing the mother's response to night-waking. But how would this affect her baby?

> I know I don't have to rush to G every time she cries. But she's trusting that I will. It's the trust that matters. If I *don't* go to her, what will she make of that? I'm hoping G can grow up with her trust still strong enough, so that she knows we are *there* for her. She'll turn into a person who feels secure because she has been heard. It's all a question of her trust. [G, 8 months]

Mothers can see little signs that their babies are learning to trust them.[110] A baby who trusts his mother is no longer alone in the world. Mother and child are coming through something together. The mother has achieved a crucial part of her work. And that is the logic supporting mothers who sacrifice sleep.

There is a 'time boundary' here. The mother knows, at the back of her mind, that night-waking won't be for ever. Her child will eventually sleep for longer and she will catch up on her own sleep.

A mother can declare she is utterly exhausted – but this changes if her child is ill. Then new resources of energy seem to arrive from nowhere. Many feel they would do *anything* to help their ill children.

B has eczema. I've made huge cuts in my diet [*because she was breastfeeding and knew what she ate might affect him*] and it seems to help. He was suffering so much. I made a vow to myself that I would be ready to exist on *water*, so long as B was all right. [B, 8 weeks]

Last week, I was feeling a bit sorry for myself. G was teething, not sleeping, and I was sleep-deprived. On my way home, I tripped and fell on my front, with G strapped to the front of me in her sling. Her head hit the pavement, which was the *worst* moment of my life. We went straight to hospital, and they said she was all right. But it changed the way I see things. I don't mind being tired – as long as G is all right. [G, 10 months]

To anyone who hasn't mothered an ill child, the lengths mothers go to may sound excessive. It might help to imagine how one would feel about a beloved friend who fell ill. The usual boundaries are waived because this is an emergency and a call to one's feelings of love. And a mother who has nurtured and given birth to her baby may have even stronger feelings for him than a friend for a friend.[111]

Mother and child have been together since conception. Together they shared the experience of birth. The mother may have been one of the first to see her child's face and to hold his body. To see that treasured body ill and suffering can rack her feelings to a degree that may be difficult for other people to understand. She may feel desperate and plead with God or Fate to let her child survive, or to suffer less. A child who dies or perhaps disappears without trace is not forgotten by his mother. This is well expressed by the title of a book, *Always With Me: Parents Talk About the Death of a Child.*[112] Of the thirty-one contributions, twenty-eight are by mothers and three by fathers. The reason for this disparity isn't clear, but it shows how a mother's connection to her child can long outlive his presence.

There are many paintings showing a mother sitting at the bedside of her ill child. Through him, she has known something of the miracle of a new life. There is a whole dimension of experience concerning birth and death that is unique to mothers. This is when mothers spontaneously resort to religious language, though they frequently add that they are not religious. A mother may feel awkward using words such as 'sacred', 'holy', 'soul', 'spiritual'. However, these words can act as doorways and allow secular people as well to enter a different 'room'.

> Having a baby is such a spiritual experience. [G, 6 weeks]

> Being a mother brings out something spiritual in me. I think about the meaning of life, and my values. And I'm not at all a religious person. [1G, 3 years; 2G, 13 months]

What could be more extraordinary than pregnancy and birth? Although each of our lives is the result of a pregnancy, it is surely a miracle every time that a woman's body can house and nurture tiny cells that mature into an entire new person. Giving birth can feel a sacred experience, bringing a mother close to the source of life itself.

> I've had a medical condition for twenty-seven years. When I was pregnant, I used to keep worrying that I'd never be able to cope. When G was born, she was laid beside me, and I couldn't *believe* I'd given birth to such a beautiful little daughter. I lay awake the whole *night*, gazing at her. [G, 17 months]

A newborn can look calm and wise. His mother may be filled with awe to look at him. Where did he come from? Who entrusted this child to her?

> You think your baby will be a sweet little person that you almost know [*from pregnancy*]. After the birth, you look at this strange person in your arms and think: Where did *you* come from? I'm

not a religious person. But I began to think about his soul. [B, 14 months]

At first, G had no personality, she was just pure *Life*. [G, 4 months]

The presence of a newborn affects visitors too. Instinctively, they soften their voices and try to avoid crashing around and banging doors. The newborn (all being well) looks calm and people seem to respect this and try not to disturb him.

When B was born, he looked very contained and peaceful. You can see a little bit of their soul when they are born. [B, 4 weeks]

'Peaceful' and 'soul' suggest a different kind of experience. It can jar with a mother's everyday mode. 'Motherhood appears to be an opportunity for spiritual awakening,' wrote Aurélie M. Athan and Lisa Miller who made a research study of the existential questions that mothers asked.[113] By spiritual, they meant an opening outwards from an egocentric position to one of feeling connected to other mothers, to the wonder of nature and to an unseen presence beyond temporal life. The researchers wanted to explore not only a mother's feelings about childbirth but the 'daily experiences of motherhood.'[114] They concluded that there was a 'lack of spiritual language' for many mothers.[115]

Mothers find it hard to explain what moves them so deeply.

First mother: Do you ever feel overwhelmed by . . . Sometimes I look at G when she's asleep and I want to cry. She looks like the *best* thing that's ever happened in the world. [G, 7 months]

Second mother: I feel that too. When G is asleep, I can picture her face, even though I can't see her. Then it makes me cry. [G, 10 months]

It's interesting to read that the philosopher Martin Heidegger pointed out in his book *What Is Called Thinking?* the resemblance between the words 'think' and 'thank' which are also similar in his native German. He thought the similarity was meaningful. 'In giving thanks,' he wrote, 'the heart gives thought to what it has and what it is.'[116] Heidegger wasn't referring to mothers when he wrote this. And mothers don't always feel thankful for what they have. Yet each child can stir up thoughts about the source and the wonder of a human life. In that sense, many of us do have moments of giving heartfelt thanks.

A mother may realise how tender she and her baby have become when they go outside. The rest of the world can be a noisy shock. Ordinary busy street life suddenly looks dirty, alien and threatening.

> Four days after my son was born, I went out into the street for a walk. I can clearly remember noticing that the world had become so *hard*. [B, 6 months]

> I keep noticing schools with concrete playgrounds and thinking that G is *never* going to go to one of those. [G, 3 months]

This tender state seems to depend on the mother's sense of closeness to her baby. For how long does it last? It must vary from one mother to another, depending on circumstances. But is there an average length of time? Apparently not. Other people may start talking loudly in a baby's presence, but the mother may still feel as if she and he are set apart.

> *Mother:* I'm wondering how I will feel when I go out into the world again.

> *Me:* Where are you now?

> *Mother:* In a bubble. A great big bubble [*gesturing that it was all around her*]. [G, 2 years]

The bubble image seems to occur to a number of mothers independently. It describes their sense of being inside a thin membrane which separates them with their babies from everyone else. A bubble is transparent, so people can see the mother and can talk to her. A mother with a baby is an ordinary sight, so it might seem as though she must feel as 'ordinary' as she looks. But, say mothers, these other people don't understand that she feels *inside* a special space with her baby.

> I'm happy inside my bubble, but I feel sad when I look out at the rest of the world. [B, 5 months]

> When I was pregnant, I felt really special. I thought people should make way for me everywhere I went. I was still in that bubble for the first three months. Then it subsided. [B, 13 months]

'You're in a bubbly cloud,' one mother said about herself. And another explained that she was talking to her baby in a shoe shop. 'What did you say?' asked the shop assistant who was walking towards her with a pair of shoes. 'He couldn't see,' she said, 'that I was inside a sort of a bubble, talking to my baby. So then I had to change my tone of voice to talk to him.' Going back to work was 'like coming out of a bubble', remarked another mother. She meant that once she left her baby for paid work, their exclusive closeness changed.[117]

Not all mothers like the sense of being enclosed with their babies. The novelist Rachel Cusk used a vivid image to convey her feelings. 'Motherhood, for me, was a sort of compound fenced off from the rest of the world,' she wrote. 'I was forever plotting my escape from it, and when I found myself pregnant again . . . I greeted my old cell with the cheerless acceptance of a convict intercepted at large.'[118] Her second child was conceived soon after the birth of her first, and this couldn't have been easy for her. Both times, she felt that having a baby set her apart from her normal life. With her characteristic honesty she compared it to being imprisoned.

At first, many mothers feel shocked to find what they have lost. Having a baby means they have less time for themselves, less contact with colleagues and reduced, or no, personal income. No wonder that many become depressed. What is harder to discover is whether they feel they have gained anything. The loss of one form of freedom often leads to the gain of another. This will be taken further in the next chapter.

Aurélie M. Athan and Lisa Miller, the researchers on spirituality quoted earlier, thought that many mothers today were missing an opportunity. They found that when they questioned a sample of mothers, they would mention spiritual experiences that they didn't seem to have discussed with anyone before. Those with religious upbringings had a vocabulary that they could use to describe them. Those with secular upbringings mentioned similar moments of awe, wonder, compassion, thankfulness, and a new sense of being on a journey, but felt at a loss about what to do with these feelings. The researchers concluded that there was a 'missing spiritual voice within motherhood'.[119]

If mothers have a 'missing spiritual voice' what kind of voice might this be? Perhaps present-day secular 'voices' have lost an ability that ordinary people used to have, to be open to experiences beyond the immediate. Without this sensitivity, once so common, the image of being inside a bubble seems to be the closest that many mothers get to articulating some of their strange experiences.

Occasionally, a mother will describe an experience that sounds like a spiritual one.

The American psychotherapist Daphne de Marneffe experienced such a moment, pushing her bicycle up a hill with her youngest son in a cart attached to the bike. She was planning the day ahead when she suddenly became aware of the present, what a beautiful morning it was, and how her son was asking questions and she was answering them. 'His thirst for knowledge and my power to slake it move me,' she wrote. 'It feels good and right to hallow this morning, this hour.'[120] 'Hallow' is an Old English word meaning to make holy. And this special memory was the way she ended her book, *Maternal Desire*.

It's moving to hear how ordinary these occasions were. No special ascetic discipline was necessary such as isolation, fasting or particular exercises. Each time it happened unexpectedly in the middle of the mother's everyday life.

> B and I go swimming together and then – I'm in *heaven*. [B, 7 months]

> B fell asleep on top of me, so I had to lie still. I felt guilty not standing up and using the time to get on with things. So I decided I'd do a meditation exercise. Only I fell asleep, and B and I woke up together. And then I really *saw* him – whole. It was wonderful. My parents were always rushing and *doing* things. I don't think they saw me whole. [B, 15 months]

I asked what she had seen. She said she couldn't explain, but she knew it had been an extraordinary moment.

The next mother had had an unhappy childhood. She received material comforts, but her parents separated and neither seemed to have been kind to her. She resolved to do better for her own children. This seemed to mean being available for them, night and day, when they needed her. Like many mothers who do this, she became extremely tired. But she felt delighted to see her children blossom and become confident and sociable. Then she found that they could give her something special for herself.

> I had a perfect day yesterday, the absolutely most perfect day. I was feeling a bit bored that morning, and then I read about a meeting of parents on a heath. I thought: We're *going*! They met by a huge, ancient, hollow oak tree and the children all climbed into it. 2B fell asleep [*in his buggy*] and the older two whispered to me: 'Is 2B asleep? Come on, you come into the tree too.' So I

did and it was wonderful. It supported all the values I believe in. And afterwards I thought: Is it okay to feel this happy? Because I often just see the dark side of things. But this time I allowed myself. [G, 5 years; 1B, 3 years; 2B, 9 months]

This kind of experience can make up for broken sleep, chaotic days, everything. It can restore us to the simple essentials we need to be joyful. It's true that our children don't know all the sad things that we do. But we may have lost touch with something that *they* know. Children seem able to be joyful in the most unlikely situations. If we spend time with them and draw close to them, they can show us how little we really need in order to get there.

And that can return us to the original meaning of that spiritual word 'sacrifice' which means to make sacred. Babies seem to revere life, just as it is. Their reverence goes beyond the everyday towards something more transcendent that people have called 'sacred' and 'holy'. Realising this doesn't mean we are slipping back into talk of a mother's 'holy duty'. Rather, inside the 'bubble' or through this loving friendship with our children, we have the chance to learn, or relearn, to experience the wonder of being alive.

CHAPTER EIGHT

Who am I?

Becoming a mother is an extraordinary change. In time, new mothers are amazed to find how much they have gained. But it doesn't usually feel like that at first. Mothers are more aware of what they have lost, especially their sense of identity. No wonder that many ask: 'Who am I?'

I'm not who I used to be, but I don't know who I am now. [G, 4 months]

I was sure I was going to *die* before I became a mother. Now I look back, I think I was wiser than I knew. I *did* 'die'. I am so different now. [B, 9 months]

Motherhood is like landing on a different planet. And I'm an alien on it. [G, 13 months]

Do all mothers start like this? Many say they do. Most seem to look much calmer than they feel. They say they no longer feel like their 'old selves'. This doesn't mean they have discovered 'new selves'. No, they feel in limbo, disorientated and confused. An eighteenth-century Jewish teacher said that all real change has a 'between stage'. He described a sprouting seed that 'does not begin to sprout until the seed disintegrates in the earth'. The 'between stage' may be a helpful way of thinking about becoming a mother, because it implies that the sense of loss is not the final outcome but a necessary midway phase.[121]

A new mother has entered a different social category. To an outsider, she may look like a mother. But it often takes a while until she feels she 'belongs'.

> I was sitting on a bus and I remember looking at all the other people and thinking: You're probably seeing a normal mother out with her baby. You don't realise that, inside, I don't feel normal at all. [B, 6 months]

An important part of our identity is appearance. Most women like to look attractive. Fashion photos tell us that an attractive woman is groomed and carefully dressed. Even with hair artfully tousled, a groomed woman will still look immaculate. Whereas a mother who has gestated a baby for nine months, given birth and is now feeding that baby round the clock doesn't look pristine. Her body has been put to a good deal of use.

In many cultures, a maternal appearance is a source of pride. But, in ours, signs of maternity tend to be seen negatively. Mothers are expected to lose their pregnancy weight quickly, so that they can fit into their usual clothes again. They want to 'get their bodies back'. Pregnancy, birth and even motherhood aren't supposed to make a lasting difference.

> People say: 'You don't *look* like a mum.' And they mean it as a compliment. [B, 8 months]

So it's quite usual to hear mothers say they feel less attractive if they look more motherly.

> I've developed large bosoms and a curvy shape. I used to wear very slim clothes and I enjoyed being flat-chested. When I look down at my body, I feel very strange. [G, 8 weeks]

There seems to be a shortage of attractive clothes designed for mothers that would show her changed shape to her advantage.

First mother: After B was born, I bought a new dress and it just covered my body up like a sack. I didn't look like me any more. [B, 9 months]

Second mother: I'm so glad you said that. I thought it was vain of me to mind how I looked. I thought I should just be grateful that I'd got a baby. I don't look like me either. [G, 8 weeks]

Mothers are often unaware of how *beautiful* they look. Many don't wear makeup because there isn't time to put it on, nor much social need. Without makeup, their faces look stronger and more sensitive. Their body movements look less constrained, more spacious. Their voices sound soft and tender. People are critical of an ungroomed 'mumsy look'. But not all beauty requires grooming. Why aren't there more well-designed clothes to set off the beauty of a woman who radiates the warm and unselfconscious loveliness of a mother?

Mothers don't usually *feel* beautiful. There's no time to think about it. They know they are responsible for the lives of their babies. Many are unprepared for how often their babies are hungry, how urgently they cry if they have to wait and how long it takes to feed them. A mother may achieve very little between one feed and the next. Even when her baby is older and feeds less often, he needs her and she doesn't have much time for herself.

I feel as if I will never have another selfish moment again in my whole life. [G, 4 weeks]

The biggest change to being a mother is the constant watchfulness. There's no room to think your own thoughts. [G, 10 months]

First mother: You just want a few minutes for your own headspace. [B, 23 months]

Second mother: And to breathe. [B, 3 years; G, 11 months]

Me: To breathe? Why, what happens to your breath?

Second mother: Well . . . you are always listening out, so your breath gets tighter. On your own, it can soften and get looser. [*The mothers present all agreed with her.*]

I had never before heard mothers say that their very way of breathing had changed. Looking back, I'm sure I would have felt this too, though I couldn't have described it as well as this mother did. And a tight way of breathing must affect the tempo of a mother's life.

There's a side of yourself, dreamy and reflective, that you can never contact when you are always in the present with your child. [B, 20 months]

It can feel strange to be caught up in the present and to have so little time to be 'dreamy and reflective'. The lack of time to think about oneself can feel a huge loss. No wonder that mothers feel disorientated and grieve for their former selves.

I miss the old me. She used to be flippant and carefree. Now I've turned into a forward planner. But have I lost her for ever, or is she just on a sabbatical? [B, 7 months]

The contrast with their previous lives is immense. Many mothers describe a complete collapse of confidence. They used to be self-assured, able to solve problems of daily life. Now they say they get stuck on the simplest questions about their babies.

I used to manage a team at work and I was always very decisive. If anyone on my team saw me now, they wouldn't recognise me. I can't make the smallest decisions. And they all sound petty. Should I put B in a jacket or a cardi to go out? Is he too hot? Is he too cold? It's endless. [B, 4 months]

The lack of confidence is understandable because the mother is inexperienced. Besides, not all her decisions are small ones. There are crucial health choices she has to make for her child – about vaccinations, for example, which may have lifelong consequences.

A new mother's uncertainty is humbling and uncomfortable. She doesn't feel like the person she used to be. Val Gillies, a researcher making a special study of working-class mothers, realised that part of their experience was common to mothers of *every* class. 'Motherhood', she wrote, 'entails a change of identity for all women.'[122]

Maybe this change of identity explains why some researchers conclude that mothers are less happy and more depressed than women without children.[123] But could the lower amount of happiness be not a final state, but part of a process of change?

In a paper with the interesting title '"Where did I go?" The invisible postpartum mother', two researchers – Jennifer Benson and Allison Wolf – have tried to explain what happens. They looked at literature for postpartum women and found that authors focused more on babies than on their mothers. They concluded: 'The message sent is that babies are important, women are not.'[124]

'Where did I go?' is a brilliant question. Something has definitely happened to a mother's sense of 'I'. Her 'I' goes through a strange metamorphosis when she becomes a mother. But it hasn't been widely recognised or understood. Lauren Porter, a mother in Australia, remembered: 'Motherhood was offering me a way to be more than just an individual. In order to accept that invitation, I had to step through to the unknown.'[125]

The 'unknown' can be frightening. Mother and baby are learning to share their lives. You can't call one of them important and the other one not. They are in transformation together, and *both* are important. The mother may have lost something of her old life.

But so has her baby. His solitary life in the womb is over. He finds that he is in a world of people, and he can't survive without their help.

For a mother, sharing her personal life with a baby is a major adjustment. Once she learns that her early difficulties are a part of a process of adjustment – a *major* adjustment, but not a threat to her entire identity – she might feel able to allow herself to change. But many mothers feel storm-tossed, frightened and bewildered. They mourn the loss of their old lives without seeing it as a necessary step towards something new. Their anxiety may be extreme and is then treated as an illness, 'postnatal depression', requiring medical intervention.[126] It might be more helpful to see the way women develop into mothers as a difficult *major* postnatal adjustment. Women have different histories. Some have good reason to find the transition to being a mother especially painful. But hardly anyone finds it easy.

Nearly every mother says: 'The beginning was very hard,' whether she had practical help from her partner, mother or a neighbour, or whether she had to manage on her own. So how do new mothers get beyond all this? The basic change is that they move from feeling almost shipwrecked to discovering that their boat is, after all, still afloat, and that they are learning – despite everything – how to manage it.

> *First mother*: I feel so lost. I've got so many questions and I don't know if I'm doing things right or not. [B, 2 months]

> *Second mother*: I can remember feeling like that, frantic and looking for answers 'out there'. But while I was looking, all the time, I was doing it. I had to learn that. [G, 5 years; 1B, 3 years; 2B, 15 months]

'I was doing it' is crucial. 'Doing it' sometimes has to be the answer, and thinking about it comes later. Doing and then reflecting on it, in that order, is exactly how mothers learn.

'But look,' some people might say, 'babies have been around for millennia. What's the problem? There are manuals and websites packed with useful information.' True, and new mothers are only too thankful for them. This is the part of mothering that *can* be taught. But, after a while, these guidelines seem limited. They are about 'average' mothers and babies. However, no mother and baby match the average exactly. So when a mother consults an 'expert', she may find that the advice she receives simply doesn't suit her own baby.

> If I could have my first year back again, I'd tell myself not to be so hard on myself. I had read a book on what to do with your baby. But B didn't like any of the ideas in the book. Now that doesn't worry me any more. [B, 12 months]

A big step forward is when mothers dare to discard ideas about babies that don't work for them. It sounds a negative step, but it clears the way for getting more in touch with their direct experience of their individual babies.

> *First mother*: My mother told me not to pick B up when he cried. But my arms *needed* B. [B, 6 months]

> *Second mother*: There's been a lot of research on how being left to cry affects babies. But there's nothing to say how it affects *mothers*. I'd feel terrible if I couldn't pick G up when she cries. [G, 12 months]

Mothers who learn to respond more spontaneously to their children report a mysterious surge of energy that helps them. There has been some research on maternal tiredness, but hardly any to help us understand maternal energy.

> One day I decided to relax and have fun with G. And after spending time with her, I found I could do all the jobs I was planning to do very quickly because my energy was different. [G, 5 years; B, 2 years]

This change of energy is a common experience. A mother may have arranged an outing and finally got herself and her baby outside their front door. Her plan is simple: buy a picnic from the corner shop and take her child to the park. She's remembered keys, cards, her baby's things – anything forgotten? Yes, she'd completely forgotten that her baby might have ideas of his own. First, he notices two wood pigeons on a fence and wants to look at them. She hadn't realised what gorgeous colours their breast feathers were. Then, suddenly, the sky clouds over and rain comes pelting down, so they have to race for shelter. Her baby finds this hilarious. There's the magic of sharing a laugh together, though they haven't even got to the corner shop and now it's too wet for a picnic.

Being able to relax, abandon her plans, and have fun enables a mother to 'tune in' to her child. It may not come easily, but it's an important part of learning to share her life.

> G notices simple things like the shape and colour of a stone. It makes me appreciate those things too. [G, 15 months]

> *And the same mother a week or two later:*

> *Mother:* I am learning to slow down.

> *Me:* In what way?

> *Mother:* I don't keep telling myself: 'I *have* to do this. I *have* to do that.' I ask myself: 'Why do I *have* to?'

It takes courage for a mother to share with her daughter the shape and colour of a humble stone. And then to question her own agenda and ask: 'Why do I *have* to?' However, many mothers complain that letting go of external pressures and learning to be in step with their children means they can't achieve their own goals. Letting go their goals depresses them. I think this reflects a widespread idea that a mother is supposed to get back to her former clothes and recover her individual life quickly, rather than take time to develop into a mother.

> People are always saying they want to get their lives back. I don't want to go *back*. I enjoy being a mother. I don't see why people can't go *forward*. [G, 4 years; B, 2 years; G, 9 months]

Going forward means that the mother isn't struggling *against* her child to lead her separate life. The two of them have connected. So, much to her surprise, she finds that learning about her child is also revealing new aspects of herself.

> I thought being a mother was about feeding and nappies. I didn't realise how much it would teach me about myself. [*Unanimous agreement from the mothers present.*] [G, 5 months]

More experienced mothers also recognise this:

> *First mother*: B has confronted me with myself. I don't mean he is a reflection of myself. It's just that when I talk to him . . . It's hard to explain. [B, 9 months]

> *Second mother*: Exactly. You discover yourself. [B, 11 months]

For mothers of several children, self-discovery becomes more complicated. But it still continues.

> Each child is different and brings out a different side of yourself. You are always yourself, but children want different things from you. My youngest is a challenge and I've got to find new parts of myself to deal with the challenges she gives me. [Mother of seven children aged 34–17 years]

What does a mother learn about herself? It emerges from the life she and her baby are creating together. It's not that she has all the answers. But when she compares what she is doing with what the 'experts' say, she notices that their advice is informed by their value systems.[127] This becomes clearer when some of these clash with hers. She may not have realised how many she has already. These are values she really believes in. She doesn't need to import a lot of advice embedded in the value system of somebody else.

> It's good to stand back and take a second look at the values you have accepted. I've had to revise many of mine. Being a mother gives you the chance to know who you really are. [B, 18 months]

This is at the very heart of what mothers learn for themselves. They start to understand their babies, but their babies are also learning to understand *them*. Mothers ask: 'How do I do my best for my child?' At first the answers usually come from someone else's advice. But, almost imperceptibly, mothers go on to make their own choices. This must be what Mary Wollstonecraft meant when she wrote that mothers need 'independence of mind'. Mothers aren't always aware how deeply they hold particular values until they begin to make daily decisions about their children. These decisions may sound pragmatic, but they have an ethical base.

> When G was four months old, I took her to a swimming class. She screamed at the water and got distressed. The teacher told me I must persevere. She said: 'Once G gets the idea that she can make you do what she wants every time she cries, you've lost the battle.' Now I know exactly what I think about that line of argument. *Now* I'd take G out of the water and go home straight away. But *then* I was new and felt intimidated. So we stayed. [G, 10 months]

> People are always telling me that I must do this and do that with my kids. And I think: *No!* Having children makes you see what your values are. [1G, 3 years; 2G, 13 months]

> It's taken me till I was a mother to be able to assert myself. Sometimes I'm completely alone in what I think is right for 1B.

If someone opposes me, I may take a step back, but I think: This is really *wrong*, isn't it? [1B, 4 years; 2B, 14 months]

Looking back, I now see that mothers have been telling me, for years, how having a baby has made them reconsider their values. I took this to mean that they now had a different outlook. But recently, I've realised that they were also trying to tell me how they had gone further than abstract thinking. Since becoming mothers, they had discovered how to put their values into practice.

'A mother runs a small country called Home,' said the writer Allison Pearson.[128] This sounds accurate. Through running her 'small country', the mother decides on her priorities, and eventually turns them into overall policies. And this must be what mothers have tried to tell me they are doing, for decades. Pearson doesn't mention fathers. But isn't the father the traditional head of the home, the *pater familias*? Yes, for centuries fathers held overt power over their families. But a closer look shows that Pearson has a point. In reality, it's usually the mother who runs the daily life of the home – and not just today, but in different eras and societies.[129] Now that fathers are becoming more involved with their families, this may change. But at the moment, mothers sound as though they are in charge.

Once mothers start identifying their personal values, they talk much less about the selves they have lost. Instead, they agonise about their decisions and the possible long-term effects on their children. No longer are they consulting other people. They can't. No other person holds the same combination of values as they do. And now they have taken steps to live by them. This means that they are really taking responsibility as mothers.

I've always been a 'good' student. That's been part of my identity. I suppose that has meant letting other people judge how good I am. Now I'm a mother, *I'm* the one that has to judge what's best. [B, 17 months]

Now, when I hear mothers talking, I notice how *often* they mention what they value. Single examples are part of the mother's larger system. 'I've never left B to cry.' 'I don't dress G in pink clothes.' 'I don't want B to have stranger anxiety.' 'I always tell G to try a new food, even if she doesn't like the look of it.' 'I always tell my children *why* I'm asking them to do something.'

One mother explained that:

> My daughter doesn't know the meaning of failure. If she's trying something and it doesn't work, she's interested and tries to find a better way. Life for her is full of amazing experiments and I've never taught her that she is supposed to succeed. [G, 5 years; 1B, 3 years; 2B, 2 years]

All these examples arise from the mother's strong ethical convictions: philosophical, religious, feminist, humanist or other basic position. These help her to formulate general principles that shape the daily life of her family. Some mothers prioritise kindness and cooperation; others individualism and competitiveness. Some believe in good manners; others prefer honesty and spontaneity. Some mothers want the safest possible environment for their children. Others think that having children shouldn't stop a family from risk-taking and adventure. And whatever a mother's priorities, situations arise when she finds two of her values collide. Then she has to unravel the issues at stake.

> I like to be tidy, and I'd shout at the children to make them tidy up. But they wouldn't. So then I thought: Do I want to be a nagging mother? Do I want them to carry memories of a nagging voice from their childhood? [1B, 6 years; 2B, 4 years; G, 18 months]

It can also be difficult taking her children to another mother's house because her values may be different. Both then worry that their children will notice the differences and be confused.

Much more problematic is when parents of the same child

disagree. Both may say they have the child's best interests in mind. Both may hold strong convictions, be overstretched and tired and find it hard to listen to one another. Mothers mention these conflicts, but don't always say how (or whether) they are resolved.

Also, either parent or both can easily abuse their power. They may be tempted to adopt values that serve their own interests, at the expense of their child's. After all, their child can't do much to stop them.

A mother whose value system includes respect for children will be sensitive to the attitude of people who think differently.

You hear people say: 'Don't talk to me like a child.' Well, I don't think you should talk to *children* like that either. [1B, 6 years; 2B, 4 years; 3B, 7 months]

If a mother talks respectfully to her child, he seems to sense it, long before he can talk himself. A mother will sometimes say that her baby is 'assertive' or has 'a strong will'. Does that mean that she has a special kind of headstrong baby? Probably not. A pre-verbal baby who communicates his likes and dislikes has learned that his mother is willing to 'listen' to him. He has already worked out one of her values. She wants him to have a 'voice'.

One thing I've learned is that children aren't completely malleable. Not at all. G's got her own personality and she tells me what she wants. [G, 7 months]

First mother: To me, the most important thing is to let your child have their own feelings. [1G, 3 years; 2G, 11 months]

Second mother: Yes, when B gets angry, my mum always tries to distract him. I say: 'B's *angry*. Don't distract him. Let him have his moment.' [B, 13 months]

I try to take time to listen to what my children are telling me, though that's not the same as doing everything they ask for. [B, 7 years; 1G, 4 years; 2G, 2 years]

When a mother quietly listens to her child, she allows him to feel safe with her. She needs self-discipline for this, and an onlooker is unlikely to realise how much silent energy she is giving to support her child.

I hope G will grow up to be herself. I'm just hoping I don't knock it out of her. My feeling is that if she can be herself, like she is now, then, no matter what difficult things happen to her, she's going to be all right. [G, 22 months; 32 weeks pregnant]

As her child develops, so does she. Mothers sometimes describe how they have changed by saying: 'Being a mother has made me . . .' and then adding a moral quality. But being a mother doesn't automatically *make* anyone a better person. Rather, it is part of a humbling journey during which a mother struggles with a good deal of uncertainty. She usually emerges gradually with a stronger sense of what she believes. But it doesn't just happen. It depends on herself.

I've become much softer as a mother. I don't mean I've turned into a softie. In many ways I'm much tougher as a mother, much more sure of what I believe in. But I worry about going back to work and having to be more hard and quick, not able to be honest with people. [G, 13 months]

From feeling like a lost beginner, a mother learns to trust herself in making choices. Many of these are experimental, not rigid. And not all mothers like having so much choice. Some develop in different ways. But the ones who say their values have changed and who create families based, at least in part, on their own priorities discover something unexpected. The early months of panic are gone. They feel stronger in themselves.

I've *found* myself, being a mother. I've become more of the person
I want to be. [B, 3 years]

It seems much easier to love when we are being ourselves. So
if someone is striving to be 'a perfect mother' by other people's
standards, love can be more difficult. Listening to mothers who
say they aren't perfect but are trying to create families that embody
some of their values, I frequently hear them say how much they
love their babies.

I love B so much. I didn't know I was going to. It's such a *strong*
love, it hurts. [B, 3 months]

My life is so different with B. There's all that love that flows through
me. [B, 18 months]

At first, babies seem intent on learning how to survive. But once
they feel secure, they start to smile and express their love too. It's
usually mothers who receive the first signs of it. It can come as a
shock to find that babies' love is completely unconditional. They
bathe us in passionate love that few of us feel we deserve. After all,
they haven't chosen us. When they are older, they will have the
right to review us, faults and all. But at first, they love without
reservation.

This morning, it was pouring with rain and I was walking along
a busy city street, carrying G. It was cold, and everyone looked
huddled, wet and miserable. Then G gave me this gorgeous smile.
I thought: I'm just so *lucky*! [G, 12 months]

As a mother, you get so much love back. It makes you feel loving –
all day. I've never loved anyone like that in my whole life. [B, 17
months]

Those of us who accept this unusual love discover that it has
the power to change us. Many of us have never in our lives been

loved like this, without judgment. The love of our babies can melt our defensiveness and give us a second chance to become more of the people we want to be.

Even so, love doesn't come easily to every mother. It can feel hard to give something which perhaps she rarely received as a child herself.

> I was afraid of having a baby. I was afraid I would love her too much. Love always leads to so much pain. And now I've got her and the beginning was very hard. I didn't think I could do it. [G, 9 months]

In any case, giving and receiving love doesn't mean our lives are permanently joyful. We bear our children in hope, but life will inevitably bring sorrow too. Because a mother gives birth to her child and sees him so new and beautiful, because she falls in love with him and yearns above all for him to have a wonderful life, no one feels quite as distraught as she does when she sees him suffer. If a child is seriously ill, maternal guilt can be very strong. Mixed with the joy of love comes a good deal of anxiety, fear and grief. These experiences are hurtful, but they can also change and perhaps even strengthen us.

> *Me:* When G was ill and you had to cope, did it help you to feel stronger as a mother?

> *Mother:* Not stronger. It reminded me that we *are* strong. We are meant to cope with things like this. [G, 12 months]

> I find when you feel as though you've got to the end of your tether that you're just about to grow a bit. You're going to become more patient than you ever thought you could be, or something like that. [B, 16 months]

Mothers do 'grow a bit'. It's easier to see when they look back on it.

G and I are happy. We've been happy for quite a long time. I think motherhood has transformed me. I feel at home with myself. I can't imagine being myself without a child. I feel proud because it was difficult at first and I know I've *weathered* it. [G, 21 months]

So now we may be able to answer that question: 'Where did I go?' Living with a baby means that a mother has to shelve a lot of her individual life to make room for him. At first, it looks like a deprivation. But it enables her 'I' to change. Her 'I' has to make space for another 'I' and, to some extent, live as a 'we'. Both mother and baby have lost some of their earlier independence. But both are learning and becoming more than they were. The mother finds she has to identify her values and her 'I' becomes much more defined. And during this time of change, both may discover how much they love one another.

Their relationship needs continual adjusting because babies develop so quickly. But their love is a constant. It's not conditional. And this gives the mother a very different feeling about her life. If she can allow herself to love and be loved unconditionally, it can warm her through and renew her energy to be joyful.

Compared to being at work, I feel really *alive*. I feel very thankful for that.' [1B, 3 years; 2B, 5 months]

Dana Raphael, quoted on page 50, coined the word 'matre-scence'[130] to describe a transitional period in which women adjust to being mothers. But there is a sense in which there is no final arrival. Being a mother seems to be a lifelong adaptive journey.

First mother: I'm not who I used to be, but I don't know who I am now. It's too early to say. [G, 4 months]

Second mother: But I find you never get to that new place. First you're the mother of a newborn, and you get used to that and what you need to know about it. Then you're mother of a growing baby, then it changes into a crawler and then a toddler. Suddenly you're the mother of a two-year-old and it changes again. I expect it will change after that. [B, 2 years; G, 8 months]

You learn some things as a mother, but you're always at the start of something new. [1G, 2 years; 2G, 4 months]

And then, after all, it seems that a mother's previous identity has not vanished but is 'waiting in the wings'. It might reassure new mothers to know that experienced ones recover their old selves.

I've found already that parts of myself have started to come back. I feel stronger. More integrated. [B, 3 years; G, 9 months]

I'm beginning to realise that my old self hasn't gone. She's still here! I'm so impatient to live more of her. [1G, 3 years; 2G, 21 months]

Then what about her 'new' self? A mother may have a much clearer understanding of her priorities. Within her family, she has made decisions and seen how they work out – how much is possible. Her family is a microcosm of larger social settings. Many mothers return to their workplaces with realistic aspirations and as capable organisers.

To me, though this metaphor might not suit everyone, a new mother is something like a fruit tree changing from spring into summer. The delicate, bee-attracting flower petals drop off and, at first, it seems that nothing more is happening. But the tree is hard at work. By the autumn, it is incredible to see the strength of the tree laden with fruit. In a similar way, it is amazing to see how the once bewildered mother and baby have matured into distinct people.

People say mothers are 'tied down' by their children. In one sense they are. But they are also freed. Surely in no other field do they supervise themselves to such an extent. In no other field are they free from the pressure of having to sell their work: their children are not for sale. And so, after feeling like lost souls in the vast terrain of motherland, they find that, after all, they have created their own 'small countries', in which they and their children can continue to develop.

CHAPTER NINE

Fathers in flux

It's not unusual, now, to see fathers with young children in the street. Their faces are pale, clothes dishevelled, and they look as exhausted as mothers. Some wear their babies in slings and take their older children by the hand. They talk in voices that sound gentle and connected. Occasionally they shout, but only in moments of panic, not with traditional male authority. They are sometimes alarmed because their child is skipping too near the kerb of a busy road, or has just picked up something dirty from the pavement. I think these fathers must be the adult sons of my generation of mothers. I feel deeply moved to see them. And their children look up at them and respond, not out of fear, but with the trust of love. These fathers are pioneering a new way. They will need to describe fathering in their own words.

This chapter will focus on how mothers are affected, especially by the changing role of fathers.

The Victorian ideal of a good father is still with us. Yet, even then, people were critical of it. The following passage is from an 1869 issue of the literary journal *The Cornhill Magazine*.

Men toil early and late for their children and think they have done well. The man who said that he had never seen his children by daylight except on Sundays, expressed with only a very little exaggeration what is a common state of things. And I say that such fathers do well in their generation as 'bread-finders'; but might they not do better, if they lived less in the counting house and a little more in the nursery and the school-room?[131]

Many fathers today are keen to have more contact with their children than their own fathers had with them. And most women have done paid work but received little preparation for becoming mothers. So both parents may feel like novices.

'Parent' and 'parenting' have suddenly become popular words. Some of the work of childcare is interchangeable and can be divided equally. Many couples plan to share all they can. However, during the pregnancy months, both can see the mother's abdomen slowly growing. She can feel the baby inside her, and may be physically uncomfortable, emotional and concerned about giving birth. So even before the baby is born, it becomes obvious that, though both of them are parents, and though the father is keen to be involved, the mother's pregnancy can't be divided and shared.

At a meeting I went to, a mother started talking about having spreadsheets, so she and her husband could plan equal parenting. I couldn't understand what she meant. It went against what I'm doing and I felt confused. For *nine* months, babies have been inside their mothers. They've known their smell, and heard the sound of their voices, and felt their mothers' rhythm. When they're born, their mothers are familiar to them. It must take fathers ages to catch up and make their own relationships. How can parents be equal? Perhaps I'm overlooking something, but I really don't understand it. [G, 20 months]

Even after the birth, it's difficult to see how parenting can be shared equally, with or without spreadsheets. Many expectant mothers assume that 'equal parenting' means they won't be caring for their babies on their own. However, if the partner is the main earner for the family, then dividing the work of babycare equally between them won't be possible. Mothers who had envisaged this find the reality unfair.

> I believed in equality. But now I'm a mother there's *no* equality. It's more like 80/20. I do 80 per cent. F keeps asking me what to do. [G, 8 months]

> F said to me: 'So what do you say to your mother friends when they do everything themselves and we are 50–50?' I said: 'We are *50–50*? When did you do . . . ?' And I listed all the parenting things I do that he never does. Then F was really upset. [B, 15 months]

'In our culture,' wrote the feminist Ursula Owen in 1983, 'mothering is a job and fathering is a hobby. It may turn out to be a lifelong passion, but it is still a hobby, and fathers who want to alter this find no real model available to them.'[132] She gives an interesting example in the book she edited, *Fathers, Reflections by Daughters*. Owen asked each daughter for a photo of herself with her father. 'Almost everyone', she wrote, 'had difficulty finding one. Why? "Because Dad always takes the photograph."'[133]

It seems as though, even in the 1980s, many fathers saw themselves as slightly removed from the inner family – not remote, but still an outsider, looking in. A frequent complaint of mothers today is that their partners *behave* as if they thought being a new father was like taking up a hobby. Fathers, they protest, continue living much as they did before.

> F had an accident on his bike yesterday. He's all right. But he doesn't wear a helmet and he sometimes listens to music while he's cycling. I'm trying to tell him that he's a *dad*. [G, 3 months]

The beginning was hard. My husband wanted a baby, but his life didn't change. He'd go to work in a beautiful suit, and come home and tell me where he'd been for lunch. And I'd be sitting on the sofa, in my pyjamas, feeling fat and unsexy, trying to breastfeed our baby. [B, 3 years]

Other fathers seem overwhelmed by their new babies and want to contribute all they can. But, especially if mothers are breast-feeding, it's not obvious what fathers should do. How is he supposed to be an equal parent? Remembering his own father may not give him the role model he is looking for.

My father was brilliant at playing with us [*herself and her brother*]. He'd invent games and it was such fun. But I can remember my mum saying: 'You've got the children all excited when it's time for bed.' [B, 9 months]

F has no template for being a father. His own father worked and was never around. F seems to go suddenly from permissiveness to authoritarian with no middle bit. [B, 4 years; G, 3 months]

It's not only the newborn who needs care. A mother who is often still recovering from the birth, and especially if she is breast-feeding, needs help too. Some fathers are glad of the chance to rally round for mother and baby. When they do, mothers proudly tell one another: 'F *always* puts the bins out.' '*He* does all the cooking.' 'I had a Caesarean birth, and for the first few weeks F did all the nappies. I didn't do *any*.'

They are all New Men, aren't they, our partners? They think they are doing so much. And they *are*. Compared to their dads, they're amazing. But there's some of it they just don't get. [G, 2 years; B, 6 weeks]

What don't fathers 'get'? A pregnant woman has had an intro-duction to mothering. She had to share her body with a lively, independent being. He may have started kicking inside her just when she needed peace and quiet to get to sleep. This difference of needs may have prepared her for what comes next. Once her baby is born, she shares not just her body, but her daily life. It's constant and tiring. Many mothers assume that their partners understand this, and are shocked when they don't.

> I was getting so tired, I asked F if he could get up one hour earlier so I could get more sleep. And he said he wouldn't. He said: 'No, if I get up one hour earlier, I would want that time for myself. I could do yoga.' [G, 3 months]

> F comes home and pours himself a beer before he's even *looked* at G and me. [G, 7 months]

> I was so tired, I said: 'Could you take G for half an hour?' F said: 'Oh, but I'm just ten minutes away from the end of my [*computer*] game.' [*Moans of recognition from the listening mothers.*] [G, 12 months]

> F never puts G first like I do. I say: 'Can you look after G while I go to the loo?' And his answer is: 'Not now. I'm just going to make myself some coffee.' [G, 15 months]

New situations keep arising, with misunderstandings when the couple make assumptions about what the other person means.

> *First mother*: On Saturday morning, we decided we'd all go out. F said: 'Is there time for me to have a quick shower?' I thought he meant ten minutes, so I said yes. But it was half an hour. By that time, G was ready for another feed. [G, 7 months]

> *Second mother*: You need your partner to orbit round you and the baby. I find it's hard when I'm with people who expect me and the baby to orbit around *them*. [B, 4 years; G, 5 months]

But the father who wanted the shower *was* trying to 'orbit round' mother and baby. He had asked if there would be time for his shower. The difficulty arose because she assumed his 'quick shower' would fit the short time span during which their baby could wait, whereas his idea of 'a quick shower' must have matched their old pre-baby sense of time.

From what mothers say, many fathers are bewildered. They can see that being a father doesn't just happen. They know they should be taking on new responsibilities. But, especially in the home, it's not obvious what these are.

Me: There's a lot for new fathers to learn.

Mother: Yes [*very tartly*]. But he should know where his socks live by now. [G, 3 months]

I think men have got a small black hole and all the things you ask them to do go straight down it. [G, 9 months]

Fathers of this present generation don't usually turn to their own fathers for advice. Instead, they turn to their partners. It's true that they have a lot to learn, and that mothers can sometimes supply the information they need. But it can change the relationship. Mothers take on the role of 'experts' while fathers are demoted to 'beginners'. This doesn't seem good for either of them.

F asks me about everything. But I don't know all the answers. I'm not an oracle. I don't always know why G is crying. [G, 3 months]

F did a lot for me and G, the other day. Afterwards he said: 'I like to help you lots.' I was furious. Then I remembered the male culture all around us. I said: 'You are not "helping me lots". You are being G's *father*.' [G, 6 months]

My partner says: 'Tell me what I can do to help you.' I say: 'I'm too tired to tell you. I need *you* to think how you can help. [G, 17 months]

It's easy then for mothers to regard their partners as helpless and incompetent. Most mothers can give countless examples. They feel unsupported and exasperated.

I don't think F is turning into a father. I think he's turning into a child. [B, 4 months]

My aim is for F to be an active daddy not just a play daddy. I want him to think about when G is tired or hungry. [G, 9 months]

I feel I put F and B in the same box. I feel I have to look after them both. I love looking after B. But when I take care of F, I resent it. [B, 11 months]

One mother admitted:

I use a really patronising voice to my husband, as if he was an errant child. I think it would be better if I got straightforwardly angry. [B, 7 months]

But don't both parents feel like errant children? Neither has had much preparation, both have a lot to learn and mothers are only a short way 'ahead'.

F and I had only known each other for a year before we had B. We're not married. We haven't got our own home. We haven't got plans for the future. Other couples have been together for years and years, and planned everything and seem so grown up. We're like two kids with a baby. [*I asked the mothers listening to her if any of them felt similar – and they all did!*] [B, 8 months]

Some mothers feel that, when they are at home and caring for the children, their partners have the more difficult role as bread-winners. They see their maternal role as providing support.

First mother: I took all three children out one morning so poor F could plaster a wall. [1G, 4 years; 2G, 18 months; B, 9 months]

Second mother: I don't know. If I had a choice, *I* might prefer plastering a wall to your work looking after three children, all under five years old. Hmmm. Nice, quiet job. No interruptions. Nice cup of tea. [G, 4 years; 1B, 2 years; 2B, 4 weeks]

In a similar exchange, two listening mothers helped an exhausted mother to see that even a husband as busy as hers could contribute a bit more.

First mother: I feel tired behind my eyes, so tired. I feel like a single mum. There, I've *said* it. F is so busy, he doesn't help at all. [G, 8 months]

Second mother: Don't do so much housework. Make him notice. [B, 5 months]

Third mother: Don't buy any loo paper! [B, 7 months]

Breadwinning fathers are doing responsible work. But so are unpaid mothers. Fathers who do take on some of it quickly learn what difficult work it can be.

My husband looked after G all day. When I got back, he said to me: 'I don't know how you do it. How do you go for a pee?' He hadn't eaten all day because he was so busy looking after G. And none of the washing-up was done, or any tidying. [G, 9 months]

I feel as though I'm on the fast track to parenthood and F's on the slow track. F looks after B more now, and he says things I *used* to say, like: 'It's relentless. I can't get anything done. I'm always being interrupted.' [B, 4 years; G, 7 months]

It's only when mothers notice what their partners *aren't* doing that they begin to see how much they have learned themselves. A person *without* a baby or a child can go from one room to another, then realise she has left something in the first room and go back for it. For a person *with* a baby or child, this simple act is more difficult. A mother learns to keep a mental list of everything she will need from one room before moving herself and her baby to the next. That way, she is organised and calm. Even if she has never enjoyed planning, she will find that everything is easier with a baby if she plans the details ahead. This is a tiny example of a way of life that she has taught herself without realising it. Her partner may not have thought of it.

> As a mother, I've learned to be two steps ahead. I don't think my husband can do that. I came into the bedroom yesterday and F had lain B down on the bed, just as he was, to sleep. I said: 'But you haven't changed his nappy.' I'd have picked up a clean nappy on the way to the bedroom. F said: 'Don't I get any credit for getting B to bed and to sleep?' I said: 'But in a few hours, his nappy will leak and he'll wake up. Feel how heavy [*with urine*] it is already.' Then F had to agree, and we changed him. [B, 2 years; 35 weeks pregnant]

There's a lot for fathers to learn. It includes tiny details of organisation – but paid work depends on this kind of pre-planning too.

A frequent complaint by mothers is that fathers don't keep their side of agreements. Typically, a father will agree to take over childcare at a set time. The mother plans and prepares everything to make the changeover easy. She looks forward to the moment when the father will arrive and she will have time to herself. Then he phones from his office, tells her he's sorry, there's a work crisis on, and he'll have to change plans and cancel for today. Mothers remember these occasions as huge disappointments. They say their partners present the change as unavoidable and seem to think that the mothers are being unreasonable to mind as much as they do. So not only are all the mother's plans thwarted but she receives short shrift for her feelings too. This is a very common example of a situation that the father doesn't seem to 'get'. As he sees it, she is making light of his work crisis. Isn't he working to support their family? He might find her more sympathetic if he tried to understand why she, doing continuous, round-the-clock, unpaid work – also for the good of their family – might feel so let down.

One mother discovered that, with her husband, it was better not to plan set times but to have a more casual arrangement in which he could choose his moments.

> My husband said he would look after G on Friday at three. I was really excited. But then he forgot. He said: 'At work, every day is full of appointments and schedules. It's nice to get home and be more relaxed.' And I've noticed that sometimes, when he's at home, he *does* take over G. [G, 7 months]

To what extent do mothers need to step back and allow fathers to make their own choices? Being a father is *not* a hobby. It never was. Some of the practical work can be done by the mother's parents or siblings, neighbours and paid help. But theirs are auxiliary roles. Being a father gives a man a unique relationship to his child. Many fathers today are sons of fathers who worked away from home and didn't spend much time with their children. But perhaps the absence of a role model can be an advantage. It leaves a new father free to pioneer his own way of fathering.

> My husband said to me: 'I'm G's father. Sweetheart, I need to be able to deal with her when she has tantrums. But I can't if you don't let me practise.' I didn't know I was stopping him. But perhaps I am. [G, 21 months]

Other mothers are desperate before they discover how capable their husbands can be.

> One evening, I couldn't cope another moment. The last straw was that B had put mud in 1G's hair, and she *hates* the hairdryer. I'd

only just washed her hair the night before. I was trying to dry her hair, and she was complaining, and I said to F: 'I've had enough. *You* take over.' 2G was already fed and asleep, fortunately. I knew the other two would be safe with F, but I didn't think he'd be much help. I went and sat in the park for what felt like ages but was probably about twenty minutes. When I got back, F was reading a story to B, 1G was in her bed with dry hair, and the washing-up was done! [B, 5 years; 1G, 2 years; 2G, 8 weeks]

It's interesting that the mother was surprised at her husband's competence, even though he'd been a father for five years. And she'd had to ask for his help. He hadn't volunteered, capable though he obviously was.

Are many fathers more capable than they seem? If a mother has done the early babycare, as many do, her partner may see her as so competent that there seems nothing much that he can offer. But fatherhood doesn't only mean being competent.

From birth, most babies enjoy being cuddled. Many fathers enjoy cuddling their babies and are awed by the tremendous sensation of peace and joy that this simple action can give. I was curious to hear, though, that there might be a special fatherly way of doing it.

Mother: I've seen F have a cuddle with B. But . . . it doesn't look the same as when I cuddle him. [B, 6 months]

Me: What's different?

Mother: I don't know.

Me: Could it be that fathers cuddle their children differently? [*All the mothers listening agreed that fathers seemed to have a different way of cuddling, but they couldn't explain what it was.*]

Dr William Sears, American paediatrician and father of eight, proudly described his own invention, the 'neck nestle' in which, he assures us, 'Dad shines'. He nestled his baby's head under his chin, held him close, and sang 'Ol' Man River' while swaying from side to side.[134] Many fathers must have improvised their own ways of relating to their babies, even though they may never have got into print.

> F carries B round the house and sings: 'The pirates are coming!' That's himself and B. [B, 5 months]

Some fathers get more drawn into parenting when a second child is born. Mothers want more help then, and get exasperated if a busy father fails to provide it. The father may not realise how desperately the mother may need his support.

> It was the last day of our holiday, but I hadn't had a holiday at all. I told F, and he took both children out. I couldn't think what to do with the time. In the end, I lay down and slept. And that was brilliant. I felt the difference for days after. [G, 2 years; B, 5 months]

A father may also overlook how important he is as a *friend* to the mother. Not many mothers mention it, but those who lack it know what is missing.

> F comes home from work and he cooks the dinner, washes up and then he goes out to do some gardening. I've been alone with G all day, and I say: 'Please, can't you sit down while I'm breastfeeding and be with G and me for five minutes?' But he won't. [G, 5 months]

> I visited a single mum, like myself, over the summer, and she talked non-stop about her teenage daughter. Completely non-stop! I hardly got a word in. Afterwards, I realised that I do exactly the same myself. If you haven't got a partner, there's no one to share it with. All the time, G does such wonderful things, I'm *dying* to share them. [G, 24 months]

The most poignant evidence of the difference that fathers make can be heard in the tears of mothers who have lost their own fathers. Many remember how their fathers walked out on their families. They struggle not to cry, but their sobs surge up from deep in their chests. Surely this depth of grief is the same for deserted sons too. The tragedy is that many fathers may never have appreciated how deeply they were loved. There is often a special pride in a child's voice saying: 'My *father* . . .' A father may think he was unworthy – but children are usually forgiving and grateful for the fathers they have.

> I had a letter from my father, four months ago. It was like a heavy grey cloud hanging over me. I've got a baby now, and there's been so much sadness in my life, I didn't want any more. [*Her father had left the family when she was a young child.*] But then I saw that my answer could be quite simple. So last night I wrote it. [*Sobs. Another mother passed her a tissue, which she took in a very casual way, as if unwilling to acknowledge she was crying.*] [G, 8 months]

> My father died when I was twelve. I'm thinking I could put together a book of photographs and stories so G will know who he was. [G, 5 months]

Some women become single mothers by choice. They may not know the identity of their child's father, and often don't want to. Others break up with their partners, or their partners with them. All these single mothers worry how their children will develop without their father.

> [*Tears*] I didn't mean to get upset. G and I are happy together. But I'm a single mother. I'm on my own, and hearing you all talk about your partners . . . I'm sorry. We're fine together. But I wish . . . I'm concerned about G's *future*. [G, 3 months]

> I'm a single mother. And I notice, when we are on the train going

somewhere, if there's a man sitting near us, B will always reach across and put his hand on the man's hairy arm. And I wonder: Is he wanting what he hasn't got? It's just him and me at home. [B, 13 months]

And in families where the father is around, mothers notice how much their children enjoy it.

I can really only relax when my partner looks after G. He has a different tempo from me. They have a lot of fun. [G, 10 months]

When F comes in, B looks up to him as if he is a rock star. [B, 21 months]

I came into our sitting room and F was throwing a huge ball at B, and sometimes it hit B. At first, I was shocked. But B loves it. He's ready for more vigorous play. [B, 3 years; G, 3 weeks]

However, cooperating as parents isn't always easy. A mother and father may not agree on what they think is best for their child. There are many decisions to make, and, for each of these, there can be conflicting views.

My mum was a single mother. And I knew F and I were having a baby together, but I didn't realise it would mean sharing the decisions. I'm not used to sharing, and it's a learning curve. My mum made all the decisions on her own. [B, 6 months]

Even a mother who grew up with two parents can be very critical of her partner's views. Sleep-training is a typical issue, with the mother wanting to comfort her child if he wakes in the night, and the father usually wanting undisturbed sleep and more night-time contact with his partner.

First mother: My husband wants to be involved in all the decision-making. He says: 'Let's talk about when B's old enough to go into his own room.' I'm terrified. I don't want to talk about it. [B, 3 months]

Second mother: But men have their own agenda, don't they? It sounds like a criticism. I hear it like that. But I can see, now, that F just wants me back in his bed. [B, 3 months]

And don't some fathers think that mothers are having too easy a time at home, while they are working flat out to pay for them? The next mother was tearful. She had breastfed her son while going through a painful week of mastitis when she had lost weight and felt weak.

My partner manages staff. He's very high-powered and, on Friday, he told me off for not doing enough. And he's right, I'm not, apart from looking after B. I know I should be doing more. [B, 11 months]

Mothers are usually distraught at being criticised. They often rely on their partners for emotional support.

I couldn't do without F. He's my moral support. If he says he's upset or worried about something, I can't cope. [G, 4 years; 1B, 2 years; 2B, 4 weeks]

Tensions often arise during 'transitional' moments, when one parent leaves for work, or comes back home. Mothers complain that their partners, when they are the main breadwinners for the family, seem to take too much time to remember that they are now fathers.

F comes home from work all tired and hot. First, he changes his clothes. He *always* does that. Then, he likes to have tea, and *then* he takes B. I teach yoga once a week. It's physical, so I come home all hot and sweaty. The underground is so hot and I'm dying for a shower. But the minute I'm through the door, B just wants me. He wants me to hold him and breastfeed him. So I never get a shower or anything. [B, 9 months]

F comes home and of course he is in a completely different rhythm from us. [B, 2 years]

F comes home from work and he's very tired, and the other day I found him upstairs, lying on the bed. 'I'm having a rest,' he said. It seems so unfair. I look after the children day and night and no one lets *me* have a rest. [G, 3 years; B, 3 months]

Then should we say that parenting is overall an unhappy experience for parents? This was one conclusion drawn by Catherine Hakim, the British sociologist. She wrote: 'Marital satisfaction declines from the time children are born up to the teenage years, then rises to former levels after children leave home and after retirement.'[135]

This conclusion surely depends on what couples understand by the word 'satisfaction'. Often, neither partner has received much preparation for the work of parenting. There is much to learn – and no end in sight. So a parent would be unlikely to reply to a researcher: 'Yes, I'm satisfied with my work as a mother/father.' That would fail to do justice to the infinite learning of being a parent.

At first, parents are more concerned for the new baby than for one another. Both have moments when everything seems unfamiliar and difficult. Both have times when they are tempted to blame the other one because they feel anxious and critical of themselves.

First mother: I'm patient with G all day. Then, when F comes home, he gets it in the neck. [G, 11 months]

Second mother: I'm going to buy F a 'Sorry' card. I've been horrible to him. I've said I'm sorry, but I want him to know that I'm *really* sorry. [B, 8 months]

I keep getting annoyed with my partner for all the things I see

him doing wrong. Then he does one nice thing and I'm feeling so
critical that I don't even *notice*. [B, 3 years; G, 5 months]

F and I both have inner critical selves, so we often turn our critical
voices against each other. I think we ought to be much kinder to
each other. [1G, 4 years; 2G, 21 months; B, 9 months]

Couples are usually drawn to each other because they share a
basic outlook. Why do they keep quarrelling simply because they've
had a baby? Often, each is attracted to the other for qualities that
are the opposite of their own: cautious/carefree, economical/
extravagant, calm/emotional and so on. But when each is tired,
anxious to do their best for the baby and aware of their own
shortcomings, it is only too easy to feel safer with their own original qualities and to blame their partners for the 'risky'
dissimilarities that once attracted them. Instead of the earlier
connection when they felt enriched by their differences, couples
seem to drive one another into opposite 'corners' with each on
the defensive.

Many couples are unsure about how to resolve their differences.
They have an 'either/or' attitude: either we both think alike, or we
can't live together.

Since B's birth, F and I quarrel a lot, most of the time in fact.
I still love him. But we're talking about splitting up. [B, 2 years]

It is extremely sad when a mother who loves her partner starts
talking about splitting up. Their quarrels can be painful because
their relationship is intimate, so each knows exactly how to hurt
the other. But why do they want to hurt one another? A quarrel
is a disagreement. It's understandable that two people who are
both responsible for the upbringing of a new person may disagree
about how to do it. Probably both of them have good points if
they can find a safe way to listen to one another. Each quarrel
may not be a sign of a relationship in ruins but a new chance to

understand the reasons for their differences and to deepen trust in one another.

However, each may feel insecure. Fathers may be puzzling over their new role. Mothers usually change physically after giving birth. And both are probably sleep-deprived. Each partner may wonder whether she or he is still loved. They now have less time and energy for the romantic and sexual side of their relationship.

We can go through a whole day without touching each other. I'm so busy, there's always too much to do. I'd never have *dreamed* that could happen. F and I have always been very tactile. [B, 7 months]

First mother: My body's a big part of my identity, and I'm two stone heavier than I was. I don't know who I am any more. [G, 8 months]

Second mother: I put on weight at first. My husband hurt my feelings so much. He was always talking about fat women who were too lazy to go to the gym. [B, 3 years]

First mother: My husband never says anything, but I think: Bet you wish I still looked like the woman I was.

Often men crave the revival of sexual love, but for many mothers, especially during the first year after childbirth, the idea of sex seems exhausting. And yet, mothers have reached a new stage of sexual maturity. Their bodies have changed.

I felt very sexual and strong after the birth. It was a wonderful birth, and I felt I could do anything. And F annoyed me because he was just the same as before. But now he has changed. I think it takes men longer to catch up. [B, 17 months]

It seems rare for mothers in our society to enjoy their maternal sexual beauty, and for partners to appreciate them. The more common idea that mothers have become less sexually attractive surely contributes to the lack of desire that so many mothers describe.

> My sexual desire has gone. My partner and I are just Team Mum and Dad. When I see him, I do still *like* him, but I don't *desire* him. There's all this pressure on you to be saying: 'I have a baby, and I have a great sex life.' And you think everybody else is having fantastic sex except for you. [G, 7 months]

> Sex is always at the bottom of my list at the moment. F loves my breasts, but after I've been breastfeeding G in the evening, I can't bear F to touch them. [G, 10 months]

> My partner would never push for sex. He says he'll wait till I'm ready. But in a way I wish he *would* push for it. I'm so far from sex at the moment. I'm breastfeeding. I worked out I must have done 2,000 breastfeeds. There are so many things I'd rather do than sex at the moment. But if he insisted, I'm sure I'd enjoy it. [G, 11 months]

Even after the first year, mothers report sexual reluctance. It sounds as if the difficulty is often more emotional than physical. Mothers now *really* understand that sex can lead to pregnancy and another baby, and may not want a second baby too soon.

> *First mother*: We tried a few months ago, and it hurt. [G, 15 months]

> *Second mother*: Me too. It's funny because I've had a Caesarean birth, but it felt as though my body was saying: '*No!* Nothing is going to go in there!' [B, 16 months]

So what can couples do? Many describe how important it is to restore a friendly relationship between the two of them, rather than rush to bed. Talking can help, if couples can go beyond blaming one another. In caring for the baby, it can be easy to overlook how much they owe each other. So often, one partner assumes that the other *knows* how grateful he or she feels for their help, and appreciation goes unspoken. Telling the partner can make a great difference.

> F puts 1G to bed, and I do 2G and B. We compare notes in the morning, and sometimes F will say: 'I think you've had a harder time than I have.' Then I feel *much* better. [1G, 4 years; 2G, 23 months; B, 11 months]

Once the couple feel closer, mothers are more willing to renew their sexual relationship.

> My husband's been sleeping in a different room to get a proper night's sleep. But he's on holiday this week and more relaxed. He came back into my bed, and it led to something nice happening. Twice. I feel so different. He had a cold, and I was *much* more sympathetic to him than I usually am. [G, 12 months]

> F and I have got closer again. Sex happened! Before that, it was [*snappy voice*]: 'You didn't do this.' 'Well, *you* didn't do *that*.' [B, 16 months]

> I always feel much too tired for sex. So when he asks, I think: Might as well. I'm never going to feel less tired. And then . . . I've forgotten this other side of me. I'd forgotten how I used to feel. [G, 20 months]

What about the resentment that many mothers feel because having a baby means much more menial work which has to be repeated, day after day? Mothers usually find themselves doing it because it is quicker than instructing an inexperienced partner. However, one mother decided to consider her husband as capable as herself. After four years as a mother, she saw a cure for her resentment.

I said to my husband: 'Whatever foreplay used to mean to us in the past, *now* it means doing *half* the clearing up.' It makes me feel much more kindly and loving towards him. [1B, 4 years; 2B, 19 months]

Mothers discover that parenting actions, even if they look like nothing, can be crucial. Fathers may take longer to appreciate that simple, sensitive responses are essential to parenting.

We were out with B and he got upset about something. It could have blown up into a scene, but F and I took turns and we managed to calm him. When we got home, I said: 'We did that well.' F was puzzled. 'What do you mean? What did we do well?' I had to explain it to him. He said: 'But that seems like *nothing*.' Then, one night, maybe a week later, B wouldn't go to sleep. It took me two hours to settle him. Finally, he was asleep and I texted F: 'I'm exhausted.' He texted back: 'You did that well.' [B, 17 months]

With some experience behind them, couples learn that they can comfort one another, even when both are worn out.

The other night, after we'd got the children to sleep, F made us both a marvellous hot white-chocolate drink with a dash of rum in it. [1G, 4 years; 2G, 2 years; B, 9 months]

By Sunday afternoon, F and I were overwhelmed. We sat down and looked at each other, and F said: 'Why don't we each give one another one hour off?' I didn't think that one hour would anywhere *near* meet my needs. But I went to the top of a very high hill and sat down and looked at the view for nearly an hour. And afterwards I felt fantastic. [G, 5 years; 1B, 3 years; 2B, 10 months]

In time, couples often create, out of the endless rotation of parenting tasks, enjoyable daily rituals and special times to celebrate.

F and I share a notebook and write things in it that G does. It's nice. My parents did the same for me. [G, 6 months]

F had a lovely idea. He said: 'When it's one of the children's birthdays, you should celebrate that it's your Birth Day too.' So when it was 1G's birthday we went out together, just the two of us, and had a wonderful time. [1G, 5 years; 2G, 2 years; B, 21 months]

Fathers often seem to feel driven to work harder to support their families. Many mothers have to slow down or drop their careers while they are looking after their children. They may compare their lives with their partners' and feel deprived.

F is starting a new course this month. It's wonderful for him, it's a whole new life opening out. But I'm just at home with G. I feel . . . I feel . . . static. [G, 24 months]

Some couples swap the traditional roles. The mother becomes the breadwinner, while the father takes daytime care of their children. But this attractive-sounding solution isn't always as easy for mothers as they'd imagined.

F will look after G when I work. I have the better-paid job, so it makes sense. But I feel jealous of F [tears]. It sounds terrible, I know. But he'll be able to see G every day, and I won't. [G, 7 months]

First mother: I wanted a big Victorian house, so now we have a huge mortgage, and I have to return to work. But I resent F [looking after their child], though the decision was mine. [B, 5 months]

Second mother: Yes, I've taken on far more work than I can do, and I resent not having more time to be with my children. I can hardly keep it all together. And I feel angry with F too. Mind you, he has stepped up well to being a father. But, as soon as I get home, he feels entitled to rest. [B, 6 years; 1G, 3 years; 2G, 13 months]

Couples are experimenting with the roles of father and mother and discovering new possibilities. Now the differences between 'male' and 'female' work no longer seem inborn, as used to be claimed, but to have arisen through social and economic pressures. Yet even today, women are still trying to liberate themselves from centuries of stunting oppression.

'It's a man's world,' people say, and it seems at first as if men have got the better deal. But have they? Despite their social and financial power, generations of men may have suffered an inverse kind of deprivation. Raging against the restrictions of being a woman in the 1840s and 1850s, Florence Nightingale protested: 'But suppose we were to see a number of men in the morning sitting round a table in the drawing-room, looking at prints, doing worsted work, and reading little books, how we should laugh!' And: 'Why should we laugh if we should see a parcel of men sitting round a drawing-room table in the morning, and think it all right if they were women?'[136]

At a glance, these women might seem to be doing pointless work, and Nightingale makes a passionate case for saying that they were. True, they might have had no direct social or political influence. But they were unlikely to be sitting round the drawing-room table in a dejected circle. No, they would be talking and generating a particular energy – the warmth of human intimacy.

Virginia Woolf had a similar impression. Looking back at female novelists of this era, she wrote: 'Then again, all the literary training that a woman had in the early nineteenth century was the training in the observation of character, in the analysis of emotion. Her sensibility had been educated for centuries by the influences of the common sitting-room.'[137]

So were these gatherings of women as pointless and as ridiculous as Florence Nightingale believed? Or were women gaining something from which *men* were excluded? Claudia Nelson, researching the role of fathers in Victorian England, wrote: 'The public sphere could work as a prison, not only as a privilege. Shut out of home and family, disconnected from the personal concerns that are the core of life, the stereotypical Victorian father remains an "invisible man".[138]

'The core of life.' Looking after a baby is more than practical work. It's work that invites intimacy. The two happen together, so fathers who leave the practical work to their partners also miss experiencing the intimate moments. In the nineteenth century, the role of father was seen as radically distinct from that of mother. Small comments, said in passing, make this very clear. For example, Sigmund Freud's oldest son, Martin, wrote: 'My mother would never expect Father to act as a nursemaid.'[139]

The distinction between men and women seemed to run right through many cultures and social classes. It seemed 'obvious', so people hardly commented on it. The political activist Walter Southgate, recalling his own working-class childhood, said: 'At christening ceremonies fathers and other males were rarely present. That would be beneath their dignity. Fathers did not push perambulators with babies through the streets, for it, too, would be considered beneath their dignity, a comedown in the realm of cockney family life.'[140] Even today, some men say they feel unmanly if they are seen pushing a pram.[141]

So for generations, men were called fathers, and indeed, they had fathered their children. But they often had minimal opportunity to get to know them. Some were called on to chastise these children when they were 'naughty', with the result that many adults still remember how much they feared their fathers.

Is the 'man's world' completely desirable? It can seem so, for anyone excluded from it. But it can be harsh, competitive and short of love, tenderness and intimacy. Perhaps men who have become more active fathers are beginning to recognise something that fathers before them have missed. It wouldn't be surprising if they felt cheated, bitter and angry in a similar way to feminists.

The difference is that women could not compel them to avoid the nursery. Men created the barriers themselves.

These are historical sexual, social and political issues that can affect a couple. Rather than fight one another, the couple can clarify what is wrong. Then they can feel close again.

> I finally told F what I thought. He works freelance, but when I'm looking after G, I'm working too. I felt he didn't understand that, and he wasn't supporting me. It was the first time I'd really let go my feelings. And it's fine, now, and I love him again. [G, 6 months]

Many couples feel closer once they have gone back and discussed the birth of their child. During childbirth, events can move quickly, and a couple may see one another apparently being unforgivably insensitive to the other's needs. It can be a revelation to hear the reasons for what the other person was doing.

> A few months ago, my husband and I had a long talk. We debriefed. We went back to the birth and talked about all the things we could do better if we have a second baby. [G, 2 years]

So do couples eventually recover their old relationship? Many say that they do. But I wonder if it is the same as before or whether it has developed and become deeper and closer.

> I can't remember what I loved in F before he became a father. I *must* have loved him. But now I love him *so* much. [B, 8 months]

> *First mother*: Children put a terrific strain on your relationship. But it comes back. Before 2B was born, F and I had six months, and we found our relationship again. [G, 4 years; 1B, 2 years; 2B, 4 weeks]

> *Second mother*: Yes, so did we. One afternoon, all three of our children fell asleep upstairs. F and I had a cuddle, and then we put on a really *adult* movie, and we were just like we used to be. [1G, 4 years; 2G, 18 months; B, 9 months]

A couple relationship tends to be stronger than it looks. Women used to be more submissive, so disagreements often went unspoken. Now, with women earning and men discovering intimacy, couples are more equally matched. They may look as if they are going through stormy weather after their children are born. But both are learning intensely. In times between 'storms', each may catch sight of their familiar partner and restore their trust in the person they had chosen.

CHAPTER TEN

'When are you coming back to work?'

Mothers used to go 'out to work'. Now they go 'back to work' and this tiny change indicates where they are expected to be.

The general view seems to be that mothers who look after their children during the day are not really working. They're 'stay-at-home mothers', as if, as a Canadian researcher put it, 'to stay at home is to spend one's days in activity that is self-indulgent and socially wasteful'.[142]

> When I go out with B, people treat me as if I'm a bit stupid. Whereas when I'm at work *without* B, it's quite different and people look up to me. [B, 11 months]

British government policy is consistent, no matter which party is in power. It aims to help mothers return to their paid jobs. A government information sheet for mothers starts: 'When you take time off to have a baby . . .' 'Time off', explains a dictionary, is 'time for rest or recreation away from one's usual work or studies.' To anyone who has done it, 'rest or recreation' is an odd description of maternity leave!

So are mothers in a hurry to finish their maternity leave and get back to their paid work again? You might think so from the frequent demands for more nurseries and crèches. But these demands only represent some mothers. The reality is a wide range of wishes. This chapter will reflect the views of mothers who have talked to me. It will differ from a general sociological study of where we are at the moment.

Many mothers plan their maternity package with their employer if they have one. But how much leave should they ask for? It's difficult for an expectant mother to imagine how she will feel by the end of that leave. She hasn't yet seen her baby. She hasn't held him. She may have been shown his uterine image on an ultrasound. But it's not the same. The unborn baby can look remote, unknown, not quite hers.

Then how does a first-time mother know before the birth how much maternity leave to ask for? The answer is simple: she *can't* know. Nor can anyone else. There's a wide spectrum of ways in which new mothers react. Most find adjusting to life with their babies very difficult. And for some, it's unbearable.

I took a year's maternity leave for my first child. But it was too long for me. After six months, I'd had enough. I felt too *enclosed*, just me and the baby. I need people, I need to be *out* there. [1G, 3 years; 2G, 2 weeks]

The poet Hollie McNish found that she could adjust, though with difficulty. Painfully, she described the slow process of trying to get her child dressed. The two-year-old would insist on dressing herself, and stomp off if McNish tried to help. She thought about it and decided that she and her child were both learning. Her child was sensitive about learning to dress herself, and so McNish had to develop new skills of patience and diplomacy. She challenged a common assumption:

People often say that parents or carers who 'leave employment' in

order to raise their kids are losing valuable skills and CV points
and job training . . . I feel that the new skills I have now acquired
as a parent should be a mandatory part of any application for a
UN or government position requiring any sort of negotiation or
discussion skills.[143]

In this light-hearted way, McNish was making a serious point.
A child's pride is easily hurt, and mothers discover that understanding and tact get results quicker than impatience and threats.
They then find how effective this same response can be in dealing
with sensitive adults. Many also learn how to adjust a schedule at
a moment's notice, and how to 'work backwards' to calculate
timings. The plans of an experienced mother tend to be practical,
with attention to detail and potential mishaps. These abilities are
not learned overnight. But it means that when mothers have
finished their maternity leave, they may return to their jobs with
a 'training' in an abundance of new skills.

> I think any employer should jump at the chance of having a part-
> time mother. They don't waste a minute of work time. I'm amazed
> at how much I managed to pack into a three-day week. I've learned
> to cut corners, and my output is just as good. [1B, 3 years; 2B, 7
> weeks]

For some mothers, an early return to employment brings relief,
complicated by a sense of guilt that they 'ought' to have stayed
with their child. However, it usually restores their social status.
Friends and colleagues may also be taking short leaves and an
early return can seem the obvious thing to do.

> I went back to work part-time when B was four months. I never
> thought about it. My mother-in-law said she would look after B,
> and I like earning my own money. But it felt too soon. My head
> was *divided*. [B, 23 months]

This mother's head felt divided because her decision to work wasn't just about herself. Her baby came into the equation. She came to realise how much her decision affected both of them. But it can be hard to say why spending time with a baby matters. Isn't an employed mother doing more important work?

What I'm doing with B feels so *huge*, but I don't know how to explain it. I can't think of the words for it. [B, 5 months]

Another mother found it easier to explain her work at home as household chores.

My husband said to me: 'When are you coming back to work? It's been such a long time.' Then I felt *so* bad. But I thought: My time is not worth nothing. I do not charge you for cooking. I do not charge you for all the cleaning and washing that I do. [B, 3 years]

But what about all the work she did for their son? That didn't seem to have struck her as worth mentioning.

One mother used an opportunity to describe her mothering as proper work.

On Saturday night, I went to a party. There was a woman there telling everyone about her new job. When she'd finished, I said: 'I've got a new job too. It's very hard work, for very long hours. You can't stop when it's 5.30, and you don't even get free time at night. There are no weekends off and no holidays. It's not even paid. But I *love* my new job, and I wouldn't want to swap it for anything.' [B, 16 months]

Another mother tried to give an honest picture of how she felt.

I don't like the way everything is so black and white about mothering. Some people say they adore being with their children all day, and other people say they could never do that. I've chosen to be at home with my three. And parts of it are good, and there's other parts I really don't like. [1G, 5 years; 2G, 2 years; B, 10 months]

Many mothers say they can't afford to stay at home with their small children. Few have saved enough money to spend time on the unpaid work of mothering. Many talk about full-time mothering as 'a luxury I can't afford'. With hindsight, they would have saved, they say, and chosen differently.

> I went back to work on Tuesday, and they said: 'It's great to have you back. We've missed you.' I thought: But I'm *not* back. I may look back. But my priority is B. [B, 7 months]

> I went back when G was a year old. It was very hard. I felt bereft. [B, 7 years; G, 15 months]

Many mothers are taken by complete surprise to discover how much they love their children. For an expectant mother, her job can feel more important than the prospect of having a baby. One of the main lessons of becoming a mother is to find how those values can reverse after the birth. 'I *love* my job,' you can hear mothers say. But they use a different tone of voice when they say: 'I love *G/B*.'

Mothers have to make the best of difficult choices. Many who resume work keep photos of their babies in their workplaces. They say they leave work promptly to get back to their children, rather than relax after work with colleagues. One mother described two supermarkets that were on her way home. She always shopped at the smaller one. It sold inferior food, but she prioritised getting home to her children as quickly as possible. She didn't want to waste any extra minutes on shopping – a good example of how there is more to mothering than providing food.

There are no easy answers for when to resume paid work. Some mothers can't afford to go back and feel trapped at home. They say that their salaries would barely pay for childcare. Others take extended maternity leave to spend time with their babies but constantly worry that their jobs might not be held for them, or that they might be 'restructured' or even that their skills might be outdated by the time they return.

> My academic achievements might not seem great but [*in tears*] they meant so much to me. I can't work now, so I'll fall behind and soon be unemployable, and I'll lose everything I worked for. I think having B was a mistake, I'm in a trap – and yet I *love* B so much. He's so wonderful. [B, 6 months]

> I panic when I see all my colleagues moving up the success ladder and I'm at home with B. But I want to know where he is and what he's doing. I'm not ready to leave him. [B, 15 months]

> I'm at home all the time with my children. And sometimes it's the loveliest thing on earth. But other times, I look at myself and think: What will happen to me? I don't know how to get back into work again. [G, 3 years; B, 15 months]

Many mothers who have greatly enjoyed their paid work suppose that a few months of maternity leave will be plenty. However, once they meet their babies, everything changes. The end of their leave cuts short their daily lives with their children.

> I don't want to go back to my job [*in tears*]. I *really* don't want to [*stroking G's head*]. G will take her first steps and I won't be there to see. [G, 10 months]

> I'm going back to work tomorrow and G will go to a nursery [*tears*]. It's a huge change for us. Everyone keeps telling me we'll be fine. But I want space for my feelings. I feel *jealous* of all those people at nursery that will hear G's laugh and get the chance to play with her. I'm the one who brought her to this stage. It doesn't seem fair. [G, 12 months]

I went back to talk to my boss at my job at the Civil Service, and they bent over backwards trying to accommodate me. It all made perfectly good sense up here [*touching her forehead*], but down here [*touching her heart*] went '*Ow!*' [G, 12 months]

Those who do manage to be full-time mothers for at least a year find that they keep being questioned about this choice. 'When are you coming back to work?' can sound like a reproach. Longer-term mothers are a minority and feel as though they are swimming against a strong social current.

I feel I'm supposed to say that I want to go back to work. I feel embarrassed to say that I want to be with B. [B, 9 months]

It's not acceptable to say you are staying at home to mother. All my group of local mothers are going back to their high-powered jobs. [G, 9 months]

I'm the only one of my friends that hasn't gone back to work. They keep asking: 'What are you doing?' I feel uncomfortable. I gave up my work when I was pregnant. I want to look after B. [B, 11 months]

None of these mothers seemed very well off, though they could afford to be full-time mothers for at least one year. Are they taking a soft option to avoid the responsibilities of paid work? It doesn't sound like it. When mothers say they enjoy being with their babies, they don't mean that it's easy – but that the work feels worth doing, for all that.

I love being with G. It's hard work, but there's nothing I'd rather be doing. I worry that it's wrong to be enjoying myself so much. [G, 15 months]

I think 2G will be my last child. Most of my friends are going back to work. I *couldn't* let someone else look after 2G. Not yet. I'm not sure if I'm allowed to say I'm enjoying it. [1G, 2 years; 2G, 8 weeks]

What *are* mothers doing? They might find it hard to put into words, but they talk about it with unmistakable passion.

> I feel weird. All my friends have gone back to work. Am I the only person looking after my own baby? Why should I *pay* someone to look after her? No one could do it as well as I do. I'd rather *die* than let someone else look after her. [G, 13 months]

> My father asks me when I'm going back to work. At first, I thought I was being with B for *me*, because I couldn't let him go. But I'm *not*. I can see that he really still needs me. [B, 23 months]

Why does a child of nearly two years old still need his mother? Isn't he supposed to be independent by this age? Are these mothers holding their children back and keeping them in a state of needless dependency?

Young children *are* dependent. Modern society is complex, and children need years of adult guidance to show them how to manage. This is responsible work. But does it have to be done by mothers? Do mothers do it best? That's difficult to answer. It's clear that mothers have done it, have not been recognised for doing it and that the 'it' in question is never properly defined. Many people have argued that others can do this work just as well. But they seem to be confusing mothering with childcare.

In her paper 'Maternal Ambivalence', Dr Keren Epstein-Gilboa, an American university lecturer and nurse-psychotherapist, noticed how hard it was for mothers to be close to their children and yet committed to their paid work:

> In my work as a psychotherapist and researcher studying breast-feeding families, I frequently encounter mothers struggling with conflicting desires to be close to their child, while simultaneously trying to fulfil western conceptualisations of self-worth, equality, and distancing from children, typically exemplified by a return to the highly valued workplace and roles outside motherhood.[144]

These 'conflicting desires' can be a problem when mothering values counter the workplace ones. A good example is given by the American feminist sociologist Sharon Hays who wrote: 'Why can't a mother be more like a businessman?' She describes Rachel, an employed mother, who was devoted to her two-year-old child. One day Rachel explained to her boss, a childless woman, that her daughter was ill and had to be hospitalised. Rachel said that she needed to be at her daughter's bedside. But her boss replied that she needed Rachel for an important assignment. Why, asked the boss, couldn't Rachel get someone else to care for her child?[145]

Hays then demonstrates how strange Rachel looks from a business point of view. She is 'over-invested in her daughter',[146] and '. . . this outlay of time, energy and capital . . . [is] in fact a net financial loss'.[147] Rachel is 'pumping vast resources of [her] time and energy into mothering', without getting any immediate 'return on investment'. Hays commented: 'The logic of Rachel's boss is . . . far more powerful, and Rachel and other mothers are fully aware of this.'[148] But the last claim isn't logical. Mothering and financial profit are two different sets of values. The boss's real power over Rachel lies simply in being her boss.

One of the ways in which Hays supports her argument is to repeatedly define what Rachel does as 'intensive mothering'. This suggests that Rachel is doing something a bit too much. Not once does Hays call Rachel's boss an 'intensive business manager', though that might be appropriate.

Hays is right to point out the conflict of interest though. This kind of predicament must be common. But if mothers always put their children first, they would be unemployable. Presumably a mother like Rachel is usually available for work, and a situation like her daughter's hospitalisation is an exception.

So how did she and her boss deal with this conflict? We don't hear how it ended. It doesn't sound, though, as if Rachel lost her job. That's not surprising. Mothers like Rachel often don't realise what a valuable role they play in the workplace. The most ruthless boss usually depends on a motherly member of the team who can quietly calm the people that boss has upset. She, on her side, needs an efficient boss who can reward her work with a regular income, on which the family depends. Rachel and her boss may have different priorities, but enough in common to build a strong working alliance. Provided neither provokes the other too much, both may find ways to compromise over their different values so that they can continue to work as a good team.

However, Hays has raised an important question. How cost-effective is mothering? Is it really worth the time and energy of millions of individual mothers? Couldn't pre-school children be looked after *en bloc* by a small number of professionals, freeing mothers up to rejoin the workforce?

Large nurseries for the daycare of young children are common in many countries. But are they the best way to bring up children? Sue Palmer, author of *Toxic Childhood*, sums up the dilemma: 'The movement of mothers into the workforce [has happened] without anyone giving proper consideration to the effects of a "mother-shaped" gap in children's lives.'[149]

And surely there must be a reciprocal 'child-shaped gap' in the lives of many mothers. There is so little recognition of what mothers are doing for their children that a 'child-shaped gap' probably sounds sentimental. But if a mother is reluctant to let a professional person care for her child, this is likely to be because she *knows* that her child isn't ready yet.

Some mothers seek out professional care. There is a lot in print about a war that is supposed to exist between so-called mothers at home and employed mothers, who resent them. Is there really such a war, or is this a controversy inflated by the media to create newsworthy stories? Mothers are often supportive of one another. Their common doubts about their choices unite them. Two American researchers examined media presentations of the

'Mommy Wars' and then conducted a survey to find out what mothers thought. They concluded that: '. . . the data failed to support claims about the dynamics of the Mommy Wars and were inconsistent with claims that the Mommy Wars exist.'[150]

Employed mothers usually have clear reasons for wanting or needing to resume their work. But mothers at home often find it hard to explain their choice. In a study of one hundred mothers in Dublin who stayed at home with their babies, 'Forty per cent of them did not want to comment on what influenced them to stay at home.'[151]

It *can* be hard to explain. Why couldn't Rachel, in Hays' example, ask a kind friend to sit by her daughter in hospital? The kindest friend wouldn't have the detailed and intimate knowledge of her daughter that Rachel had. A busy doctor or nurse might need information quickly that only Rachel could supply. She would also be able to liaise between her daughter and the staff. Without her vigilance, misunderstandings with long-term consequences for her daughter's health could arise. Her daughter would almost certainly feel lost and frightened without her mother in the unfamiliar hospital setting. Rachel would be able to calm her and help her to cooperate with the staff. For all these reasons, it makes sense for the mother herself to stay with her two-year-old in the hospital, even if it means jeopardising an important business assignment.

Then what about all those children who aren't in hospital? Why do they need the daily presence of their mothers? Won't group care do just as well?

A mother is like a sensitive bridge, linking her child to various parts of the society in which they live. At home, the child learns that some actions are allowed; some not. Out in the street, or on a bus or at a playground, he learns that what is allowed changes. His mother either explains the main rules or leaves him to work them out for himself. As she takes him to different settings, he begins to make sense of our complex social world, its logic and sometimes what looks like its unfairness. Perhaps, on an empty bus, his mother lets him sit on his own seat beside her. Then the bus fills up, and she quickly lifts him onto her lap. She doesn't explain why but her manner communicates a social message: that on a bus he and his mother have to accommodate other people.

All these experiences with his mother prepare him for the cultures of nursery and, later, school, when she won't be with him. Even if she has taken a great deal of trouble to prepare him, he may feel daunted by becoming one child in a large, noisy group. But surely his response makes sense.

> People talk about small children having 'separation anxiety'. But it isn't that at all. I've only recently put words to it. They haven't yet familiarised themselves with a new situation. As soon as they've done that, they're fine. [1B, 5 years; 2B, 2 years]

This is well observed. 'Separation anxiety', a term coined by professionals, is now in common use. It suggests that the child is over-anxious. This mother noticed that her children were being reasonable. There are a lot of 'rules' for a child to learn about a new situation, which adults may not realise. 'New-situation anxiety' might be a much better term for the process.

How does a child familiarise himself with a new situation? He may notice details and think of questions which the staff are far too busy to answer. It helps if his mother can continue to be his 'bridge' to the unfamiliar situation.

> I can't just leave B at nursery. He needs me. He likes to know what all the rules are. Like: 'Can you touch this? Or play with that?' The other day, he told me he wasn't allowed to talk at nursery. He'd heard the teacher tell another child not to talk. But I found out that was when the teacher was reading them a story. [B, 3 years; G, 10 months]

There are physical problems to surmount too. One mother who had been a primary-school teacher before having her own children remembered:

> The ones who enjoy school most are the ones who don't have practical worries to hold them back. They are curious and eager to learn something new. But you see three-year-olds, and their little fingers aren't strong enough to undo their coat buttons or put their shoes on without pressing down the shoe-heels. They have to keep asking for help from an adult that they hardly know. There is too much to worry about for them to enjoy it. [B, 3 years; G, 12 months]

Readiness is not only having the physical skills, but also the confidence to get help from a busy teacher. Sometimes the ones who cling most vehemently to their mothers, while teachers are assuring them that they will be fine, seem to have high aspirations of the independence they want to reach. So they hold on to their mothers as if for dear life, and then amaze everyone once they are ready by how capable and resourceful they can be.

Sometimes, a child can't cope. To the staff of a busy nursery or playgroup, the child might seem happy, well-adjusted and able to enjoy being there. But the mother may see more intimate signals.

> G goes to a very large playgroup. But I need to take her out of it. I've just made that decision. G comes home with her face closed tight, like a little *mussel*. I want G. I want to get G back. [G, 3 years; B, 12 months]

And sometimes a mother has no choice but to resume paid work while her child is young. She may wish it was not so soon, but because she is understanding and sympathetic to her child, the child seems able to manage.

> G cries whenever I reach up to ring a doorbell. She remembers that that's what I do when I leave her at the childminder's. I *have*

to work, so I've got to leave her, and I'm told she only cries for a
bit and then she starts to play. [G, 12 months]

Once a mother has helped her child to become familiar with
the new situation, make sense of its structure and understand the
new rules, he will be ready to enjoy being in a group of his peers.
Then his mother will be able to return to her paid work with
satisfaction. She created a bridge, her child used it and can now
cope with the far side.

Some of these children who have been helped by their mothers
go on to help their peers.

There are about six children at B's childminder's. If one child is
crying, they've told me that B will always go and fetch that child's
favourite toy. He knows exactly which it is. I thought maybe he's
doing that because F and I have been kind to him. [B, 19 months]

Is it necessary to be either a mother at home or one at work?
Can an employed mother keep her child with her? Some do. This
is very useful if a mother is breastfeeding. La Leche League has
published a book, *Hirkani's Daughters*, in which seventy-nine
mothers from more than thirty-five countries all over the world
describe how they do this. They do a wide range of work in careers
that vary from a stand-up comedian to a maid and a professor.
With planning and organisation, these mothers have found all
kinds of interesting solutions. However, once babies grow into
toddlers, they need a lot of looking after, and mothers find it more
difficult to attend to them as well as their jobs.[152]

For an experiment, the *Guardian* newspaper suggested that its
staff who had children should bring them to work for one day.
The children were of different ages, and it proved chaotic. The
journalist Zoe Williams reported it in 'Bringing in baby' (8 April
2008). I don't think the experiment was repeated. But the principle
of having children at their parents' workplace sounds enterprising.

For other mothers, doing a small amount of their former work is a useful stepping stone.

> I met someone to talk about some voluntary work I could do for her. I felt really unprofessional. I'd come without a notebook, which I *never* used to do. I was like: 'Can you give me some paper? Can I use your pen?' But I *love* my work. I did the voluntary written work yesterday and thought: *Yeah!* I can still do this. [G, 7 months]

> I found a girl to look after my children and went to my art studio. I only had an hour and a half. But it was wonderful. I need to work with my hands. I wanted to cry afterwards because I knew the work was important, so important to me. [G, 4 years; B, 18 months]

A mother may feel excited by how much she has learned during her maternity leave. But, if she is working for a high-powered company, her motherly abilities are unlikely to be valued. Her colleagues will probably talk about her child as an impediment. He will make his mother late for work schedules, they say, or keep her up at night, and will need extra looking after if he is ill. From a fast-paced business perspective, he is a '"focus killer"'.[153]

So when a mother meets her employer, or even chats to colleagues, she can feel as if she no longer lives in their world.

Many mothers fear that they have lost skills by being at home with their children. At one meeting, mothers were saying how hard it was to find jobs because now they had so little to offer. I questioned this and immediately got a more positive response.

> *Me*: What do you think you can offer employers when you go back to work that you couldn't have done before becoming mothers?

> *First mother*: Contingency planning! If Plan A doesn't work, I'll have a Plan B ready and a Plan C. [G, 7 months]

Second mother: Time management. Organising a whole day effi-
ciently. It's all got to work. My friend says she only wants to employ
mums because they are so efficient with their time. [B, 11 months]

Third mother: I don't think I'll be so interested in office politics
when I go back. [G, 10 months]

Fourth mother: I'm a psychotherapist, and I can 'hold' my clients
much better. I've learned a lot, having G. [G, 6 months]

It's interesting to hear that nearly every mother, once she returns
to paid work, reports back how much easier her work seems and
how much more capable she feels since having children.[154]

Work is such a cinch after three months of looking after a baby!
[G, 3 months]

Allison Pearson observed: 'When a banker friend of mine was
asked why she dealt so well with difficult clients, she shrugged:
"I'm the mother of fifteen-year-old twins. No client can faze me."'[155]

Another mother returning to work after fifteen long years with
her family remarked:

How to work in the new on-line environment can be learnt rela-
tively quickly. What cannot be learnt so easily are the plethora of
non-technical skills gained while being a mother and running a
family. These skills are difficult to teach, but are essential to
management and succeeding in business: understanding people,
flexibility, compromise, negotiation, conflict resolution, teaching
others, to name but a few.[156]

And one mother didn't seem to have had a career before having
children. However, she said: 'My first career as a stay-at-home
mother prepared me for my second career as a technical writer. I
learned . . . management skills through raising six strong-willed
children . . .'[157]

Mothers often become good at multitasking. This requires concentrated thought as well as visible action. I noticed my doctor typing a referral letter for me while also advising the parent of an ill child on the telephone. 'How did you do both?' I asked her afterwards. 'I've got three children,' was her reply.

People who work full-time don't necessarily focus on their tasks from the beginning to end of their working day. They take breaks, chat to one another, surf the web and devote a lot of emotional energy to office politics. Mothers who return to office work notice this and may be critical of it.

> I'm going back to work in two weeks. And I feel differently about it. I'm not going to get into those conversations everyone thinks are so important. I'm going to go in, focus on the work, and be out by 4.30, so I can get back to G. [G, 8 months]

> There is so much in-fighting at my work. I have no time for it. Some people are *sharks*. [B, 10 months]

There are also other insights learned from mothering that can be very useful.

> I've been back to work – and what an eye-opener it's been. I'm a lot calmer than I used to be before I had a child. What I've found is that people at work waste so much time over petty quarrels. They behave just like toddlers. And I think: Well, I've learned how to deal with that! [G, 2 years; 27 weeks pregnant]

Being able to recognise toddler-style reactions must be very helpful. A mother who doesn't take her colleagues' behaviour personally, and can see it instead as a 'toddler reaction', may be able to defuse a situation, and make sure that the work gets done.

From a mother's perspective, an office environment can also seem quite peaceful.

> I've taken on some part-time work. It's great. You get to sit in a

nice office, and there's no one tugging at you every few minutes to do something with them. You get loads of time to think and to get on and *finish* what you're doing! [G, 2 years]

Mothers have also learned about their own resources of energy, and how to find more, even when they are tired.

Children can challenge you so you think: I don't think I can do this. I've got no energy left. I'm depleted and there's no more I can draw on. But somehow, you do; you *have* to because your child needs you, and you realise there's always more you can draw out of yourself. [B, 2 years; 20 weeks pregnant]

Having children can also help a mother who works with children.

I teach, and now I've got a baby, I think of the children as another mother's girl or boy. It helps me to understand their behaviour much better. [B, 9 months]

Mothering can be an education in seeing another person's point of view. If the mother has an argumentative child, she may be able to hold his viewpoint in mind together with her own while deciding what to do about them. If she gets good at this, she may find that she can transfer this ability to her workplace.

G was high-need. Very demanding. I found it easiest if I did things her way, at least at first. I learned to see things from her point of view – and now I'm very good at seeing other people's points of view. [G, 4 years; B, 8 months]

And mothering doesn't only teach women how to understand other people. A mother who has discovered her own values while being with her child may feel stronger and more clear-sighted about what she believes, and where her priorities are.

I'm going back to my work when G is one year. G has helped me to see what is important. I can see work in perspective. I don't think I will take work setbacks so personally now. [G, 6 months]

Business managers are only just beginning to recognise some of the truths that mothers have always known. One manager advised: 'Every leader will likely say that they listen to their employees. But are they really? When I say listen I mean something deeper than simply hearing others. **Leaders should listen to truly understand their employees**. Then they should be willing to be moulded by what those employees tell them.'[158]

If you substitute a mother for 'leader' and children for 'employees', it all makes sense. The ability to listen 'deeper than simply hearing' is exactly what many mothers learn to do.

All this means that mothers shouldn't have to plead with employers or the government for family-friendly terms. If mothers become more conscious of their own worth, employers will seek them out. Anne-Marie Slaughter, international lawyer and author, wrote:

> . . . the United States has an enormous pool of unused talent composed precisely of women in their forties and fifties who are willing and ready to get back into the workforce and pour the same energy into their work that they have poured into their families, but employers simply do not recognise their value and potential.[159]

This must be equally true of other countries.

Not all mothers want to pour energy into their families. Mothers differ. But those like Hollie McNish, who recognise what they have learned, may find that they can use it in their paid work. *Every* mother who has poured energy into her family will have a great deal to offer. Their challenge is to negotiate levels of payment that reflect their new worth.

CHAPTER ELEVEN

About grandmothers

A grandmother is a significant member of her family.

She might not think she is. Some grandmothers feel sidelined. Many react by being overly assertive. After all, they have had years of mothering experience. Now they see their children consulting their peers or medical research for the latest information about childcare. So the new grandparents may be instructed by their children about recent theories and practical tips, rather than the other way round. A grandmother might feel unimportant, and not very useful, except for babysitting and financial help.

Mothers discover that, to their parents, mothering has become more difficult. Grandmothers often comment that new parents today are inundated with contradictory views of what is good for babies. In retrospect, their own mothering looks far less complicated.

> Things seem much harder for mothers today. We had no Internet and not so many books. We just got on with it. We were able to go with our instincts. [Daughter; grandson, 8 months]

> We used to put the babies in those large prams we had, and then

we'd go for a walk over the hills, and that was the afternoon, and
then we'd come back home for tea. [4 children, many grandchildren]

Another major difference that mothers notice is that many of
their mothers' generation stayed at home and did their intense
mothering during their children's early years. Then many would
take on part-time work, once the youngest started school. But
mothers today are under pressure to return to work long before
their children start school. Most schools now have nursery classes
and take on younger children. No wonder that grandmothers
thought their own mothering had been simpler. Mothers today
regard the teenage years as especially challenging. But many of
their mothers considered that by the time their children reached
their teens, it was time to let go and allow them to grow into adults.

> It gets harder as they get older. It's easy to give babies what they
> want. But in their teens . . . you have to let go. You have to let
> them make their own mistakes. It's very hard. You love each one.
> [11 adult children, many grandchildren]

And some of this modern complexity and weighing of decisions,
grandmothers believe, gets passed on to their grandchildren. One
grandmother admitted a concern that seems common for her
generation:

> Shall I say this? Is it all right to say what I really think? Modern
> mothers give children far too much choice. Like: 'What would you
> like for dinner tonight?' Because that means choosing from
> everything [*making a huge circle with her hands to indicate vast
> choice*]. But if you say: 'You can either have fish fingers or an egg
> on toast', a child can manage that. [4 children, many grandchildren]

As new mothers discover how much work it takes to look after
a baby, they think about when they were babies themselves.

> Until you have a baby yourself, you don't realise all your mum did

for you. I didn't, and now when G wakes up at night I feel amazed at her [*her mother*]. [G, 10 months]

My mum had four of us, so she knows what to do. She arrives in the morning, looks round the room, takes in the situation and within half an hour she's done all the washing up, brought me a cup of tea and asks what I'd like her to do next. She didn't have anyone to help when we were little. [B, 3 years; G, 11 months]

Most of the mothers who talk to me are on maternity leave. Others return to their paid work promptly, and some ask their own mothers to provide daytime care of the baby. This means the mother now depends on her own mother in a new way. The two have to renegotiate their relationship.

Although mother and daughter may have grown apart, a common pattern is for the daughter to turn back to her mother, once she becomes a mother herself. Listening to new mothers talking, it is immediately obvious how much their own mothers matter. New grandmothers often want to have a say in questions of babycare, but their daughters may not want it. It's something else they are looking for.

All you want from your own mum is for her to tell you that you're doing all right. [B, 3 months]

I'm scared of my mum. She's a powerful woman. She gives me a shower of advice, when what I probably need is a hug. [B, 6 months]

I keep hoping for mothering. But I never get it. How do you stop hoping? My mum said: 'Come home for some TLC.' I thought: Yes, *please*! I went home that weekend. But there wasn't any. [G, 5 years; 1B, 3 years; 2B, 14 months]

In a gathering of mothers, once one of them makes this kind of comment about her mother, most of the others will join in. They tell anecdotes to give examples of what they mean and respond to one another's stories with laughter that sounds almost like crying. So have all these women got horrible mothers? Or are they a generation of ungrateful daughters?

They don't sound ungrateful. Instead, they convey an overwhelming sadness at their disappointed hopes. New mothers seem to long for warm, kind, appreciative, supportive mothers. Even if a grandmother hasn't been a particularly caring mother, even if a daughter has quarrelled bitterly with her mother in the past, once a woman is a mother herself, she often hopes she can be loved by her own mother at last, and be held safe in her arms to receive compassion and understanding.

Some grandmothers are able to do this, even if they live a long way away, perhaps on another continent. These grandmothers may feel as though they are offering their daughters very little, just a listening ear and a word of encouragement. But, as so often, small gestures can mean so much.

> My mum's wonderful. I phone her up every morning and she never complains when she hears me grumbling about how little sleep I've had. [B, 8 months]

It's much easier for a grandmother to see her daughter's situation from a wide time-perspective. The daughter may think she is having a difficult time and that nothing is going right. But her mother may see that, in spite of the daily problems, her daughter is mothering well.

> Sometimes I feel as if we've had a really bad day when B seems to keep crying. But I think I tend to focus on the crying times. Because on one of those days my mum was here and she said: 'I can't believe B has been so calm and happy all day.' That helps a lot. [B, 6 months]

> My mum visited and said: 'Look how happy and confident B is. You are a good mother. You are awesome.' And I thought: Really? Am I? Say it all over again! [B, 9 months]

Ideas about mothering change. Some grandmothers seem to expect their daughters to follow the same ways they did and feel personally criticised if they do things differently. But others admire their daughters, despite these differences.

My mum totally respects me as a mother. She doesn't advise me unless I ask her something. But she's *interested*. She likes to see what I'm doing with G. [G, 8 months]

My mum said G is very responsive. She said she could see it was because of the way I mother her. I was so moved because the way I am to G isn't at all what she did with us as children. I tried to hold on to that because she quickly moved on to talk about something else. [G, 11 months]

However, listening to what mothers say, it seems that grandmothers often question the details of their daughters' daily lives. Then, once they've been told some details, they've got something definite that they can worry about, and this can be unnerving for their daughters.

Mother: Mum always worries about us so much. She still does, she still worries.

Me: How does it feel to be worried about?

Mother: I *wish* she wouldn't. Just let us get on with our lives. [B, 5 months]

My mother keeps worrying that B is getting too hot, but F keeps worrying that he will get cold. [B, 7 months]

From worrying about her daughter's choices, it seems only a small step to criticising her, and that's exactly what many worried grandmothers do. They either make comments or give advice with a critical edge to it. Very often, the new mother wasn't asking for an opinion. So it can be especially hurtful if her own mother proffers unasked-for negative messages.

I haven't got a problem looking after B. It's easier than I thought. [*B was born prematurely, so he was very sleepy.*] My problem is with my mother. She is from abroad and staying with us. She follows me around everywhere and tells me what to do in a way that seems a bit aggressive. Five times in one day she says to me: 'You must give the baby water.' And she says: 'In my day, we always listened to our mothers and aunts.' And I say: 'Well, we have the Internet!' [B, 3 weeks]

My parents did everything by rule. Our family had many rules. I'm doing it differently with G. Now my father [*sudden tears*] and my mother too have telephoned me and told me I'm doing everything wrong. [G, 15 months]

My mother and my mother-in-law both kept criticising what I was doing with B at first. Now he's a lovely little boy, so happy, smiley and talkative. So they can't criticise me any more. They can see how he has turned out. [B, 2 years; 36 weeks pregnant]

One new father had a good way of helping his wife to deal with her mother's criticisms.

My mum is so critical. Last time she came, I was in tears. After she had gone, my husband sat down and made a list of all her criticisms. It came to *ten* things! [B, 5 weeks]

Because this father sat down with his wife, listened to what she said and reduced her mother's complaints to a finite list, they were then able to consider each complaint and evaluate it. This enabled the new mother to rally instead of just feeling overwhelmed.

Other criticisms can be non-verbal. A daughter who knows her mother will understand the 'message' only too well.

B and I have had the *worst* week. My mother came to stay with us. She cleaned everything. She cleaned the whole house. She washed all my clothes – she said they were filthy – and she even found and polished all our shoes. I feel *so* inadequate. [B, 6 months]

A daughter who has been criticised a lot as a child and perhaps has learned to be self-critical, may anticipate parental criticism. She may respond to it even though her parents haven't said anything.

We have a special atmosphere in our home when we are all together. It's very relaxed. I wish I could extend it to my mum and dad, but I don't seem able to. When they come to see us, I feel that I'm too big, my flat is too small and I become clumsy and awkward. [1B, 7 years; 2B, 4 years; 3B, 1 year]

And sometimes the grandmother, coming into the new family with fresh energy, may intend to be helpful without realising that her actions take no account of the feelings of her exhausted daughter.

I sometimes feel jealous of my mum. She comes to visit and she's very lively. And then she cranks it up and makes a lot of noise and drama. G loves it. She's sad when Granny goes. And I feel like a dull, boring person in the background. [G, 18 months]

'Grandmothers seem hard wired for loving grandchildren,' wrote the feminist philosopher Sara Ruddick.[160] If this is true, some must be giving their grandchildren a tough version of their love. These grandmothers seem to believe their daughters are being naïve about their babies, whereas they themselves are more astute and can see what is 'really' going on.

My mum says: 'Let B cry. Just dissociate from it. You'll make a rod for your own back if you keep picking him up. He's manipulating you already.' I said: '*Mum!* He's only two months old. He's *not* manipulating me. It's called sur*vival*.' [B, 8 weeks]

First mother: My mother sometimes says G is being naughty and getting away with it. But she *isn't*. She's not capable of it. [G, 10 months]

Me: How can you tell?

First mother: It's obvious. She's so *pure*. Later on, she may lose that, but not now.

Second mother: I can tell G wouldn't be naughty, and she's not even my daughter. [G, 7 months]

Two mothers compared notes and said their mothers-in-law were extremely critical of the way they were bringing up their babies. Both were boys, one aged two months, and the other fourteen months. Both mothers-in-law had commented that 'B looks *exactly* like F at that age'. They then made critical remarks, as if to be helpful, which began: 'Aren't you going to . . . ?' or 'You surely won't . . . ?' Both new grandmothers conveyed to their daughters-in-law that *they* knew the right way to mother and had little confidence that their daughters-in-law could be good mothers to their grandsons.

New grandmothers don't always recognise how sensitive their daughters are to the comments they make. Negative comments can hurt, even when they are intended to be helpful. Daughters and daughters-in-law aren't always looking for advice on how to be good mothers. Rather, they may be looking for comfort, and reassurance that their mothers think well of them. (No wonder a book on *Contemporary Grandparenting* includes a chapter titled 'Being there, yet not interfering'.[161])

My mother is thousands of miles away. But she still makes her presence very much felt. She used to be my go-to person. But now, especially after having G, I began to realise that, after every conversation with her, I felt much worse. It can take me *four* days to get over the conversation. [G, 2 years]

It's a pity that more grandmothers don't realise how influential they are. They don't have to fight to be heard. Mothers are listening. Some grandmothers may feel guilty that they can't afford a generous financial outlay, or hours of practical help. But a few kind words, a sort of blessing from mother to daughter, doesn't cost money or much time. It's a loss on both sides if she is unable to articulate them and give them to her daughter.

At other times, it may be the new mother who is critical of her own mother. Grandmothers who may have been very aware of the dangers of sugar on their children's teeth and waistlines or too many toys on their imaginations seem to waive this knowledge when it comes to their grandchildren.

> My mother keeps wanting to feed B something sugary. She *knows* I don't want him to have sugar. I'm embarrassed – I don't know why she keeps saying it. [B, 9 months]

> *First mother*: My mum gives us far too many presents. I suppose it's her way of showing her love. [1G, 3 years; 2G, 8 months]

> *Second mother*: My mum's like that too. Even if she comes to visit, we go shopping. [G, 5 years; 1B, 3 years; 2B, 12 months]

One reason for this frequent complaint may be that the grand-mother may have more money now than she ever did as a mother. She may be thrilled to be able to give her grandchildren treats that she could not have afforded to give her own children.

Once a daughter becomes a mother herself, she often has a new interest in what she was like as a baby. Her own mother is usually the only person who can provide details.

> My mum gave me a diary she used to keep for the first three months of my life. I've only looked at a bit of it. It's just a few lines for each day. But it says things like that I had a taste of peach, or that I smiled that morning. [G, 5 months]

Sadly, if a grandmother has died, any information she hasn't written down has died with her. No one else knows the minute early details about her daughter as she did. One mother, whose baby daughter was eleven weeks old, explained that her daughter had an uncommon digestive problem that she too had had as a baby. It seemed to be an allergy to both dairy food and soya, which came through the mother's breastmilk. The baby kept crying from discomfort. The mother longed to be able to ask her own mother about it, but she had died a few years earlier, and her father couldn't remember much about it.

And a grandmother who has died might be longed for, not only for her knowledge but simply for herself.

My mum died about five years ago. She never knew G which is sad. But we didn't have a close relationship. She was an alcoholic and wasn't a good mother to me in many ways. But I was looking through a box of her things yesterday and . . . I could smell her perfume, and there was one of her hairs [*trying hard not to cry*], and . . . I *miss* her. [G, 13 months]

As children grow older, they too may be curious about the grandparents who died before they were born.

My parents passed away several years ago. B never knew them. But one evening he was lying in bed and he asked me: 'My grandparents – what did they look like? What were their names? How old were they?' And I thought: Where did all these questions come from? I had to get out all my old photos to show him. [B, 3 years]

Times change, and grandparents can pass on precious stories about the family history. These stories have a particular meaning for the grandparents, but may be transformed when told to a new generation. Values can reverse. A shameful skeleton in the family cupboard (perhaps about a sexual secret or a wartime pacifist) may sound interesting and even admirable to a new generation, while a family hero (perhaps a military or a financial one) might seem less impressive today. 'Grandmothers', wrote Sara Ruddick, 'are able, and likely, to speak in a generational voice.'[162] They convey very personal family stories, and through them their children and grandchildren can learn where their family fits into national and international events.

When there are several generations of family members in a room together, a mother can get a sense of family patterns.

> My grandmother thinks G is a boy and always calls her 'he'. I think it's quite sweet. My grandmother is ninety-five and has always been very nice to G. But my mother can't stand it! It reminds her of when she was growing up and her mother preferred her brother to her. [G, 7 months]

Some new grandparents relate to their grandchildren in ways that show mothers how they themselves were brought up. This can be revealing.

> When B was two days old, he was crying and my mum was like: 'Well, let him cry.' And I said: '*Mum*! He's only two days old. I can't let him cry.' I said: 'Is that what you did to me and . . . [*her brother*]?' She said: 'Yes.' I found that quite heavy, quite hard to bear. [B, 2 months]

> My mother keeps saying to me: 'Have you got B into your routine yet? Make sure you are not into his.' But *that's* what she did to me. I never had any voice. *My* voice was never heard. But I don't want to go to the exact opposite and go to the other extreme. I've got this constant battle going on inside myself. [B, 11 months]

Many women have strong-willed fathers, but these men rarely seem to play with small children. The next grandfather seemed happy to spend time with his young granddaughter, though on his own terms. This gave the mother a new insight into the strong influence he had had on herself.

My dad came over and G said: 'Let's make a den.' He said: 'I'll show you how to do it.' But she said: 'No, I know what to do.' So she pulled some cushions across and made a perfectly usable den. She's only four. But afterwards my dad took it apart and made his own den. In the evening, he said: 'I've had a very good day. Now G knows her grandfather can build a *proper* den.' I saw a pattern, then, of how he used to be with me and how I got the message that nothing I did was ever good enough. And maybe he had grown up thinking the same about himself. [G, 4 years; B, 3 months]

However, some grandmothers behave quite differently with their grandchildren from how they were with their own children. As grandparents, they seem to find it easier to be relaxed and playful.

First mother: My mother used to be very impatient with me. She was twenty-one, in a new country, and I can understand that now. But she came to see us, last weekend, and she was very patient with B. The strange thing was that, after her visit, I was impatient with B. And that's quite unlike the way I usually am. [B, 7 months]

Second mother: Could you have a jealous 'inner child'? It might sound odd, but perhaps the little girl who used to be you feels jealous to see your mother being more patient with your son than she ever was with you. [G, 12 months]

G loves my mum. My mum is very good with her. I heard them playing a game about a 'magic strawberry' in the kitchen. It was out of nothing, and it sounded such fun. My sister and I looked at each other in amazement. We didn't know Mum could be like that. Where was her sense of fun, all those years ago? [G, 16 months; 23 weeks pregnant]

Other grandmothers develop intense relationships with their grandchildren. A number of mothers describe how their mothers seem to bypass them and relate to their grandchildren as if they were their own children.

> It's as if my mother has a relationship with B that leaves me out. When B cries, I say: 'I'll go.' But she always gets up quicker than me and takes him. Once I came into the room and she was holding B and she did *this* [*leaning back, clutching the baby so M could not take him*]. [B, 10 weeks]

> *First mother*: My mother-in-law won't accept that I'm the mother. She decides she'll take G for a walk any time she likes and for as long as she likes. She never asks me, and it doesn't suit me at all. I'm trying to get some authority back. [G, 7 months]

> *Me*: How do you do that?

> *First mother*: I say she can take G to the local supermarket.

> *Second mother*: Yeah, tell her to buy ice cream! [*Because the grand-mother would have to bring G back home quickly, before it melted.*] [B, 3 months]

'The grandparent relationship is at least triangular,' wrote Sara Ruddick.[163] But the triangle may not be a benign one.

> My mother says: 'I've come to see my darling.' That's B. She some-times forgets she's not his mother. Or she says: 'It's like having an affair with a man who belongs to someone else.' [B, 11 months]

This last quote sounds incestuous, and a strange way of relating to a grandson. The grandmother may be fond of him, but it sounds confusing to imagine he is someone with whom she could have an affair. Nor is her daughter an inconvenient 'someone else' who owns her grandchild. She did some useful babysitting for her daughter, but never sounded as if she accepted herself as a *grandmother*.

Sometimes a grandmother will overlook the new mother in a

seemingly trivial way. Mothers frequently complain how hurt they feel.

> I remember in the early days when I was sitting and breastfeeding G, my mother-in-law came to visit. She made herself a cup of tea and she didn't offer to make me one. She's been a mother herself. How could she have forgotten? [G, 10 months]

That memory still hurt, months later. Breastfeeding uses a lot of liquid and mothers are constantly thirsty. Possibly, the grandmother assumed that she shouldn't give a cup of hot liquid to her daughter-in-law while she was breastfeeding. But perhaps there was a safe surface beside her. In any case, it would surely have been kind to make her the offer.

Mothers often look back at their childhoods. They notice all kinds of problems and resolve to treat their children differently.

> *Me*: You realise that about two hundred years ago a wilful child would have been seen as sinful, and you would have to get your whip out and use it to break your child's will?

> *Mother*: We were brought up like that. It wasn't two hundred years ago. And that's the one thing I *don't* want to do. I don't want to break B's will. [B, 9 months]

> My mum used to get depressed when we were children. She'd go quiet and we'd get that feeling, you know, when you know something's not quite right. I don't want B to have that. [B, 9 months]

> My mother wanted a doll. She liked buying me clothes and dressing me up. Before G was born, I tried not to have any expectations of what she would be like. [G, 11 months]

Thinking about childhood, and resolving to bring up her own family differently, gives a mother a strong incentive to make changes. It's not easy but it does seem possible not to repeat her upbringing with the next generation.

> F and I have both had difficult childhoods. But we seem to have broken the pattern. Our children haven't got the problems that we have. [G, 5 years; 1B, 3 years; 2B, 14 months]

When mothers become most emotional in complaining about their own mothers, they often paint a similar picture. They describe them as too self-absorbed to be fully aware of them, both when they were girls and even now that they have become mothers themselves. They say their mothers also seemed to eschew responsibility for their own actions and blamed their daughters instead, for 'making them' feel and do wrong things. Their daughters had grown up feeling overly responsible and constantly guilty.

One mother used the word 'narcissitic' to describe her own mother. The response to this word was immediate. All the listening mothers agreed that this one word summed up their mothers too. They compared notes about how little attention they had received from their mothers as girls. Yet in each case the mother had demanded quantities of attention for herself from her daughter.

I was impressed by the strength of their feelings. If, I asked, they had been brought up by narcissistic mothers, how would they make sure they didn't become narcissistic mothers themselves? To my surprise, they all agreed on a simple answer: 'We ask questions.' 'We don't take things for granted. Narcissistic mothers never doubt themselves.' 'We question what we are doing as mothers. Narcissistic mothers never do that.'

If this is true, it means that all the uncomfortable questions and self-doubts that new mothers describe (see Chapters One and Eight especially) have a positive outcome. They ensure that mothers are not self-absorbed. They are able to make space for their babies, and to think about them.

New mothers often complain that their 'world' seems to shrink.

Now they are absorbed in the minutiae of daily life. But the mothers' 'shrinking world' is not permanent. As children grow, and especially once their children have children of their own, some older mothers and grandmothers experience their world as 'expanding' again. They are able to give their attention to international events in a new way. They have learned from being mothers, and their understanding has often become deeper and more realistic. Recently, groups of grandmothers have banded together to found organisations. They usually focus on international peace and cooperation. They have learned, from being mothers, about our common humanity. This is a new development. There are now more grandmothers in good health living to their eighties and nineties than ever before.

In 1982, American mother and grandmother Barbara Wiedner founded Grandmothers for Peace which soon spread and is now an international organisation. She visited the Soviet Union and was deeply moved to meet Russian mothers and grandmothers who were as concerned about peace as she was. She died in 2001, but Grandmothers for Peace is slowly growing, and groups are organising in several countries. As Wiedner said: '. . . [In] today's dangerous world we can no longer keep or promote peace by sitting in our rocking chairs!' Part of her organisation's mission is 'to address the issues of violence and injustice that continue to plague our planet and the human family . . . We believe it is imperative to foster in the next generation of world leaders the **principles of non-violence and responsibility** for their community and the world.'[164]

In Austria and Germany, which have seen the rise of far-Right parties, grandmothers have come together since 2017 in many small local groups under the banner of 'Omas Gegen Rechts' (Grannies against the Right). These grandmothers are looking ahead to the kind of future they want for their grandchildren. As mothers, they were busy with their children and getting by. But as grandmothers they find they have time and energy to be activists, protesting against intolerance and violence.[165]

There is also the International Council of Thirteen Indigenous Grandmothers. These thirteen grandmothers first met in Phoenix, a village in upstate New York, in October 2004. In a statement, they wrote: 'We, the International Council of Thirteen Indigenous Grandmothers, believe that our ancestral ways of prayer, peace-making, and healing are vitally needed today. We come together to nurture, educate and train our children.'[166]

Other groups and movements may not have 'grandmother' in their titles, but grandmothers seem to have the time and energy to promote them. They are nearly always working for unity. In order to work for these movements, grandmothers have to be able to cooperate with one another. Humans are unbelievably argumentative, if not quarrelsome. Different ways of mothering can make mothers feel alienated from one another. How is it that so many grandmothers learn to cooperate?

It is this important question that takes us to the last chapter.

CHAPTER TWELVE

No mother is an island

It's easy for a mother to feel like an island. If she is with her baby night and day, her timetable may be affected not so much by clock time as by when her baby is hungry or tired. By evening, he is usually tired though still excited, so she has to help him relax into sleep. But that is exactly when her childless friends have time to phone and visit her.

> It's hard to stay in touch with friends who haven't had babies. Our timetables are out of sync. The best time for me to talk is in the afternoon. But my best friend's at work then. She likes to phone in the evening as she's walking home from work. But that's the *worst* time for me. [B, 15 months]

Mothers often miss their friends and colleagues from work. At work, their efforts were part of a cooperative output. This gave everyone reasons to contact one another. Contact is not only essential for work progress – it also gives each person a reminder that his or her contribution matters. That sense of connection is exactly what new mothers say they have lost.

'Mothers seem to me to be little islands adrift,' wrote one mother. 'Adrift' is a good word for how mothers feel. They say they are disconnected not just from their work colleagues but from one another. One mother might meet another for a walk and a coffee – but each is looking after her own baby and can't give the other her full attention.

> *First mother*: I found loneliness was the hardest part of being a mother. When my partner's there, it's easier, and when we went on holiday with my parents there were four adults and everything was so *easy*. [G, 5 months]

> *Second mother*: But that's the whole trouble, don't you think? Whenever other people are there, they see you having an easy time with your child. They never see how *hard* it is when it's just you. [1B, 4 years; 2B, 9 months]

> I don't think mothers are meant to do this alone. [G, 17 months]

But how alone are we? The poet and cleric John Donne wrote that human isolation is an illusion.

> No man is an Iland, intire of itselfe; every man is a peece of the Continent, a part of the maine; . . .'[167]

Is this true of mothers? Is every mother 'a peece of the Continent' too? In traditional societies, mothers created local 'networks' that would welcome a new mother. In today's Western-style cultures, these neighbourly networks are rare. Experienced mothers and grand-mothers often spend their days far from home, at their paid work. The Internet enables mothers to contact one another across a distance. But not everyone has access to it. Besides, a mother has to turn her attention away from her baby while she is clicking links and reading.

A different challenge is that our society is culturally diverse. This can be exciting for an *experienced* mother. She may be curious about different mothering customs. For a new mother, wanting to find her place in this new category of people she has just joined, contact with other mothers can be unnerving.

You have all your mother friends saying they are doing something that you are *not* doing. And it makes you think: Am I being stupid? Why don't I do what they're doing? And it takes me a *long* time to think: No! [*Kissing G*] I am doing what works for me and my child. I am doing what works for us. [G, 8 months]

First mother: I never meet mothers who are parenting like I do. So then I doubt myself. [G, 8 months]

Second mother: It helps to find your 'tribe'. [B, 16 months]

Third mother: Yes, and once you find similar mothers, you discover who *you* are. You can't learn it on your own. And after that you can talk to *any* mother. [B, 18 months]

I come to meetings and I get a wider perspective on my mothering. It helps me to see the kind of mother I am. [B, 16 months]

How do mothers discover what kind of mothers they are? If they are 'a peece of the Continent', they first seem to seek out one another in a kind of local 'mother-continent'. Mothers have always found ways to gather round and talk. As the feminist philosopher Sara Ruddick wrote, mothers '*think* differently'.[168] This different way of thinking gives mothers a great deal to discuss. Because it is all so new, mothers who don't know one another start by looking for common ground.

First mother: The beginning was hard. I didn't realise what mothers meant when they talked about 'lack of sleep'. [*Roars of sympathetic laughter.*] [B, 7 months]

Second mother: Yes, without sleep, you're in a different world. [G, 4 years; 1B, 2 years; 2B, 4 weeks]

There should be a new word for tiredness when it's a mother feeling it. [G, 10 months]

I'm tired. I'm *really* tired, not just tired. Does everyone know the difference between tired and *really* tired? [*The mothers listening all nodded or made affirmative noises.*] [B, 10 months]

In this kind of conversation, mothers aren't trying to find solutions to one another's tiredness. Those conversations can easily become competitive and leave each mother feeling unsure of what she is doing. Instead, they describe problems that the listening mothers recognise. No one mentions a solution. But that doesn't matter. It's the sharing that brings them together.

I was wondering what to say as I was walking up to get here [*to a meeting*]. Now I'm here, I realise why I come. It's to listen to all the mothers' stories so I can say: '*Ditto!*' It stops me feeling I'm going mad. [B, 9 months]

I took home something another mother said here last week. She said there were some parts of being a mother that she didn't like. I wasn't enjoying all of it, last week. It felt very hard. But then I thought: I don't have to like all of it. *She* doesn't. [B, 11 months]

This is my fourth meeting and, each time I come, I can relate to every point the other mothers talk about. I can relate to all of it [*indicating her heart*]. It helps me to feel better as a mother, more than I do after two years of psychotherapy. And he is a very good psychotherapist. [B, 3 years]

Once mothers discover some experiences that they share, they feel safer about trusting the others with more difficult feelings. Even over these, they are simply sharing, not solving anything.

First mother: I feel so guilty because I have a half-thought. I don't exactly think it. But when I am doing something while B is asleep, I think: Don't wake up now! And then, if B does wake up, I think: Couldn't you sleep a little longer? [B, 6 months]

Second mother: *I've* thought that. You shouldn't feel guilty. I don't think *any* mother could *ever* not have that thought. [G, 12 months]

Is it normal to worry about your child dying? I mentioned it to my mother and she sort of gave me to understand that it's *not* normal. [*The mothers of children up to the age of four in the circle quickly assured her that they worried too: whether the child was still breathing when carried in a sling; when asleep in another room; when the mother was going up and down concrete steps; or walking under a builder's ladder.*] Oh, I see. Maybe I should accept the worry then, insead of fighting it. [B, 8 months]

In one large circle of mothers, a toddler was teething and cried. He cried for the entire length of the meeting. His mother tried to comfort him at the far end of the room. At the end of the meeting, she said:

I don't mind it when B cries. I try to comfort him and feel very sorry for him. But what felt really nice was knowing that all the other mothers here understood what I was going through [*in being unable to comfort her son*]. It was like a big, soft cushion for me. [B, 16 months]

If some mothers find this kind of meeting so helpful, why don't all mothers come to them? One reason is that there is always a risk of getting hurt if negative feelings are not confirmed by the other mothers.

One afternoon, I was feeling a bit tired and I did something I was ashamed of. I got angry with B. And there was a voice inside me saying: you can't do that. He's only little. He doesn't mean to make you angry. [*I can't remember how mothers responded. Motherly anger is a common theme at these meetings, but she said to me afterwards:*] I'd have felt better if other mothers had said they felt that too. [B, 14 months]

How much courage does it take to come to a group and trust the other mothers in it?

First mother: Being a mother is a huge change. I think it's similar to becoming an adolescent. You meet all these mothers whom you don't know, but you are also sleep-deprived, so you can't talk properly. And it brings back all those adolescent insecurities, like: did I say the right thing? How am I coming across? Are the others going to talk about how they don't like me? It's silly, but I've lain awake at night, worrying about it. [B, 5 months]

Second mother: I'm glad you said that about mothers' meetings. I worry too. [1B, 3 years; 2B, 14 months]

It can feel safer to join a forum online, and exchange views from the security of home. At the dead of night, when a mother needs information urgently, these exchanges can be very helpful. But there is a gentle quality about embodied meetings that mothers like.

First mother: I think B is teething. He never sleeps more than an hour and a half at a time. I've hardly slept for five days and nights [*tears*]. I feel so terrible when I can't comfort him. He moans and it sounds like one long litany of complaints of things I'm not doing right. [B, 4 months]

Second mother: But when you brought B this morning he was smiling. His eyes were sparkling, and he looked full of joy. You *must* be doing something right. [G, 15 months]

Many conversations are confessional. When a mother is confessing something, it's reassuring to *see* the mothers she is talking to. And it's helpful for them to see her.

First mother: I've failed at doing things to improve our house. There's just so much I've failed to achieve. [*She was sitting on a*

floor cushion, managing to breastfeed 2G and B at the same time.]
[1G, 4 years; 2G, 18 months; B, 9 months]

Second mother: If you could see yourself *now*, you wouldn't say you'd failed. You are doing so much. I don't know how you can. [B, 7 months]

First mother: I don't want to put anyone off having three children. But some evenings are just so *hard*. I don't get anyone's needs met and . . . [*Long, detailed account of her failures with each child. She burst into exhausted tears.*] [B, 5 years; 1G, 2 years; 2G, 5 months]

Second mother: Your tears reach my heart. All I can say is, and of course I haven't got three children, that so often, those times you agonise over – they don't matter. In the end, you come through and it's all right. [G, 21 months]

It can also be helpful for the listening mothers to see the effect of a conversation on a struggling mother.

First mother: What do you do when you've given all you can, everything, every bit of yourself, and your children need more. Where do you find that more to give? [*Pointing to her chest, looking very white and strained.*] There's no more to give. [1G, 3 years; 2G, 21 months]

Second mother: If you are feeling like that, it must be because you are giving your children so much already. [*The first mother said nothing, but we could see her relax, and her facial colour and smile came back.*] [1G, 4 years; 2G, 9 months]

Mothers often don't realise how much they have learned until they listen to another mother who feels confused and lost. Then they realise that they can see the other mother's dilemma from a different perspective.

First mother: G cries all day. I think it's reflux. But I've got a voice in my head saying she *shouldn't* cry, and *I* should know how to make it better. [G, 3 months]

Second mother: I used to think like that. But I read that it can be good for a baby to let feelings out, if you've checked that it's not hunger or a dirty nappy. I find that comforting. G cried and her grandparents kept saying: 'Be a good girl. Don't cry.' Basically, they were telling her that they only liked *bits* of her, the smiley bits. I want G to feel accepted as a whole person. I don't want her to be a people pleaser. [G, 22 months; B, 4 months]

First mother: That's a completely different way of looking at it.

First mother: B has been waking up every hour for weeks. Sometimes I think: That's okay. That's what he needs to do. But sometimes I keep asking myself questions. Is it me? Have I failed to help him? Will he always be like this? [B, 6 months]

Second mother: My baby's the same age. [*It turned out that the babies were born on the very same day, in different hospitals, twenty minutes apart.*] I have exactly the same questions as you, and the same doubts. But, on some nights, I can enjoy it. It's the only time B and I are alone together. It's just us. [B, 6 months]

[*The first mother said, at another meeting, that the second mother's words had stayed with her and helped her.*]

Mother: Last week, a mother was saying here that you didn't have to wait till your baby was asleep to do what you wanted. You could do a lot of things while they are awake. So the other day I took ten minutes to read an article. It was *great*! [B, 9 months]

Me: Could you concentrate?

Mother: Oh yes. And I said to B: 'You can't talk to Mummy now. I'm *reading*.'

And often, one mother's experience can be a useful corrective to the assumptions of another.

> *First mother*: G may be breastfeeding and just about to drop into sleep when suddenly she jerks and she's wide awake. I think it's because she was a Caesarean birth, and she doesn't know how to do slow transitions. [G, 17 months]

> *Second mother:* I don't think the birth has anything to do with it. B was a normal vaginal birth, but he dozes off and then jerks himself wide awake in just the same way. [B, 19 months]

Comparing experiences and then refining their understanding of them is an important way in which mothers learn.

If the group feels a safe one, a mother can risk opening up a dilemma for which she *does* want a solution.

> *First mother*: I don't like weekends. I'm a single mum and I feel alone then because all the mums I know are on Family Time. [B, 5 months]

> *Second mother*: We could have a girls' night *in*. I'll come round to your place. I'm sure [*two other mothers*] will come. The boys can mind the babies, and we'll cook. [G, 6 months]

> *First mother [cheering up]*: And we'll watch some inappropriate films.

> *First mother:* I've lost confidence in my parenting style. I was fine until four months ago. Now B has gone wild, running everywhere, climbing up everything. [B, 2 years]

> *Second, more experienced mother*: Sometimes you only need to make a small adjustment. [G, 5 years; 1B, 3 years; 2B, 12 months]

> *Third, also experienced mother*: Yes, often a little change is all you need. [1G, 3 years; 2G, 8 months]

Group discussion of an issue, once the mothers have agreed on some common ground, can go much further than an individual churning it over at home. At home, a mother's thoughts are likely to be interrupted and left unresolved. In a group of mothers – at a meeting, in a park, outside a shop – ideas can be shared, questioned, refined and, to some extent, sorted. A group can generate a sense of warmth and an almost electric kind of excitement.

> That was an amazing meeting. Every mother said things that were so rich in content. You could spend two weeks discussing the issues those eight mothers brought up. [G, 5 months]

Even walking to a meeting, a mother can feel affected by memories of the previous times.

> On my way here, I realised: I'm doing all right. I can see that. But that's not the way I always see myself. [G, 4 years; B, 3 months]

Afterwards, mothers 'take home' whatever impressed them during the meeting. They usually have more energy. It's as if they are leaving the 'mother-continent' and carrying back something from the meeting to their 'island homes'.

> It's been a hard week. I carry this group around with me all of the time, and it helps me to feel I am doing all right. [B, 10 months]

> Last week, I felt much lighter after the meeting. I *skipped* home. I cried at the meeting and I felt I was held, and it was lovely. [G, 14 months]

> I feel nurtured here, so then I can go home and go on being giving to my son. [B, 2 years; 25 weeks pregnant]

> This is a necessary group. It is good for grandmothers too. [Grandmother; daughter; grandson, 4 months]

These groups depend on mothers putting aside their surface

differences and connecting to the shared experience of being mothers. However, if they venture from their islands to a mother-continent where the common ground hasn't been agreed, they can easily feel insecure and isolated.

What should a mother do when she meets another one who sounds lonely and hard on herself? It isn't always easy to know how to react.

> I went to a meeting where some mothers were breastfeeding and some were bottle-feeding. B was hungry, so I started breastfeeding him. Then I heard the mother next to me say to her baby: '*That* mother is giving her baby *proper* milk. That's better than what *you're* getting.' I felt terrible. I wanted to make it all right for her, but I couldn't think of anything to say. I just bent my head over my son. [B, 4 months]

Maybe no words would have been effective in that situation, but possibly touching the other mother or putting an arm round her might have helped, so that both mothers could feel connected.

When mothers don't feel comfortable with one another, conversation quickly becomes competitive. Then a mother can return to her island feeling inadequate, lonely and deeply hurt. Allison Pearson gives a fictional example, but one probably based on experience: 'In the sitting-room, a handful of non-working mums are in animated conversation about a local nursery school. They hardly seem to notice their kids whom they handle with an enviable invisible touch, like advanced kite-fliers, while Mothers Inferior like me over-attend to our clamorous offspring.'[169]

At more formal meetings, it helps to have a facilitating person who can welcome all mothers, whether full-time or in paid work, of any political creed, race, class, level of education or anything else – and open out the conversation, so that everyone is included. Without this, the opportunities for a genuine meeting can be wasted.

Some meetings don't work for me. I went to one and I think I was just too tired for it. There were about thirty mums there, all as tired as I was, all trying to keep it together. I didn't have enough energy to smile at other mothers, and no one seemed to smile at me. [G, 23 months]

Thirty mothers could have been divided into smaller groups, given a warm drink each, and made comfortable. It doesn't take much for mothers to feel glad they came.

I started Mothers Talking in 1991 and wasn't sure how to plan it. Perhaps mothers would think it was a waste of time to come and talk to one another. After all, there is always so much catching-up to do at home. Then I remembered having a similar thought at my first job. I was a copy-editor at Penguin Books, and we were always trying to keep to schedules, hurrying through our proofs to meet publication dates. However, a new editor took over the department and announced that he would hold a departmental meeting to discuss our progress. I was dismayed. Wouldn't it be better to use the time *to* progress, instead of *talking* about progress?

We met in an attractive room with comfortable chairs, and were offered coffee in flowery mugs. Everything felt different from the usual rush. The editor asked each of us to say which books we were editing and how we were getting on. I discovered that the copy-editor at the desk next to mine was editing an interesting psychology series, and that the draughtsman who used to sing loudly in our open-plan office had produced some very high-quality diagrams. We looked at one another with new respect. We were each a useful part of a hard-working organisation. The energy changed completely. I felt impatient to get back to work – not to meet a deadline, but because I suddenly felt a new excitement about the manuscripts on my desk.

So when I started Mothers Talking, I made sure that the seating was comfortable, and that everyone had refreshments. Then, like

my editor, I asked each mother to say her name and, instead of
the titles of the books she was editing, the name of her baby or
child, and how she was getting on as a mother. And then that
same wonderful transformation happened. Mothers began to feel
safe to share what they thought. They were able to listen to one
another without feeling they had to be the same as each other. At
the end of a meeting, some of them exchange telephone numbers,
or arrange to go for a coffee together.

Mothers Talking is an open group. Any mother can come,
whether she has a newborn baby or a large family of children. So
one mother might bring her twins, or a baby and a toddler. A
mother of several children has a lot to think about. Mothers with
a single baby are usually careful to share time fairly. Mothers of
multiples, and of second or third children often have so much to
say that they get carried away and forget that there are others
waiting to speak. They are very apologetic when they notice.[170]

What are the babies doing for an hour and a half while we're
talking? The youngest ones usually sleep for most of it. At about
two or three months, they start to look around them. There's a
box of toys and oddments on the floor. Once a baby can sit up,
he or she will sit beside the box and almost fall into it from
eagerness to touch everything. Babies are constantly learning. They
seem especially adventurous here because they know their mothers
are not rushing about but sitting in the circle.

It's good coming here because we all sit still for an hour and a
half. At home, I'm always so busy, there's always something to do.
Here, I can give G my undivided attention and she loves it. [G, 3
months]

B: [*Loud yelp.*]

Mother: What do you want, B?

B: *YOU!* [B, 3 years; mother, 38 weeks pregnant]

Just as mothers learn from one another, so do the children.

Me: G can crawl. Surely she wasn't crawling last week?

Mother: That's right, she wasn't. Last week, she watched another child crawling right across the room. So she thought: Okay, maybe I'll try that too. So this week she did it. [G, 6 months]

Me: Did you 'see' her having that thought?

Mother: Yes [*in an 'of course' tone*].

In a similar way, a boy watched a girl of his age, about eleven months, walking unsteadily around the circle. Perhaps her unsteadiness encouraged him because she wasn't too accomplished. He stood up and walked several steps which his mother said were his first.

At one meeting, a two-year-old boy was eating an oatcake. Another boy, only nine months, grabbed the oatcake and stuffed a big chunk into his mouth. His mother rushed to help him. She said later that he'd never eaten anything so hard before and had no teeth. The younger boy spluttered a bit, swallowed the lot, and was keen to go on playing. He must have sensed that his gums were strong enough for oatcakes – and he was right.

Mother: B will only breastfeed when I'm lying down. It's so annoying.

Me: But I've seen him breastfeeding when you are sitting upright.

Mother: Yes, I know. He only does that here. He must have looked around and seen the other children breastfeeding in that position and decided it's the correct way to breastfeed when he's here. But he won't do it at home. [B, 11 months]

The children are usually too young for shared games and don't often play together. They are very active in non-stop exploring – either the objects in the toy box or running around the room and climbing up everything possible. Or they offer something to another mother, but they don't like her to take it. They like offering without losing the object offered. By the end of the meeting, they are very tired.

> G always has her best nap of the week when we go home after our meetings. [G, 13 months]

Occasionally a child will bite, push or smack other children. My impression is that this child is not aware of causing pain. He or she uses the behaviour for its effect. The hurt child will immediately drop the toy that the first child wants, and run to his or her mother. The mother of the first child is often a gentle person herself, and feels mortified if she has been too slow to anticipate and stop her child doing this. The mother of the hurt child is also shocked because she hasn't been quick enough to protect her own child. It's difficult to know what the hurt child makes of it all.

> When we left the meeting last week [*she named a boy*] bit G's hand really hard. His teeth marks went deep. They were still visible three hours later. I know his mother felt terrible. She apologised immediately. But I couldn't look at her. G really loves [*name of the boy*] though. Even after this, at home, she often says his name. [G, 20 months]

This period of hurting other children seems to be a phase that usually ends as children learn to talk. It becomes clearer then how gentle they often are.

Mothers and children learn a lot from meeting together, whether by arrangement or by chance. But what about fathers? Individual fathers often describe difficult moments. I remember a father, years ago, relating how his partner had miscarried at a local hospital. He could still recall how much sympathy his partner had received from the nursing staff. But not one of them had thought to ask *him* how *he* was. Other fathers have described the experience of being over-looked or regarded as superfluous after a birth crisis. Should fathers have their own meetings where they can come to talk?

First mother: On Friday night, F had a panic attack. [G, 5 months]

Second mother: But I think a lot of fathers must feel in a panic, especially if they are the sole breadwinner and it all depends on them. Maybe they need opportunities to talk about it. [G, 17 months]

A father may have issues to discuss that arise more often for men than for women. Some of these are practical.

Which children's loo should a dad use if he's taking his daughter to a children's toilet? F took G to the children's playground, and she needed to go. G is very conscious of being a girl. She wouldn't feel right, going into a boys' toilet. So my husband took her into the girls' one. First it was empty, but then a woman came in. This woman was angry with F and said it wasn't appropriate for him to be there. He said he was accompanying his daughter, but the woman said she was a police officer. F was *very* upset and started shouting. He said he was made to feel like a sexual abuser. [G, 3 years; B, 6 weeks]

It seems to suit mothers more than fathers to sit in a circle, sharing questions and anecdotes. I've tried setting up meetings for fathers, and so did two men at different times at the Active Birth Centre. But fathers complain that it feels artificial. Men, one father told me, like to chat informally as they pass one another, for example, in the gents. Even so, don't fathers need a comfortable place to come and talk? They may feel like disconnected islands too. I hope that a father will soon think of a solution to this.

Discussing questions about mothering (and surely fathering) highlights the social importance of what we are doing. We begin to get glimpses of a much larger picture. Mothers affect not just their own children but, to some extent, their generation.

> If this important work [*of bringing up children*] goes wrong, the cost to our society will be very great. [B, 2 years]

In traditional societies, mothers teach their children practical skills on their homesteads, such as weaving, or daily care of the family animals. In our complex society, practical skills that the mother uses may have become outdated by the time her child has become an adult. So the most effective work she does is to prepare her child to communicate with different people, in different situations. She brings him up within her value system, so he starts with a moral base. And together they can develop an intimate relationship in which both can feel safe. All this work helps her child to move on to the 'mainland' of our very communicative society.

For how long does her influence last? Life expectancy has increased. The person who is a baby today has a good chance of living for a hundred years. He may find that the older he gets, the more important are his abilities to communicate. If he becomes disabled or simply weak in old age and depends on others, he will again be in a similar position to that of a small child. Elderly people often say with great feeling: 'I don't want to be a *burden* to anyone.' Is that because, as small children, they sensed that their mothers *did* find them burdensome? Are they now reluctant to ask for help, as adults, for fear of repeating that familiar experience? Yet many able-bodied people get satisfaction from helping a needy elderly person. So the mother's early pleasure in relating well to her child may have a century-long benefit. It may free him to ask for help in old age when he needs it, and make him a much easier elderly person to look after.

A child's memory of his mother may last his whole life.

> We have such responsibility. It's awesome. We have the power to create life, and we have the power to abuse it and to ruin our

children's lives for *ever*. After all, when people are dying, they don't call out: 'Parent!' They call: '*Mother!*' [1B, 7 years; 2B, 3 years]

A dying person may call for his mother because he remembers how strong she once seemed when he was young, and how comforting she was through his childhood pain. She may think she could have done better. But a dying person may be seeing his mother at her best.

Mothers are sometimes accused of being too absorbed in their families and too little engaged with the human 'continent' to which we all belong. But this seems an extraordinary generalisation. Many express remarkable sensitivity and compassion. They cry easily as they hear about international crises, and the hardships suffered by other mothers and babies.

When I was pregnant, I read about young refugees. Some women were pregnant – many had been raped. How did they . . . ? You think you're having a difficult time being pregnant in ordinary times. I cannot imagine how it feels when times are difficult. [G, 4 months]

I work with children who have been expelled from school, from five years old to fourteen. Since having B, I have become much more sympathetic to the parents, especially their mothers. A lot of them have drink, drug and housing issues. It's hard enough bringing up a child when you haven't got problems like that. [B, 12 months]

We are in temporary accommodation until we can move into our new place and it made me realise that we have money and can buy a flat. But what do homeless mothers do with their children? How much stress must they feel? [G, 4 years; B, 9 months]

The actor Cate Blanchett visited a refugee camp and described her shock at the appalling stories she heard: 'I am a mother and I saw my children in the eyes of every single refugee child I met. I saw myself in every parent.'[171]

Just as John Donne realised that he was affected by the fate of each person (see page 277, note 167), so mothers often feel deeply affected by one another.

Mothers can support one another. I've learned that. Even if our families are far away, we're one big *mother* family. [B, 21 months]

Becoming *active* outside her family can be more difficult. Compared to the strength of their compassion, their actions may sound modest. Mothers describe them shyly.

I'm much kinder than I was before I had B. Having B showed me his vulnerability, and now I can extend that understanding to other people too. [B, 14 months]

Having G makes me see the world differently. Not in a grand way, but seeing how we all are to each other. I *feel* much more than I used to. If I get on a bus with G and the driver is nice to us that really *matters*. [G, 16 months]

Being a mother has made me much more friendly. I'm less judg-mental. When I'm by myself, I can still be . . . [*she gestured striding forward, pushing people out of her way*]. But being with B has made me a better person. And I find other mothers are like that. [B, 23 months]

And her child's actions can inspire a mother to try something new.

I took G to a crèche, but she cried so I stayed with her. There was a little boy crying and he wasn't so lucky. No one asked what he wanted, and the staff put him in his pushchair, pushed it to face the wall and left him. G was very upset. She went up to him and stroked him and then she tried to give him toys.

I felt very uncomfortable. I'm not a protesting kind of person. I'm quite shy. But in the end, I went up and turned the pushchair to face the room again. I felt I had to support all that G was doing. [G, 2 years]

These may sound tiny, insignificant steps. But, however small, they show mothers taking their new identities with them as they join the great human continent. How we relate in our daily lives does matter. And early steps can lead to larger ones. When these mothers become more experienced, and perhaps as grandmothers, they may be ready to work together for local, national and international humane causes.[172]

But how are the majority of mothers today going to have enough experience? Many feel under pressure to return to paid work sooner than they want. Mothering is unpaid, and many families depend on double incomes to get by. These mothers feel angry and guilty at sending their children to professional carers whom they can barely afford. But how else, they say, can they earn enough money to survive? Why is there so little financial support for mothers? Why are there no proper tax-relief schemes and special grants to enable them to continue mothering their children until the children are mature enough to enjoy nursery and school? I've been to many meetings and conferences where mothers protest that their mothering is undervalued, that no one understands how much they are doing and that financially they are often in hardship. Yet these complaints seem to go unheard.

Why is no one listening? Our mothering is undervalued, yes. But perhaps we aren't presenting it with our best foot forward. We are asking for respect for the work of mothering. But do we honestly respect this work ourselves?

Often, we don't do it justice. We are not 'just being at home with the baby' nor 'not back in real work yet'. Our mothering goes further than making cupcakes and wiping runny noses.[173] Those actions are visible, and I suppose that's why people keep talking about them. Why don't we mention the less visible work we do?

> I try to explain to my partner what G and I do all day, only the words don't come out right. I suppose being a mother, you are in a different mode. [G, 14 months]

A 'different mode' is exactly why mothering is hard to explain. Surely our main insight as mothers is to discover how we relate. Love emerges out of chaos, as mother and baby start to make sense of one another. It grows once the two find they can trust one another (a big step for a newborn) and can accept the other (a big step for a mother). The mother wields a special power. She can create a good emotional connection that is hard to describe. If she comes in too close, her baby will feel smothered. If too distant, the baby is likely to feel unwanted, rejected. Both these extremes have been described at length by psychotherapists. However, between the extremes is a wide amount of comfortable space, where mother and baby can enjoy being together and sharing the wonder of ordinary life. This wide space is hardly ever described. Their relationship seems to cycle. They have some moments of closeness and other moments when they are a little apart. Fathers and other family members communicate with the baby too, though the mother's relationship is usually primary. A baby who has had a good experience of it will have a strong base for creating warm childhood friendships, and eventually, as an adult, to feel safe to fall in love. Adult love can feel risky without this early preparation. So – how ever can we convey all this?

Until now, there hasn't been a pressing need for mothers to describe what they do. As an adult daughter tried to explain: 'My mother is illiterate, and she won't need to know big words like the "attachment theory", but she just did her parenting so naturally with wisdom.'[174] This is probably what mothers have been doing for millennia. And perhaps *we* don't need big words or abstract theories either.

How can we explain the different mothering mode to ourselves and then to others? One 'causeway' from our mother-islands to the mainland is through simple, everyday memories of good moments with our children. If we can describe some of these, we will be carrying across some valuable discoveries.

Those of us who are mothers are sure to have memories of the time we spent 'on our islands' with our children. What did we do? What were some of the good moments? This isn't just about *other* mothers. You and I have something to contribute. There's a fine line between bragging about special moments with our children – and doing ourselves justice. Were you really 'getting nothing done' when you were spending time with your child? Or were those together-moments so full of an alive 'something' that they were almost unbearable?

We aren't being fair to ourselves if we present ourselves to employers or the government as poor supplicants. We are rich in our experience. Nor are we victims of social expectations. Mothers make up approximately one third of society. If our society makes demands on us that feel unfair, we have the numbers to press for changes.

Women have had a long struggle to prove that they are capable in all the fields traditionally seen as male. Mothering, the traditional female role, has got left behind. It's not inborn. It's difficult for each of us to learn. And we have to un-learn many popular assumptions as well.

The origin of the word 'learn' comes from a Teutonic root and means getting information on a subject or skill. It's a practical word, connected to 'lore', which means the information learned. I discovered in a dictionary that there is a medieval word, 'lore-child', meaning a scholar or apprentice. Another term, 'lore-father', describes a master of learning.[175] When I saw this, I wondered if there was a 'lore-mother' too. I read up and down the dictionary columns in great excitement. But I didn't find anything. Lore-mother isn't there.

It's odd – because mothers learn so much. They notice details about their children that other people overlook. For example, an Australian activist, known as Maybanke Anderson (1845–1927), wrote a small book called *Mother Lore* (1919). She bore seven children, and fought for the rights of women and children. In her book, she noted: 'The baby, as soon as he can see, watches a ray of sunlight or a waving curtain, and gurgles with delight.'[176] How similar this sounds to Mme de Saussure's observation (see pages 53–4) about a baby who liked a bright metal button, and a mirror lit by sunlight, and seemed to communicate with them.[177] Both mothers noticed babies' pleasure in bright things and their desire to respond to them. Both were writing educational books about caring for children. Yet both dropped their 'educational voice' to write in a loving motherly tone. And, no doubt, many loving mothers have made independent but similar original observations that show us how we begin our lives.

Mothering will always be mysterious. But we can be more explicit about our lore. It's true that mothers sometimes describe mothering in their professional capacity as journalists, researchers, teachers and psychologists. But what about writing with the warmth of *mothers*? And for those of us who love meeting and talking, more discussion groups could be set up. Through simple words, spoken and written, we would soon get a collective picture of the richness of mother lore.

If enough of us value our mothering, we will be able to change the prevailing negative attitude we see around us. Whether we are mothers full-time, part-time or mostly employed, each of us has learned on many levels. Once we are conscious of the irreplaceable value of our mothering, we can present ourselves differently to the human continent. And that enhanced awareness of ourselves is the first step we need to take. The human continent is in denial – but it *needs* us. So, if we decide to, it is we who can bring about a change.

Notes

1   Sara Ruddick, 'What do mothers and grandmothers know and want?' in *What Do Mothers Want?* ed. Sheila Feig Brown. Hillsdale NJ/London: Analytic Press, 2005, p. 74.

2   'The psychic landscape of mothers' by Daniel N. Stern in *What Do Mothers Want?* ed. Sheila Feig Brown. Hillsdale NJ/London: Analytic Press, 2005, p. 4.

3   Leigh Minturn and William W. Lambert, *Mothers of Six Cultures: Antecedents of child rearing*, New York, London, Sydney: John Wiley, 1964, pp. 291–2.

4   For example, see Sharon Hays, *The Cultural Contradictions of Motherhood*, New Haven: Yale University Press, 1996, p. 121.

5   Shraddha Kapoor, 'Interviewing in qualitative research' in *Researching Families and Children*, edited by S. Anandalakshmy, Nandita Chaudhary and Neerja Sharma, New Delhi: Sage, 2008, p. 135.

6   'Field Observations from Rural Gujarat' by Monika Abels in *Researching Families and Children*, edited by S. Anandalakshmy, Nandita Chaudhary and Neerja Sharma, New Delhi: Sage, 2008, p. 216.

7   *The Complete Works of Geoffrey Chaucer*, edited by F. N. Robinson, London: Oxford University Press, 1957, p. 24. [General Prologue, lines 731–38.]

8   Naomi Stadlen, *What Mothers Do – especially when it looks like nothing*, London: Piatkus, 2004. *How Mothers Love – and how relationships are born*, London: Piatkus, 2011.

9   Carol Sarler, 'The mother myth: there is no such thing as a full-time mum', *Spectator*, 19 January 2013.

10 Clover Stroud, 'Stay-at-home mums tell Cameron: Ignore us at your peril', *The Sunday Times*, 31 March 2013.

11 Lucy Cavendish, 'The war at home', *Observer Magazine*, 28 March 2010.

12 Allison Pearson, 'Ignore the snipers. Unsung mothers everywhere know this is their movie', *Daily Telegraph*, 16 September 2011.

13 Adrienne Rich, *Of Woman Born: Motherhood as Experience and Institution*, London: Virago, 1977, p. 38.

14 Rebecca Asher, *Shattered: Modern Motherhood and the Illusion of Equality*, London: Vintage, 2012, p. 3.

15 *Ibid.*, p. 4.

16 *Ibid*, p. 4

17 *Ibid.*, pp. 3–4

18 Mary Wollstonecraft, *A Vindication of the Rights of Women* [1792], London: Penguin, 1975, p. 272.

19 Sara Ruddick, 'Maternal Thinking' in *Maternal Theory*, ed. Andrea O'Reilly, Toronto: Demeter Press, 2007, p. 106.

20 Sara Ruddick, *Maternal Thinking. Towards a Politics of Peace*, London: The Women's Press, 1989, p. 24.

21 Eds. Camille Peri and Kate Moses, *Mothers Who Think*, New York: Washington Square Press, 2000, p. xviii.

22 Katherine Ellison, *The Mommy Brain, How Motherhood Makes Us Smarter*, New York: Basic Books, 2005, p. 79.

23 Unnamed mother in *Maternity: Letters from Working Women*, ed. Margaret Llewelyn Davies [1915], London: Virago, 1978, p. 74.

24 S. T. Azar, E. B. Reitz, M. C. Goslin, 'Mothering: Thinking is Part of the Job Description' in *Journal of Applied Developmental Psychology* 29 (2008), p. 295.

25 Mary Field Belenky et al., *Women's Ways of Knowing. The*

development of self, voice and mind, New York: Basic Books, 1986, p. 189.

26   W. D. Wall, 'Learning to Think' in *How and Why do We Learn?* ed. W. R. Niblett, London: Faber, 1965, p. 74.

27   Quoted by Lucy Cavendish, 'The War at Home' in *Observer Magazine*, 28 March 2010.

28   Sara Ruddick, *Maternal Thinking. Towards a Politics of Peace*, London: The Women's Press, 1990; and Marcy Axness (*Parenting for Peace. Raising the Next Generation of Peacemakers*, Boulder, CO: Sentient Press, 2012). Both make cases for helping the next generation of children to be peaceful. However, they both assume that a mother has to teach her child. But children may first learn these values from experience – from the way their mothers relate to them.

29   There is an interesting study by Orna Donath, *Regretting Motherhood* (US: North Atlantic Books, 2017) of interviews with mothers who loved their children but were certain that, for them, becoming mothers had been a mistake.

30   Sara Ruddick, 'Maternal Thinking' in *Maternal Theory*, ed. Andrea O'Reilly, Toronto: Demeter Press, 2007, p. 102.

31   Nancy Folbre, *The Invisible Heart*, New York: New Press, 2001, p. 111. Also *Valuing Children: Rethinking the Economics of the Family*, Camb, Mass: Harvard University Press, 2008.

32   Marilyn Waring, *Counting for Nothing: What Men Value and What Women are Worth*, Toronto, Buffalo: University of Toronto Press [1988], 1999, p. 1.

33   Ina May Gaskin in conversation with Nick Olow, 25 March 2017.

34   Frederick Leboyer, *Birth Without Violence*, London: Wildwood House, 1975, p. 85. [Recent reprint by Pinter and Martin, 2011.]

35   Some mothers find cleaning up after their babies unpleasant. This is described by Sherri Irvin, 'Motherhood and the

Workings of Disgust' in *Philosophical Inquiries into Pregnancy, Childbirth and Mothering*, eds. Sheila Lintott and Maureen Sander-Standt, New York and Abingdon: Routledge, 2012.

36   'In a survey of 1,500 parents, more than two thirds of parents of babies of nine months and over said they wished they had spent more time cuddling their newborns. Instead, they spent time "cleaning the house, losing their pregnancy weight and getting the baby into a strict routine."' *Daily Telegraph*, 14 January 2014. Parents? Surely *fathers* aren't losing their pregnancy weight! It sounds as though these 'parents' are mostly mothers. In other words, many new mothers are spending their first days in practical chores rather than enjoying their babies, but regret this later on.

37   Maeve Haran, *Having It All*, London: Michael Joseph, 1991, p. 50.

38   Sue Gerhardt, *Why Love Matters*, London: Brunner-Routledge, 2004, p. 208.

39   'Gillian' in *Tales From the Edge: Experience of Post-Natal Depression*, North Lancashire Manic Mums Group: 2008, p.16.

40   Paula Nicholson, *Post-Natal Depression: Psychology, science and the transition to motherhood*, London: Routledge, 1998 pp. 108–9.

41   Molly Van Den Brink, 'Breastfeeding through oversupply' in *Breastfeeding Matters*, La Leche League Great Britain, July/August 2019, p. 13

42   M. Sara Rosenthal, *Women and Depression: a sane approach to mood disorders*, Los Angeles: Lowell House, 2000, p. 20.

43   Dana Raphael, *The Tender Gift: Breastfeeding*, New York: Schocken Books, 1973.

44   Mme de Saussure, afterwards Necker, Albertine Adrienne de, *Progressive Education*, vol.1, London: Longman, 1839. [*L'Education Progressive*, 1828.] This is discussed again on p. 258

45 The poet Fiona Benson seems to have realised that her baby daughter was looking at corners too, and mentions her staring at them in *Bright Travellers*, London: Cape, 2014, p. 54.

46 Allan N. Schore, *Affect Regulation and the Origin of the Self*, Hillsdale, New Jersey/Hove, Sussex: Erlbaum, 1994, p. 351.

47 Sam Leith, 'Our Economy can't deal with full-time parents', London: *Evening Standard*, 29 October 2012.

48 An account of how one-year-old babies were tested to see if they could remember a simple action one week later is recorded in Gopnik, A.,Meltzoff, A., Kuhl, P., *How Babies Think*, London: Weidenfeld, 1999, pp. 33–4.

49 Ian Sample, '60% of psychology research "cannot be replicated"'. The *Guardian*, 28 August 2015.

50 Agatha Christie, *The Murder of Roger Ackroyd*, Penguin 1926, pp. 135–6.

51 Florence Nightingale, *Notes on Nursing* [1859]. London: Duckworth, 1952, pp. 132–3.

52 Jo Baker Watson, 'There's no formula for survival', *Guardian*, 26 February 2009.

53 Quoted in Family Section, *Guardian*, 30 March 2013. From Saira Shah, *The Mouseproof Kitchen*, Harvill Secker, 2013.

54 Personal communication, 12 March 2019, quoted with permission.

55 University of Dundee: Reports of rising-five-year-olds starting school barely able to speak are coming through. This is not because the children are from immigrant families who speak a different language, but because parents are working long hours and have reduced time for talking. [*Daily Telegraph*, 14 February 2014.]

56 A. Weisleder and A. Fernald, 'Talking to children matters: Early language experience strengthens processing and builds vocabulary', *Psychological Science*. New York: Sage Publications, 10 September 2013.

There is an earlier research study by Frances Fuchs
Schachter with the attractive title *Everyday Mother Talk to
Toddlers: Early Intervention*, New York: Academic Press, 1979.
This distinguishes between 'advantaged' and 'disadvantaged'
children, showing how mothers of disadvantaged children
responded minimally to them, often reprimanding them for
their behaviour without explanation, whereas mothers of
more advantaged children engaged in dialogue, and when
they did give a command added an explanation. These results
seem to confirm the more recent studies.

57   David Attenborough, *Life on Earth, a natural history*, London
      and Glasgow: BBC and Collins, 1979, p. 308.

58   R. T. Mercer and S. L. Ferkerich, 'Experienced and inexperi-
      enced mothers' maternal competence during infancy' in
      Research in Nursing and Health, vol. 18, no. 4, August 1995.
      New York: John Wiley, pp. 340–1.

59   Dante Alighieri [early fourteenth century], *Purgatario*,
      London: Dent, 1901. Canto XXX, lines 76–80.

60   Translated R. A. Kaster and M. Nussbaum [2010], *Seneca: Anger,
      Mercy, Revenge*, Chicago: University of Chicago Press, p. 16.

61   *Ibid*. p. 54.

62   Louisa M. Alcott [1868], *Little Women*. Many editions.
      Chapter 8.

63   *Ibid*.

64   This is corroborated by the work of Ana Villalobos who wrote:
      'In an atomised world where stay-at-home mothers are often
      alone with their children, difficulties from simple frustrations
      to all-out rage can be trapped within the family walls and can
      easily turn into a source of self-doubt.' 'The Free Gift' by Ana
      Villalobos in *Stay-at-Home Mothers*, eds Elizabeth Reid Boyd
      and Gayle Letherby, Bradford, On: Demeter Press, 2014 p. 306.

65   Rachel Cusk, 'The simmering but stymied rage of stay-at-
      home mums' in *Guardian*, 9 October 2010.

66   Vanessa Olorenshaw [2015], 'The Politics of Mothering'. Available online, pages 10–11.

67   Elizabeth Gaskell, *My Diary*, London: privately printed by Clement Shorter, 1923, p. 11.

68   Alison Uttley, *Ambush of Young Days* [1937], Maidstone, Kent: George Mann, 1974, pp. 30–1.

69   Vanessa Olorenshaw, *Liberating Motherhood, Birthing the Purplestockings Movement*, East Cork, Ireland: Womancraft Publishing, 2016.

70   Rebecca Walker, *Baby Love. Choosing Motherhood After a Lifetime of Ambivalence*, London: Souvenir Press, 2009, p. 47.

71   Simone de Beauvoir, *The Second Sex*, translated by Constance Borde and Sheila Malovany-Chevallier, London: Vintage Books, 2011, p. 565.

72   *Ibid.*, p. 768. The ungrammatical switch from plural 'women' to singular 'she' is in the original.

73   Anthony Stadlen, 'Locked Up: "Patients" and their Gaolers'. 2: Kate Millett, Inner Circle Seminar 163, 8 May 2011.

74   Betty Friedan, *The Feminine Mystique* [1963], London: Penguin, 2010, p. 5.

75   Rebecca Asher, *Shattered*, London: Vintage, 2011, p 1.

76   Susan J. Douglas and Meredith W. Michaels, *The New Momism*. Cited in *Maternal Theory*, ed. Andrea O'Reilly, Toronto: Demeter Press, 2007, p. 621.

77   'Self-Soothing' by Clare Potter in *Writing Motherhood*, ed. Carolyn Jess-Cooke, Bridgend, Wales: Seren, Poetry Wales Press, 2017, p. 51.

78   For example, in a paper 'But One Gets Tired' on breastfeeding in rural Guatemala, the researchers offer the misinformation: 'Delayed introduction of solid foods contributes to high child malnutrition rates, as breastmilk alone cannot adequately nourish children beyond six months of age.' There is ample evidence that breastmilk alone has nourished children for

much longer than six months. The constituents of breastmilk change and keep pace with the child's development. So breastfeeding provides good protection against malnutrition. It also contains antibodies, and is sterile, so may be safer for a child than solid foods. But *mothers* need good nourishment to enable them to maintain their own strength while they breastfeed. The researchers show how poorly nourished these rural Guatemalan mothers were. The problems lay in an unfair social 'infrastructure', not in any inadequacies in breastmilk after six months. 'But One Gets Tired' by Anita Chary, Shom Dasgupta, Sarah Messmer and Peter Rohloff in *An Anthropology of Mothering*, eds Michelle Walks and Naomi McPherson. Bradford, On: Demeter Press, 2011, p. 175.

79   Élisabeth Badinter, *The Conflict*, translated by Adriana Hunter, New York: Metropolitan Books, Henry Holt, 2011, p. 76. It is not clear whether her anger was motivated by business as well as ideological interests. Her father founded the advertising and public relations company Publicis in 1926. She has chaired the board since 1996. One of the clients of Publicis is Nestlé, the largest makers of baby formula milk.

80   'The *Lancet* series on breastfeeding: LLLGB comments' on www.laleche.org.uk, 2016.

81   *Hirkani's Daughters: Women Who Scale Modern Mountains to Combine Breastfeeding and Working*, ed. Jennifer Hicks, Schaumburg, Il: La Leche League International, 2006.

82   *Encyclopaedia of Motherhood*, ed. O'Reilly, Thousand Oaks, Calif: Sage, 2010, vol. 2, p. 629.

83   *Ibid.*, p. 630. The main criticisms are that the League positions 'women as radically different from men [*and*] League philosophy implicitly suggests a commonality among women'. The words 'implicitly suggests' are not very helpful. It's not clear what Boon means. She also thought the League 'threatens to exclude fathers as active and equal partners in parenting'. But

La Leche League has a statement devoted to the importance of fathers: 'Breastfeeding is enhanced and the nursing couple sustained by the loving support, help and companionship of the baby's father. A father's unique relationship with his baby is an important element in the child's development from early infancy.' This concept can be found on any La Leche League website as part of its philosophy.

84   Sheila Kitzinger, *The Experience of Breastfeeding*, Harmondsworth: Penguin, 1979.

85   Vanessa Olorenshaw, *Liberating Motherhood*, East Cork, Ireland: Womancraft Publishing, 2016, p. 81.

86   Sheila Kitzinger, *A Passion for Birth*, London: Pinter & Martin, 2015, p. 92.

87   Daphne de Marneffe, *Maternal Desire*, London: Virago, 2006, p. 4.

88   Val Gillies, *Marginalised Mothers, Exploring working-class experiences of parenting*, London/New York: Routledge, 2006.

89   Heather Jackson, 'Mothering in Poverty' in *Mothers, Mothering and Motherhood*, ed. Andrea O'Reilly, Bradford, On: Demeter Press, 2014, p. 338.

90   Daphne de Marneffe, *Maternal Desire*, London: Virago, 2006, p. 315.

91   Vanessa Oloronshaw, *Liberating Motherhood*, East Cork, Ireland: Womancraft Publishing, 2016, p. 185.

92   Nancy Folbre, *Valuing Children. Rethinking the Economics of the Family*, Cambridge, Mass: Harvard University Press, 2008, pp. 1–2.

93   Andrea O'Reilly 'Feminist Mothering' in ed. O'Reilly, *Maternal Theory: Essential Readings*, Toronto: Demeter Press, 2007, p. 802.

94   Andrea O'Reilly, 'That is what feminism is' in *Feminist Mothering*, ed. O'Reilly, Albany NY: State University of New York Press, 2008, p. 195.

95   'Feminist Mothering' in *Mothers, Mothering and Motherhood*,

ed. Andrea O'Reilly, Bradford, On: Demeter Press, 2014, pp. 190–1.

96   Andrea O'Reilly, Preface to *Toni Morrison and Motherhood*, Albany NY: State University of New York Press, 2004, p. x.

97   Entry for 'Toni Morrison' by Andrea O'Reilly in vol. 2 of *Encyclopaedia of Motherhood*, ed. Andrea O'Reilly, Thousand Oaks, Calif: Sage, 2010, p. 802.

98   Sarah Blaffer Hrdy, *Mother Nature*, London: Vintage, 2000, p. x. She developed this idea in *Mothers and Others*, Cambridge, Mass: Harvard University Press, 2009. Alloparents she believed were not only a convenient solution for mothers. They were important for children too. In order to develop cooperative skills, says Hrdy, young children need to be able to 'read' not just one mother but a variety of human faces. From her scholarly studies of animals and humans, she concluded that this was how early human societies must have been organised. Because babies develop so slowly, their mothers would have needed to depend on cooperative help from other women.

99   Daphne de Marneffe, *Maternal Desire*, London: Virago, 2006, p. 49.

100 *Ibid.*, p. 156.

101 Anne Manne, *Motherhood*, Crows Nest NSW: Allen & Unwin, 2005, p. 4.

102 Keren Epstein-Gilboa, 'Maternal ambivalence' in *Stay-At-Home Mothers*, ed. Elizabeth Reid Boyd and Gayle Letherby. Bradford, On: Demeter Press, 2014, p. 34.

103 Miriam González Durántez, as quoted in the *Daily Telegraph*, 8 October 2013.

104 Virginia Woolf, 'A Room of One's Own', Chapter II in *A Room of One's Own and Other Essays*, London: The Folio Society, 2000 p. 39.

105 Many moving examples of the self-sacrifice of poorer mothers in ed. Margaret Llewelyn Davies, *Maternity: Letters from*

Working Woman [1915], London: Virago, 1978. Also eds Christine Gowdridge, A. Susan Williams, Margaret Wynn, *Mother Courage: Letters from Mothers in Poverty at the End of the Century*, London: Penguin, 1977.

106 Margot Sunderland, *The Science of Parenting*, London: Dorling Kindersley/Penguin, 2006, p. 250.

107 D. W. Winnicott, *The Child, the Family and the Outside World*, Harmondsworth, Middx: Penguin, 1964, p. 27.

108 Liz Fraser, 'I miss the early years', *Guardian*, Family Section, 31 October 2015.

109 Rozsika Parker, 'The production and purposes of maternal ambivalence' in *Mothering and Ambivalence*, eds. Wendy Hollway and Brid Featherstone, London: Routledge, 1997, p. 22.

110 The psychoanalyst D. W. Winnicott also recognised the importance of building up a trusting relationship. He was writing at a time when nearly all mothers were at home with their children, and today he would undoubtedly have phrased it less dogmatically. This is the end of the first part of his book *The Child, the Family and the Outside World*: 'The period in which one is called on to be a mother or father is certainly a time of self-sacrifice. The ordinary good mother knows without being told that during this time nothing must interfere with the continuity of the relationship between the child and herself', D. W. Winnicott, *The Child, the Family and the Outside World*, Harmondsworth, Middx: Penguin, 1964, p. 109.

111 The novelist George Eliot considered this question in *Daniel Deronda*. She didn't have children herself, but created the character of a loving mother, Mrs Meyrick. Daniel asks her whether friends aren't as good as mothers. '"We must not let mothers be too arrogant,"' he says. And she replies: '"Friendships begin with liking or gratitude – roots that can be pulled up. Mother's love begins deeper down."' George

Eliot, *Daniel Deronda* (1876), ed. Barbara Hardy, London: Penguin, 1967, p. 424 Chapter 32.

112 Donna McCart Sharkey, ed., *Always With Me: Parents Talk About the Death of a Child*, Bradford, On: Demeter Press, 2018.

113 Aurélie M. Athan and Lisa Miller, 'Motherhood as Opportunity to Learn Spiritual Values: Experience and Insights of New Mothers', in *Journal of Prenatal and Perinatal Psychology and Health*, 27(4) summer 2013, p. 248.

114 *Ibid.*, p. 220.

115 *Ibid.*, p. 248.

116 Martin Heidegger, *What Is Called Thinking?* translated by F. D. Wieck and J. G. Gray (1968), New York: Harper & Row, p. 141. (*Was Heisst Denken?* Tübingen: Max Niemeyer, 1954.)

117 The American paediatrician T. Berry Brazelton noticed that mothers seemed to relate to their babies 'inside' something: 'The mother is having to learn how to enclose the baby, how to keep him in what we call an envelope, so he can learn about himself.' T. Berry Brazelton, 'Four Early Stages in the Development of Mother-Infant Interaction' in *The Growing Child in Family and Society*, eds. Noboru Kobayashi and T. Berry Brazelton, Tokyo: University of Tokyo Press, 1984, p. 29. I haven't heard a mother use the word 'envelope', but it sounds similar to the 'bubble' that mothers describe.

118 Rachel Cusk, *A Life's Work, on becoming a mother*, London: Fourth Estate, 2001, p. 2.

119 Aurélie M. Athan and Lisa Miller, 'Motherhood as Opportunity to Learn Spiritual Values: Experience and Insights of New Mothers', in *Journal of Prenatal and Perinatal Psychology and Health*, 27(4) summer 2013, p. 248.

120 Daphne de Marneffe, *Maternal Desire* [2004], London: Virago, 2006, p. 336.

121 The Maggid of Mezritch, 'The Between-stage' quoted in

Martin Buber, *Tales of the Hasidim*, translated by Olga Marx, New York: Schocken Books, 1975, p. 104.

122 Val Gillies, *Marginalised Mothers: Exploring Working-Class Experiences of Parenting*, London/New York: Routledge, 2006, p. 118.

123 Catherine Hakim, *Work-Lifestyle Choices in the Twenty-first Century*, Oxford: Oxford University Press, 2000, p. 181. 'Overall, studies have always found that happiness, however measured, is lower, on average, and depression and mental health problems are more common among women with children than among women without children . . .'

124 '"Where did I go?" The invisible postpartum mother', Jennifer Benson and Allison Wolf in *Philosophical Inquiries into Pregnancy, Childbirth and Mothering*, eds. Sheila Lintott and Maureen Sander Standt, New York: Routledge, 2012, p. 45.

125 Lauren Porter, Unpublished work, 2019.

126 See also p. 49–50 for mothers' experiences, and Naomi Stadlen *How Mothers Love – and how relationships are born*, London: Piatkus, 2011, Chapter Two.

127 This is confirmed by Sharon Hays who wrote: 'I would call these child-rearing manuals hesitant moral treatises.' *The Cultural Contradictions of Motherhood*, New Haven: Yale University Press, 1996, p. 65.

128 Allison Pearson, 'A Mother's Worth'. Talk given to Mothers at Home Matter, 8 November 2018.

129 This fascinating topic should have a book to itself. There are countless examples, often mentioned by historians in passing. 'The daily tasks of maternity were recognised as women's business: among themselves, they [women] exchanged information and advice . . . Not surprisingly, men knew little about maternal knowledge, and they were inclined to dismiss women's talk as "gossip"'. Patricia Crawford, 'The construction and experience of maternity in seventeenth-century England'

in Valerie Fields, ed., *Women as Mothers in Pre-Industrial England*, London: Routledge, 1990, p. 27.

130 Dana Raphael, *The Tender Gift: Breastfeeding*, New York: Schocken Books, 1973.

131 From *The Cornhill Magazine*, 1869, quoted in Claudia Nelson, *Invisible Men: Fatherhood in Victorian Periodicals 1850–1910*, Athens, Georgia: University of Georgia Press, 1995, p. 45.

132 Ursula Owen, *Fathers, Reflections by Daughters*, London: Virago, 1983, p. 13.

133 *Ibid.*, p. 14.

134 William and Martha Sears, *The Fussy Baby Book*, New York: Little, Brown & Co., 1996, p. 68.

135 Catherine Hakim, *Work – Lifestyle Choices in the 21st Century*, Oxford: Oxford University Press, 2000, p. 181.

136 Florence Nightingale, *Cassandra*, New York: Feminist Press, 1979, p. 32.

137 Virginia Woolf, 'A Room of One's Own' in *A Room of One's Own and Other Essays*, selected by Hermione Lee, London: Folio Society, 2000, p. 70.

138 Claudia Nelson, *Invisible Men: Fatherhood in Victorian Periodicals 1850–1910*, Athens, Georgia: University of Georgia Press, 1995, p. 210.

139 Martin Freud, *Glory Reflected*, London: Angus & Robertson, 1957, p. 55.

140 Walter Southgate, *That's the way it was*, Oxted, Surrey: New Clarion Press, 1982, p. 12.

141 This is also confirmed in a chapter on laughter in *Fatherhood and the British Working Class*, Professor Julie-Marie Strange wrote: 'Jokes about men's helplessness at "mothering" acknowledged and approved the gendering of parental tasks.' Cambridge University Press, 2015, p.170.

142 'Seeing themselves' by Hester Vair in *Stay-at-Home Mothers*, ed. Elizabeth Reid Boyd and Gayle Letherby, Bradford, On:

Demeter Press, 2014, p. 280.

143 Hollie McNish, '31 May' in *Writing Motherhood* ed. Carolyn Jess-Cooke, Bridgend, Wales: Seren Poetry Wales Press, 2017, p. 101.

144 'Maternal Ambivalence' by Keren Epstein-Gilboa in *Stay-at-Home Mothers*, ed. Elizabeth Reid Boyd and Gayle Letherby, Bradford, On: Demeter Press, 2014, p. 31.

145 Sharon Hays, 'Why can't a mother be more like a businessman?' in *Maternal Theory: Essential Readings*, ed. Andrea O'Reilly, Toronto: Demeter Press, 2007, p. 408.

146 *Ibid.*, p. 409.

147 *Ibid.*, p. 415.

148 *Ibid.*

149 Sue Palmer writing in *Juno Magazine*, issue 30, winter 2012, p. 8.

150 'Are "Mommy Wars" Real?' by Brianne Janacek Reeber and Paula J Caplan in *Stay-at-Home Mothers*, ed. Elizabeth Reid Boyd and Gayle Letherby, Bradford, On: Demeter Press, 2014, p. 63.

151 'Integrating Choices' by Noelia Molina in *Stay-at-Home Mothers*, ed. Elizabeth Reid Boyd and Gayle Letherby, Bradford, On: Demeter Press, 2018, p. 147.

152 *Hirkani's Daughters: Women Who Scale Modern Mountains to Combine Breastfeeding and Working*, ed. Jennifer Hicks, Schaumburg I1: La Leche League, 2006.

153 Quoted by Anne-Marie Slaughter in *Unfinished Business*, New York: Random House, 2016, p. 73.

154 Many examples of this are reported in the media. One mother said: 'Having kids means now I work better – sometimes I may be working flexibly or at home but I'm far more productive and much more disciplined with my time. Others in the office have commented on it too.' *Evening Standard*, 22 January 2014. Louise Doughty, a British

novelist said: 'I think I have become a better writer since having children. It improves creativity particularly because once you have children it makes you realise the story isn't about you.' *Daily Telegraph*, 13 June 2013. And an Icelandic economist who wasn't a mother remarked: '. . . the value you bring *[to work]* as a woman is the maternal aspect, the strength that comes from motherhood.' *Observer*, 22 February 2009.

155 Quoted by Allison Pearson in *Daily Telegraph*, 18 July 2018.

156 Ronnie Cloke-Browne, 'Being a mother – a valuable career break' in *Newsletter*, Mothers At Home Matter, spring 2017, p. 10.

157 'Making it Work' by Catherine Fournier in *Stay-at-Home Mothers*, ed. Elizabeth Reid Boyd and Gayle Letherby. Bradford, On: Demeter Press, 2014, p. 246.

158 Mike Kaeding, President at Norhart: 'Great leadership is about influence, not authority', published online, 8 August 2018.

159 Anne-Marie Slaughter, *Unfinished Business*, New York: Random House, 2016 edition, p. 262.

160 Sara Ruddick, 'What do mothers and grandmothers know and want?' in *What Do Mothers Want?* ed. Sheila Feig Brown, Hillsdale NJ/London: Analytic Press, 2005, p. 78.

161 *Contemporary Grandparenting: Changing Family Relationships in Global Contexts* eds. Sara Arber and Virpi Timonen, Bristol: Polity Press, 2012.

162 Sara Ruddick, 'What do mothers and grandmothers know and want?' in *What Do Mothers Want?* ed. Sheila Feig Brown, Hillsdale NJ/London: Analytic Press, 2005, p. 70.

163 *Ibid.*, p. 78.

164 www.grandmothersforpeace.org. The bold type is in the original.

165 See *Omas Gegen Rechts* on German and English websites.

166 Carol Schaefer, *Grandmothers Counsel the World. Women*

Elders Offer their Vision for our Planet, Boston: Trumpeter Books, Shambhala Publications, 2006, p. 1.

167 'No man is an Iland, intire of itselfe; every man is a peece of the Continent, a part of the maine; if a Clod bee washed away by the Sea, Europe is the lesse, as well as if a Promontorie were, as well as if a Mannor of thy friends or of thine owne were; Any mans death diminishes me, because I am involved in Mankinde; And therefore never send to know for whom the bell tolls; It tolls for thee.' John Donne, Meditation XVII from *Devotions upon Emergent Occasions*, 1624. This is echoed by the Chinese dissident artist Ai Weiwei: 'When abuses are committed against anyone in any society, the dignity of humanity as a whole is compromised', Ai Weiwei, 'Human dignity is in danger' in *Guardian*, 1 January 2019.

168 Sara Ruddick, 'Maternal Thinking' in *Maternal Theory*, ed. Andrea O'Reilly, Toronto: Demeter Press, 2007, p. 106.

169 Allison Pearson, *I Don't Know How She Does It*, London: Chatto & Windus, 2002, p. 100.

170 Mothers often contact me to ask if I can help them to start a discussion group like Mothers Talking. I always reply that it helps to start small, and that a lot of group facilitating can be self-taught. The art is to enable mothers to feel accepted and safe. In an ideal world, there should be facilitated meetings within walking distance of every mother. They don't need to be centrally organised. They just need to be there.

171 Cate Blanchett, 'Rohingya testimony' in *Guardian*, 30 August 2018, p. 26.

172 Examples are in the previous chapter.

173 Quoted on p. 13.

174 Personal communication, 13 March 2019; quoted with permission.

175 'Lare child' (1300AD) and 'larefadirs' (1340AD) referenced under 'Lore' in *The Oxford English Dictionary*, second edition,

prepared by J. A. Simpson and E. S. C. Weiner, Oxford: The Clarendon Press, 1989, vol. IX, p. 31.

176 Maybanke Anderson (Mrs Francis Anderson), *Mother Lore*, Sydney, Angus & Robertson, 1919, p. 77.

177 '... [His] soft murmurs are sometimes addressed to a bright metal button; sometimes to a mirror lighted up by the rays of the sun; he seems to tell them how beautiful they are, and how much pleasure they afford to his newly awakened sight; sometimes he utters shrill but joyful screams as if to attract their attention.' Saussure, afterwards Necker, Albertine Adrienne de, *Progressive Education*, vol.1, London: Longman, 1839. [*L'Education Progressive*, 1828.]

Bibliography

Writing by mothers

Bellamy, Teika, ed. (2012), *Musings on Mothering, An anthology of art, poetry and prose*. Nottingham: Mother's Milk Books.

Cusk, Rachel (2001) *A Life's Work, on becoming a mother*, London: Fourth Estate.

Davies, Margaret Llewelyn, ed. (1915, 1978), *Maternity: Letters from working women*. London: Virago.

Dyer, Traci, ed. (1999), *Mother Voices, Real women write about growing into motherhood*. Naperville, Il: Sourcebooks.

Gaskell, Elizabeth Cleghorn (1923), *My Diary*. London: Privately printed by Clement Shorter.

Gowdridge, Christine, Williams, A. Susan and Wynn, Margaret eds. (1977) *Mother Courage: Letters from Mothers in Poverty at the End of the Century*, London: Penguin.

Grace, Pippa, ed. (2019), *Mother in the Mother, a thoughtful anthology of women's voices exploring their maternal lineage*. East Cork, Ireland: Womancraft Publishing.

Hicks, Jennifer, ed. (2006), *Hirkani's Daughters: Women Who Scale Modern Mountains to Combine Breastfeeding and Working*. Schaumburg, Il: La Leche League International.

Jess-Cooke, Carolyn, ed. (2017) *Writing Motherhood*. Bridgend, Wales: Seren, Poetry Wales Press.

Kitzinger, Sheila (2015), *A Passion For Birth*. London: Pinter & Martin.

North Lancashire Manic Mums Group (2008), *Tales From the Edge: Experience of Post-Natal Depression*.

Peri, Camille and Moses, Kate, eds. (2000), *Mothers Who Think*. New York: Washington Square Press.

Shah, Saira (2013), *The Mouseproof Kitchen*. London/New York: Penguin/Harvill Secker.

Sharkey, Donna McCart, ed. (2018), *Always With Me: Parents talk about the death of a child*. Bradford, On: Demeter Press.

Walker, Rebecca (2009), *Baby Love. Choosing Motherhood After a Lifetime of Ambivalence*. London: Souvenir Press.

Writing about mothers

Anandalakshmy, S., Chaudhary, Nandita and Sharma, Neerja, eds, (2008), *Researching Families and Children*. New Delhi: Sage.

Anderson, Maybanke (Mrs Francis Anderson) (1919), *Mother Lore*, Sydney: Angus & Robertson.

Arber, Sara and Timonen, Virpi eds. (2012), *Contemporary Grandparenting: Changing Family Relationships in Global Contexts*. Bristol: Polity Press.

Arnold-Baker, Claire, ed. (2020), *The Existential Crisis of Motherhood*. London: Palgrave Macmillan.

Asher, Rebecca (2012), *Shattered: Modern Motherhood and the Illusion of Equality*. London: Penguin/Vintage.

Axness, Marcy (2012), *Parenting for Peace. Raising the Next Generation of Peacemakers*. Boulder, CO: Sentient Press.

Badinter, Élisabeth (2012) *The Conflict*. New York: Metropolitan Books, Henry Holt.

Belenky, Mary Field, et al. (1986), *Women's Ways of Knowing: the development of self, voice and mind*. New York: Basic Books.

Boyd, Elizabeth Reid and Letherby, Gayle, eds. (2014), *Stay-at-Home Mothers*. Bradford, ON: Demeter Press.

Brown, Sheila Feig (2005), *What Do Mothers Want?* Hillsdale, NJ/London: Analytic Press.

De Marneffe, Daphne (2006), *Maternal Desire*. London: Virago.

Donath, Orna, (2017), *Regretting Motherhood*. US: North Atlantic Books.

Ellison, Katherine (2005), *The Mommy Brain: How motherhood makes us smarter*. New York, Basic Books.

Folbre, Nancy (2001), *The Invisible Heart*. New York: New Press.

Friedan, Betty (1963, 2010), *The Feminine Mystique*, London: Penguin.

Gerhardt, Sue (2004), *Why Love Matters*. London: Brunner-Routledge.

Gillies, Val (2006), *Marginalised Mothers, Exploring working-class experiences of parenting*. London/New York: Routledge.

Hakim, Catherine (2000), *Work-Lifestyle Choices in the Twenty-first Century*, Oxford: Oxford University Press.

Haran, Maeve (1991), *Having It All*. London: Michael Joseph.

Hays, Sharon (1996), *The Cultural Contradictions of Motherhood*. New Haven: Yale University Press.

Hollway, Wendy and Featherstone, Brid, eds. (1997) *Mothers and Ambivalence*. London: Routledge.

Hrdy, Sarah Blaffer (2009), *Mothers and Others*. Cambridge, Mass: Harvard University Press.

Jones, Julia (2018), *Newborn Mothers. When a baby is born, so is a mother*. www.newbornmothers.com

Knott, Sarah (2019), *Mother, An Unconventional History*. New York/London: Viking, Penguin Books.

Leigh, Minturn and Lambert, William W., eds, (1964), *Mothers of Six Cultures, Antecedents of Child Rearing*. New York: Wiley.

Lintott, Sheila and Sander-Staudt, Maureen, eds. (2011), *Philosophical Inquiries into Pregnancy, Childbirth and Mothering*. New York and Abingdon: Routledge.

Manne, Anne (2005), *Motherhood. How should we care for our children?* Crows Nest NSW: Allen & Unwin.

McMahon, Maddie (2018), *Why Mothering Matters*. London: Pinter & Martin.

Necker, Albertine Adrienne de (1828, 1839), *Progressive Education*, Vol.1. London: Longman.

Nicholson, Paula (1994), *Post-Natal Depression: Psychology, science and the transition to motherhood*. London: Routledge.

Olorenshaw, Vanessa (2015), *The Politics of Mothering*. Available online.

Olorenshaw, Vanessa (2016) *Liberating Motherhood, Birthing the Purplestockings Movement*. East Cork, Ireland: Womancraft Publishing.

O'Reilly, Andrea, ed. (2010), *Encyclopaedia of Motherhood*. Thousand Oaks, Calif: Sage.

O'Reilly, Andrea, ed. (2007) *Maternal Theory: Essential readings*. Toronto: Demeter Press.

O'Reilly, Andrea, ed. (2004), *Mothers, Mothering and Motherhood*. Bradford, On: Demeter Press.

O'Reilly, Andrea, ed. (2008), *Feminist Mothering*. Albany NY: State University of New York Press.

Pearson, Allison (2002), *I Don't Know How She Does It*. London: Chatto & Windus.

Raphael, Dana (1955), *The Tender Gift: Breastfeeding*. New York: Schocken Books.

Rich, Adrienne (1977), *Of Woman Born: Motherhood as Experience and Institution*. London: Virago.

Rosenthal, M. Sara (2000), *Women and Depression: a sane approach to mood disorders*. New York: McGraw-Hill.

Ruddick, Sara (1990) *Maternal Thinking. Towards a politics of peace*. London: Women's Press.

Schaefer, Carol (2006), *Grandmothers Counsel the World. Women Elders Offer their Vision for our Planet*. Boston: Trumpeter Books, Shambhala Publications.

Slaughter, Anne-Marie (2015), *Unfinished Business*. New York: Random House.

Walks, Michelle and McPherson, Naomi, eds. (2011), *An Anthropology of Mothering*. Bradford, On: Demeter Press.

Waring, Marilyn (1988, 1999), *Counting for Nothing: What Men Value and What Women are Worth*. Toronto, Buffalo: University of Toronto Press.

Winnicott, D. W. (1964) *The Child, the Family and the Outside World*, Harmondsworth, Middx: Penguin.

Wollstonecraft, Mary (1792, 1975), *A Vindication of the Rights of Women*. London: Penguin.

Index

four-month changes 31
fractiousness 53
Fraser, Liz 139
Freud, Martin 197
Freud, Sigmund 197
Friedan, Betty 121, 122
friendship 48–9, 77–80, 88, 101–2,
     111–12, 128, 131, 135, 176, 210
   childhood 256
   childless 236
   couples 192
   mother–child 145, 147, 154
   mother–father 185
   work 202, 206–7, 215, 238
frustration 2, 87, 99–103, 106,
     111–12, 115, 117, 130, 139, 143
future relationship 38
fuzzy feeling 33

G
Gaskell, Elizabeth Cleghorn 115
Gaskin, Ina May 32
Gerhardt, Sue 39
getting it 85, 177–8, 182–3, 221
Gillies, Val 127, 159
'gloomily lit aquarium' 39
goals/goal-setting 161–2
Grandmothers for Peace 234
grandparent relationship, triangular
     nature of 231
grandparents i, viii, 89, 90, 101, 183,
     219–35, 237, 243, 245, 255
Grannies against the Right 234
great-grandparents 89
group discussion, benefits of
     236–59
growing up, speed of 36–7
grumbling 104, 112, 222
Guardian 89–90
Guardian experiment 213

Gujrati mothers 6
Guatemalan mothers 267–8

H
Hakim, Catherine 189, 273
happiness 20, 24, 46, 60, 70, 80–1,
     84, 117, 140–1, 145, 151,
     153–4, 159, 171, 186, 212,
     222–4
Haran, Maeve 38
Hays, Sharon 208, 210, 273
Heidegger, Martin 149–50
Hirkani's Daughters (LLLGB) 125–6,
     213
Hitting, by children 65, 67, 69
holiday 12, 74–5, 185, 193, 203, 237
horizons, baby's 36
housework 37, 122, 181, 184, 203
Hrdy, Sarah Blaffer 129, 270
hugging 38, 221 (*see also* cuddling)
human 'Continent' 222, 237, 238,
     253, 255, 259
humour 73–4, 76, 83, 99, 139
hunger, how to read signs of 21

I
identity, change of, through
     motherhood 155, 156, 159,
     171, 172
ill health, mother's 46
illness 146, 148, 214
imagination 74–5, 144, 227
immediate present, living in 32
immersion 39–41
immigration 7, 91
inactive 12
independence of mind 14–15, 120,
     125, 164, 171, 212
insensitivity 198
instrumental activity 68